INTRODUCTION TO DISTRIBUTED SYSTEMS

Shubham Gupta

TAP

Toronto Academic Press

Introduction to Distributed Systems

Shubham Gupta

Toronto Academic Press
224 Shoreacres Road
Burlington, ON L7L 2H2
Canada
www.tap-books.com
Email: orders@arclereducation.com

ISBN: 978-1-77469-767-2

Toronto Academic Press publishes wide variety of books and eBooks. For more information about Toronto Academic Press and its products, visit our website at www.tap-books.com.

ABOUT THE AUTHOR

Shubham Gupta is a highly skilled software engineer with over seven years of experience in the field. He holds a Master's degree in Software Engineering from KIET Group of Institutes, where he gained a deep understanding of software development methodologies and best practices. Throughout his career, Shubham has worked with a variety of clients, from small startups to large corporations. He is dedicated to delivering high-quality software solutions that meet the unique needs of his clients and help them achieve their business goals. Shubham is well-versed in a wide range of programming languages, frameworks, and technologies. He has a particular expertise in web development, and has worked on numerous projects involving the development of web-based applications and services. In addition to his technical skills, Shubham is also a strong communicator and team player. He enjoys collaborating with other professionals to develop solutions that are both technically sound and user-friendly. Shubham is passionate about his work and is always looking for ways to improve his skills and stay up-to-date with the latest industry trends and technologies. His commitment to excellence has earned him a reputation as a trusted and reliable software engineer.

Contents

List of Figures

List of Abbreviations

AFS	Andrew File System
API	Application Programming Interface
AWS	Amazon Web Services
CB	Citizens Band
CBC	Cipher Block Chaining
CDNs	Content Delivery Networks
CIFS	Common Internet File System
CIFSDN	Common Internet File System Distributed Namespace
DES	Data Encryption Standard
DFS	Distributed File System
DFSR	Distributed File System Replication
DNS	Domain Name System
EOF	End-of-File
EOR	End-of-Record
FTP	File Transfer Protocol
GFS	Google File System
GUI	Graphical User Interface
HDFS	Hadoop Distributed File System
HPC	High-Performance Computing
HTTP	Hypertext Transfer Protocol
IMAP4	Internet Mail Access Protocol, Version 4
IP	Internet Protocol
ISO	International Standards Organization
IV	Initialization Vector

JDBC	Java Database Connectivity
LAN	Local Area Network
LDAP	Lightweight Directory Access Protocol
MAC	Message Authentication Code
MAN	Metropolitan Area Network
NAS	Network-Attached Storage
NFS	Network File System
NIS	Network Information Service
NTP	Network Time Protocol
NVT	Network Virtual Terminal
OFB	Output Feedback
OSI	Open Systems Interconnection
PINS	Personal Identification Numbers
PKC	Public Key Cryptography
RPC	Remote Procedure Call
RSA	Rivest, Shamir, and Adleman
SKC	Secret Key Cryptography
SMTP	Simple Mail Transfer Protocol
SNMP	Simple Network Management Protocol
URL	Uniform Resource Locator
WAN	Wide Area Network
WWW	World Wide Web
XML	Extended Markup Language

PREFACE

Distributed systems have become an integral part of modern computing, enabling applications to run efficiently and reliably across multiple machines and networks. From cloud computing to social media platforms, distributed systems play a critical role in delivering the performance, scalability, and availability that users demand. As such, the study of distributed systems has become a fundamental area of research and development in computer science and engineering.

The study of distributed systems is an important area of research in computer science, with many challenges and opportunities for innovation. As computing systems become more complex and distributed, the need for effective methods of managing and coordinating these systems becomes increasingly important. Distributed systems provide a powerful framework for building highly scalable and fault-tolerant systems that can handle large-scale data processing and storage tasks. However, designing and implementing distributed systems requires careful consideration of a variety of factors, including network protocols, data consistency, security, and performance. The field of distributed systems is constantly evolving, with new techniques and technologies emerging to address the challenges of building and managing large-scale distributed systems. As such, studying distributed systems is a valuable pursuit for computer scientists, engineers, and researchers who are interested in developing the next generation of distributed computing systems.

Chapter 1 introduces the fundamentals of distributed systems, including the concepts of nodes, networks, and communication protocols. It covers topics such as system models, architectures, and challenges of distributed systems. Chapter 2 explores the various distributed computing paradigms, including message passing, remote procedure calls (RPC), and distributed objects.

Chapter 3 focuses on data communication and networking, examining the principles of network protocols, routing, and addressing. It covers topics such as socket programming, reliable communication, and network security. Chapter 4 delves into data consistency and replication, examining the principles of consistency models, distributed transactions, and replication protocols.

Chapter 5, authored by Chat GPT, provides an in-depth analysis of distributed file systems (DFS), including the concepts of naming, caching, and access control. It covers topics such as the design of distributed file systems, file replication, and fault tolerance. Chapter 6 discusses the challenges of storing data in distributed systems, including the principles of data partitioning, indexing, and query processing.

Chapter 7 explores the techniques used to enhance the scalability and performance of distributed systems, including load balancing, caching, and distributed caching. Finally, Chapter 8 discusses the principles of distributed security and privacy, examining the concepts of access control, authentication, and encryption.

The authors of this book are experts in the field of distributed systems, with years of experience in both research and teaching. They have designed this book to be a comprehensive resource for anyone interested in learning about the fundamental principles of distributed systems. It is suitable for students studying computer science at all levels, from undergraduate to graduate, as well as for professionals in related fields who want to expand their knowledge of distributed systems.

Overall, Introduction to Distributed Systems is an essential resource for anyone seeking to gain a deeper understanding of the fundamental principles that govern the behavior of data and communication in distributed systems. Whether you are a student of computer science, a professional in the field, or simply someone with a passion for technology, this book will provide you with the knowledge and skills you need to succeed in the study of distributed systems.

—***Author***

CHAPTER 1

INTRODUCTION TO DISTRIBUTED SYSTEM

UNIT INTRODUCTION

The most dramatic change in information technology over the past two decades has been networked workstations' expansion and the centralized mainframe's decline. This change has distributed hardware resources and gives end users access to more processing power. A network of connected computers can use the combined power of all connected computers to carry out complex tasks (Lamport, 2019). Centralized or distributed computations are two categories for computation in the connections of processing nodes. In a centralized solution, one node is chosen as the computer node that locally processes the entire application, and all users constantly share the central system. As a result, there is a single point of failure and a single point of control (Barker & De Mello, 2000) (Figure 1.1).

A networked system is a program that implements a set of protocols to synchronize the activities of numerous processes on a network of communications so that all parts work together to complete a single or a limited number of related tasks. The cooperating computers can access local and remote resources in the distributed system through the communication network. In a distributed system, the user is unaware that there are numerous autonomous computers. The user is unaware that multiple computers are used to execute the jobs in different locations. This indicates that, like centrally managed systems, every device in the system is responsible for all the system resources needed to run a typical computer program (Kim & Kim, 2001).

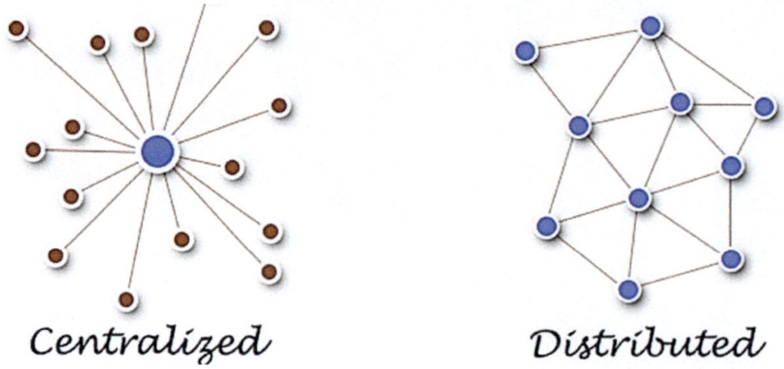

Figure 1.1. Illustration of centralized and distributed computation.

Source: Tharinda Dilshan Piyadasa, Creative Commons License.

Learning Objectives

At the end of this chapter, the reader will be able to understand:

- The concept of distributed system planning and its importance;
- The features and challenges of distributed systems;
- The eight fallacies of distributed computing and their implications;
- The client/server computing model and its advantages and disadvantages;
- The world wide web (WWW) as an immense distributed system;
- The advanced models of distributed systems.

Key Terms

- Bandwidth
- Centralized architecture
- Client/server computing
- Distributed planning
- Distributed system planning
- Eight fallacies of distributed computing
- Security
- Topology
- Web information retrieval
- World wide web

1.1. DISTRIBUTED SYSTEM PLANNING

Distributed systems are constructed on top of already installed operating and networking software. A computer network and its distribution middleware connect a group of independent computers to form a distributed system. There must be a distinct master/slave connection between two computers in a network to become autonomous. Computers can coordinate their actions and share system resources thanks to middleware, which gives users the impression that the system is one big, integrated computing facility (Gönen & Ramirez-Rosado, 1986). Therefore, middleware links distributed applications running in various physical locations and on various hardware platforms, networks, operating systems, and programming languages. The development of the middleware software complies with established standards and procedures. It offers common services like naming, tenacity, concurrency control (which ensures that accurate results are produced for concurrent processes and obtains the results as quickly as possible), event distribution, authorization (which specifies access rights to resources), security, and so on. The middleware service spans several computers (Khattam et al., 2005) (Figure 1.2).

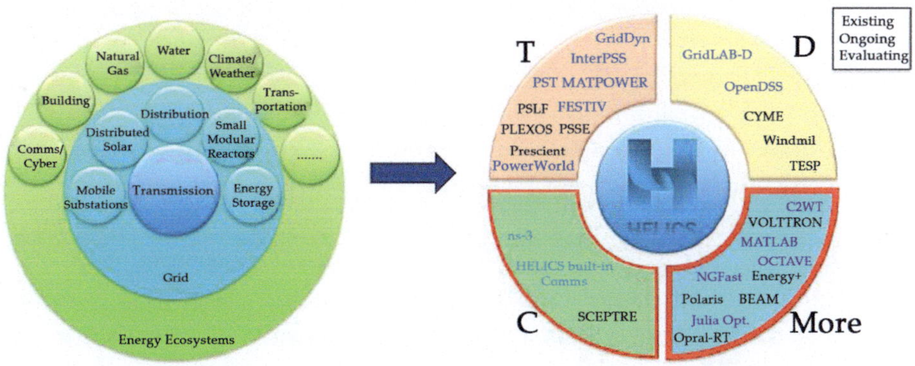

Figure 1.2. Schematic of distributed system planning.

Source: National Academies, Creative Commons License.

The distributed architecture can be considered from the perspective of the users or the computation, as well as from the perspective of the physical components. The physical view is the first, and the logical view is the second. A distributed system is made up of a collection of nodes (computers) connected by a network of communication. The network's nodes are not tightly coupled to one another and have no shared memory (Lotero & Contreras, 2011). The system's nodes exchange information by sending messages across the communication network. Protocols for communication are used to transfer messages from a single node to another. The logical model represents the application's perception of the system. It has a number of concurrent processes as well as channels for communication between them. It is assumed that the fundamental network is fully connected. Processes communicate with one another by sending messages. A system is concurrent if, when properly executed, it consistently carries out the intended action at the predetermined time; otherwise, it is asynchronous. The failure of a synchronous system is discernible by an absence of an answer from the system. As a result, failure discovery techniques based on timeouts are used (Ganguly et al., 2013).

Complete or partly connected networks can be used to build a distributed system [HUAN05, MIN04, NELS01]. A network with all of its nodes connected to one another is called a completely interconnected network. The issue in such an arrangement is that incorporating new nodes causes the number of nodes associated to the node to increase. As a result, the complexity of each node's connection implementation and the number of file descriptors are greatly increased (Lavorato et al., 2010). As a result, the scalability of such systems is constrained by each node's ability to open file descriptors and capacity to manage new connections. Scalability is the capacity of a system to keep running well when the system's size or volume changes. Because a message delivered from one computer to a different computer only travels through one link, the communication cost—the message delay—of delivering a message from its origin to the destination is minimal. Fully interconnected systems are dependable because the remaining computers remain in touch even if some links or computers fail (Naderi et al., 2012). Direct connections exist between some computer pairs in a partially connected network, but not all of them do. Star-structured networks, multi-access bus networks, ring-structured networks, and tree-structured networks are partially connected network models. The network topology for some conventional distributed systems, like the client/server paradigm, is a star. The issue with such an arrangement is that it will collapse as a whole if the central node fails (Jain et al., 2017). A group of clients are linked in a multi-access bus network by a common communication channel known as a bus. When the bus link breaks, the entire system's nodes are unable to communicate with one another, making it the bottleneck. Another drawback is that performance suffers when there are more computers added or when there is a lot of traffic. Each node forms a single continuous process for signals through every link in a ring network by connecting to precisely two other nodes. The network's diameter expands as the number of points in the system does, causing a longer delay in message transmission (Chowdhury et al., 2002). A node failure or cable break could isolate every node connected to the ring. The connections between the nodes form a tree-like structure in a tree-structured system (hierarchical network). Every point in the network is connected to a fixed number of other nodes at a lower level of the hierarchy. Since new nodes can be stated as the child nodes of the leaf nodes or within the nodes, the tree-structured network can scale more easily than the fully connected network. However, only messages sent between a parent node and its child node identified in such systems use a single link; all other messages sent between two nodes must pass through one or more intermediary nodes (Liu et al., 2015) (Figure 1.3).

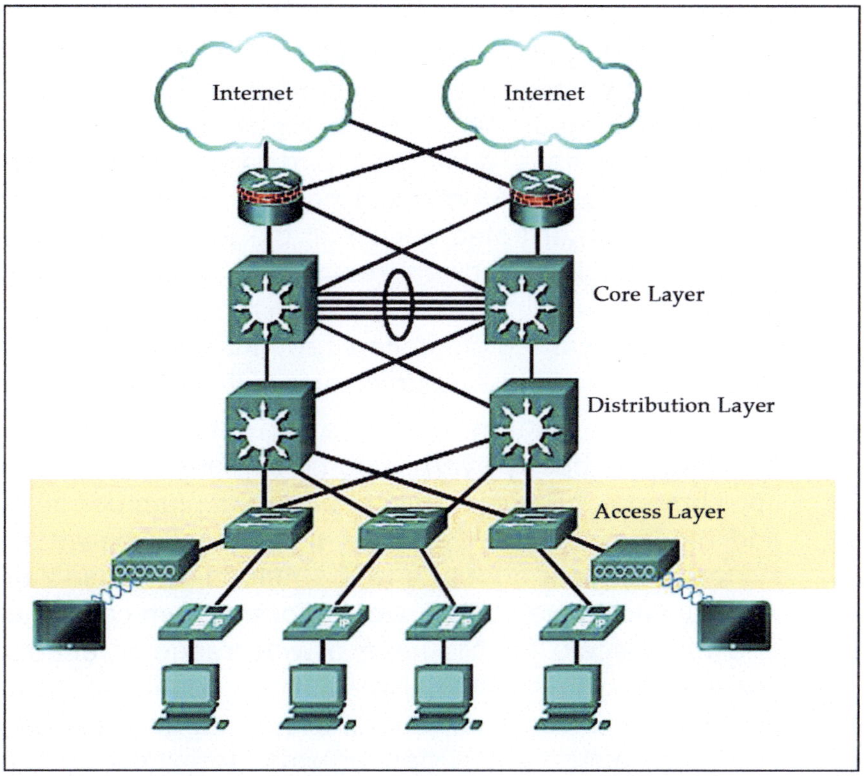

Figure 1.3. Image of hierarchical network design.

Source: Cisco Press, Creative Commons License.

1.2. FEATURES OF A DISTRIBUTED SYSTEM

To give users the best performance, a distributed system needs to have the following qualities:

- **Fault-Tolerant:** Distributed systems are made up of numerous hardware and software components, all of which eventually fail. Such component malfunctions may lead to service interruptions. As a result, the systems ought to be capable of recovering from component failures lacking to take the wrong course of action. Fault tolerance aims to prevent system failures to maintain service even when faults are present. If a system can hide the existence of faults, it is considered to be fault tolerant. Any fault-tolerant system seeks to improve availability or reliability (Leonini et al., 2009). The likelihood that a system will last until that point is what a system's reliability means. Even when a component fails, a reliable system avoids information loss. The percentage of time that a system is usable is known as availability. Redundancy is typically used to achieve fault tolerance. The term "redundancy" refers to unnecessary system components for the system to function properly. It comes in three varieties: time, software, and hardware. In order to achieve hardware redundancy, a system must have additional hardware components that can step in for malfunctioning ones if necessary. In order to ensure uninterrupted service in the event of a hardware component failure, software redundancy includes additional management instructions and code. The identical instruction is repeatedly carried out in time redundancy. This is utilized to address transient system errors (Edwards et al., 2006).

TIPS

Consider the trade-offs between consistency, availability, and partition tolerance when designing a distributed system.

- **Scalable:** A system that is distributed can continue functioning properly even as some components are scaled up. Three factors make upscale: the total number of users and other system participants, the distance between the system's farthest nodes, and the number of organizations with administrative control over various system components. The three scale factors have a wide range of effects on distributed systems. Name resolution, identity verification, authorization, communication, use of remote resources, and user observation mechanisms are some impacted components. The three methods of replication, distribution, and caching are used to manage scale (Beschastnikh et al., 2016).
- **Resources:** These are replicated to produce multiple copies. Its application to file, naming, and authentication services lessens the burden on each server and raises the general dependability and accessibility of the services. The two most crucial replication-related issues are the locations of the versions and the methods used to maintain their consistency. Resource replication's goal determines the replicas' location within a distributed system. The replicas are dispersed throughout the system if a service is being duplicated to decrease network latency when the service is accessed. Replicas may be placed close to one another if most users are local, and the service is

being replicated to increase availability or distribute the load across multiple servers. Everyone using the system should be able to tell if the object is altered. For instance, the system sends changes to any replica, and as they become available, that replica sends the updates to the others. Timestamps (the date/time the update was created) are used to distinguish the copies when across various orders (Shukur et al., 2020).

- **Distribution:** A further tool for controlling scale in distributed structures, enables the extension of a distributed service's data across multiple servers. Distributing data among several servers makes it easier for each server to maintain a smaller database, reducing the time required for searching the database. Additionally, distribution divides the workload among the servers, dividing the volume of requests that each must handle. The demand on servers can be efficiently handled if requests are distributed among servers according to their processing capacity. The upper levels can be skipped if cached copies are available from lower-level servers in a tree-structured system.
- **Caching:** Another crucial method for creating scalable systems is caching. The burden on servers and networks is lessened by caching. Accessing cached data is quicker than making a new request. The distinction between caching and replication is that cached data is temporary data. Consistency remains intact when consistency cannot be ensured by nullifying cached data rather than propagating updates. The client typically performs caching, which decreases the number of times the network service is requested. On the servers running those services, caching can also take place. It is quicker to read a file from the file server's memory cached copy than from the user's local disk (Francalanza et al., 2018).
- **Predictable Performance:** Several performance metrics, including speed (the pace at which a network sends or receives data), system consumption, network capacity, and others, are used to evaluate the performance. Response time, for example, measures how long a computer system responds to an inquiry or demand. The capacity to respond as quickly as desired indicates predictable performance.
- **Openness:** The attribute 'openness' guarantees that a subsystem is always available for communication with other systems. Web applications are software programs created to support interoperable networked machine-to-machine communication. These protocols make it possible to expand and scale distributed systems. An open system that can scale has an advantage over a wholly closed and independent system. The attribute of openness is attained by a distributed system that is not dependent on the heterogeneity underlying environments, such as software and hardware platforms. As a result, every client in the

system, whether local or remote, has equal access to every service. Implementing, installing, and debugging novel services shouldn't be overly difficult in a system with an openness characteristic (Christofides, 2001).

- **Security:** By enforcing the necessary security measures, distributed systems should enable communication between applications, users, and resources on various computers. The main goals of the security features are to ensure confidentiality, integrity, and availability. Privacy and confidentiality are safeguards against disclosure to unauthorized parties. Confidentiality violations can range from unpleasant to disastrous. Integrity offers a security against corruption and alteration. The resource remains available and accessible. Numerous hacking incidents jeopardize the reliability of databases and other assets. Attacks referred to as "denial of service" target availability. Control of access and nonrepudiation are two more significant security issues. The users can access only the assets and services they are authorized by maintaining access control. Additionally, it guarantees that users won't be denied access to resources they are legally entitled to. Nonrepudiation shields a communication from being denied by one of the parties involved. The security measures implemented should ensure the proper utilization of resources by various system users (Figure 1.4).

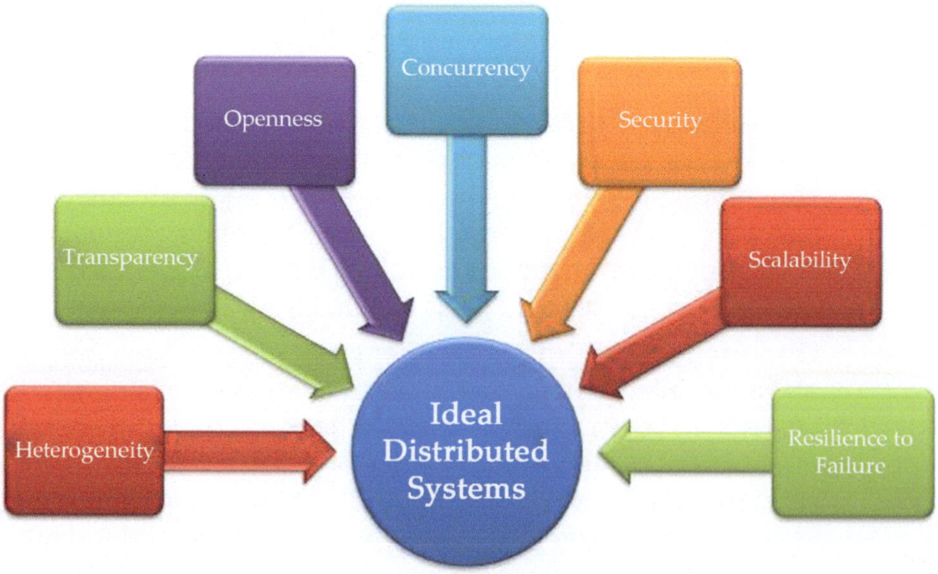

Figure 1.4. Illustration of characteristics of distributed system.

Source: Prasangi Blog, Creative Commons License.

- **Transparency:** Members and application developers should view distributed systems as a whole rather than a group of interdependent parts. Users are not shown where the computer systems are located in the operations, in tandem operations, copying of data, resource discovery from various locations, failures, system recovery, etc. Transparency allows users to see the system as appearing and functioning normally, while hiding the system's distributed nature from them. A distributed system can use transparency in a variety of ways [KAZI00, PRAD02] (Rodden & Blair, 1991):
  - Thanks to access transparency, a distributed system's users can access local and distant assets with the same operations (for instance, web navigation).
  - Location transparency refers to names that identify network resources (such as IP addresses) without considering the user's location or the location of the resource. Location transparency, in other words, enables a user to get to resources from any place on the network, lacking being aware of the location of the resource. The user's computer or servers located thousands of miles away from it may host the file.
  - Concurrency transparency makes it possible for multiple processes to use shared information objects concurrently without interfering with one another (such as an ATM network). Users will only become aware of other individuals in the system if they access the same resources.
  - Replication transparency allows the system to create extra copies of files and other assets without the users noticing to improve performance and/or reliability. If a resource has been copied in multiple places, it should display to the users as one source (for example, mirroring, which offers multiple sources of identification information to ensure dependable availability for large downloads) (Iwanicki, 2018).
  - Failure transparency makes it possible for applications to finish work even when certain system components fail. The system is said to exhibit high failure transparency. For instance, if a server fails, but users receive a redirect to a different server, the user is unaware of the failure. One of the most challenging kinds of transparency to implement is failure transparency because it is difficult to tell if a server has collapsed or simply very slowly. Furthermore, because networks are unreliable, achieving complete failure transparency in a distributed system is typically impossible (Xue & Xu, 2003).
  - Migration transparency makes it easier for resources to switch

between locations without changing their names (for instance, web pages). Users shouldn't be aware of a resource's or a computing entity's capacity to change its logical or physical location.

- Performance transparency guarantees that the load variation won't impair performance. Automatic reconfiguration in response to changes in the load could accomplish this (for instance, load distribution).
- Scalability transparency enables the system to continue operating effectively even as the number of users and connected resources (such as the world wide web (WWW) and distributed databases) increases significantly (Shrivastava et al., 1991).

1.3. EIGHT FALLACIES OF DISTRIBUTED COMPUTING

Architects and designers of systems that are distributed are anticipated to make 7 presumptions [ARNO06, INGR04] that turn out to be false, according to a 1994 document by Peter Deutsch of Sun. A further example of this fallacy was the eighth erroneous of distributed computing, which was added in 1997 by James Gosling, the creator of the Java computer programming language (Umbrich et al., 2013).

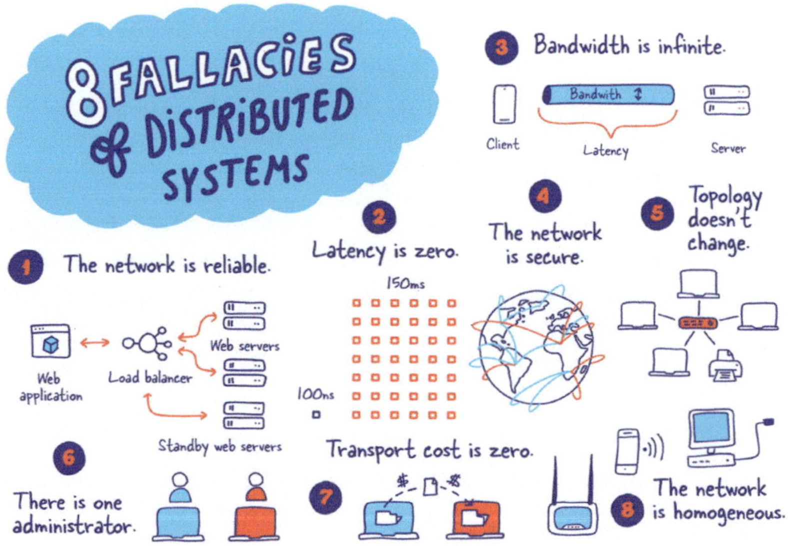

Figure 1.5. Image of eight fallacies of distributed system.

Source: Architecture Notes, Creative Commons License.

The eight fallacies of computer networking are the name given to the group of assumptions. The falsehoods of distributed systems are a collection of frequent but incorrect assumptions that programmers make when creating distributed applications for the first time. These assumptions led to the development of many distributed systems, many of which were unnecessarily complex due to errors that later needed to be fixed (Bigo, 2019) (Figure 1.5):

- The network is trustworthy;
- There is no latency;
- There is infinite bandwidth;
- The networking system is safe;
- The topology stays the same;
- One administrator is present;
- There is no transport fee;
- The network is uniform (Shi, 2016).

1.3.1. Reliability

The network will cause problems when it begins to drop packets for software developed under the assumption that the network is dependable. The autonomy of a system's nodes can frequently be increased while maintaining reliability. Replication can also increase a system's dependability (Kartik & Murthy, 1997).

1.3.2. Latency

The latency duration is the interval between the start of a data request and the start of the data transfer.

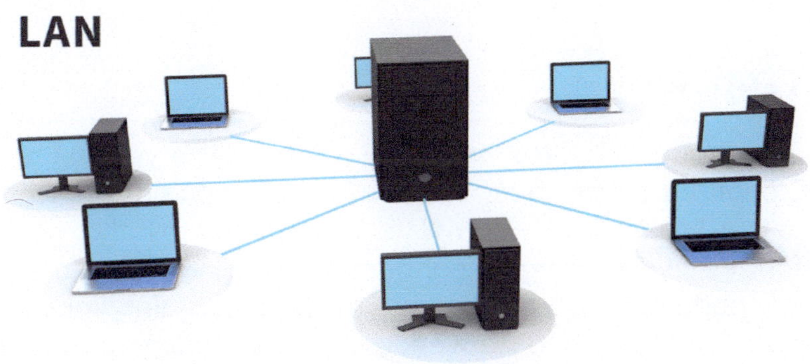

Figure 1.6. Picture of local area network (LAN).

Source: Tech Terms, Creative Commons License.

On a LAN, latency can be reasonably good, but it quickly degrades when a user switches to WAN or internet scenarios. If latency is assumed to be zero, scalability issues will undoubtedly exist as the application expands geographically or relocates to a different type of network (Reisizadeh & Pedarsani, 2017) (Figure 1.6).

1.3.3. Bandwidth

A measurement of a communication channel's capacity or the amount of data we can send over it in a given period of time. A channel can carry more data the higher its bandwidth. However, this assumption continues to be false due to two factors (Kumar et al., 2015). One is that as bandwidth expands, so does the volume of data we try to fit through it. Some recent applications that use bandwidth include VoIP, videos, and IPTV. Packet loss is the additional factor causing bandwidth to be reduced along with frame size. We must make an effort to reduce the amount of information we deliver over the wire due to bandwidth restrictions (Ghosh et al., 2007).

Remember

Bandwidth is like a highway, the wider it is, the more data can flow through it.

1.3.4. Security

The network is rarely safe because the systems are constantly being attacked from many directions. Therefore, the developer must conduct threat modeling to assess the potential dangers. The next step is determining which risks must be mitigated and how (a balance between costs, risks, and their probabilities). Network, infrastructure, and software layers all play a role in modern security architectures. The software architect needs to be aware of how crucial security is and the potential effects it can have on the project (Wang et al., 2012).

1.3.5. Topology

When discussing networks, topology refers to the various possible layouts, such as a ring, bus, star, or fully connected. For instance, the physical topology of a LAN is determined by the geometric shape formed by mapping its connections and nodes onto a graph. Each LAN node can potentially have multiple outgoing links to other LAN nodes. Similarly, the network's logical topology is established by mapping the data flow between the nodes (Batten, 2001). The physical and logical layouts in some networks will be the same, but in others, they will be different. Organizational networks may undergo change whenever new applications are introduced. The operations staff will occasionally alter the network by adding or removing servers. Last but not least, server or network infrastructure disruptions can result in a routing shift. From the client's perspective, things are much worse. Moving laptops, new mobile devices, wireless ad hoc networks, etc. In short, a distributed system's topology is dynamic and constantly shifting [NELS01] (Bredon, 2013).

1.3.6. Administrator

"There is one administrator" is the sixth computer networking fallacy. Having specialists in charge of the company's databases, web servers, networks, OSes, and so on is a straightforward solution. The issue arises when the company works with third parties, such as a partner in business, or when the application is hosted on a third-party server and made available over the Internet; in both cases, it must access services provided by organizations outside the company. In such cases, the company administrators have no say over the other administrators, who may operate according to their own policies. Therefore, the idea that there is "one administrator" to oversee everything is debunked (Antamoshkin et al., 2014). The administrators are usually not the ones who create the software. Therefore, developers should equip users with means of self-diagnosis and problem location. Tools for real-time monitoring of operations, such as those that help administrator's spot minor issues before they balloon into catastrophic outages, are also a practical addition. The users, assets, nodes, networks, etc., that comprise a growing distributed system will increasingly operate in different jurisdictions. This means there will be a greater diversity in the types of actors exercising administrative authority over the system. Resources, payments, security, and more can all run into trouble in an infrastructure that doesn't handle expansion well (Beberg et al., 2009).

1.3.7. Transport Cost

The price of transportation will never be free. Network installation and maintenance do not come for free. Purchasing routers, investing in network security measures, leasing bandwidth for internet access, and keeping the network online all incur expenses (Babay et al., 2017).

1.3.8. Homogenous Network

"Network is homogeneous" is the eighth computer networking fallacy. A homogeneous network consists of nodes that do not vary in their configuration or protocol setup from one another (Al-Amri et al., 2010). No network is completely uniform except for a handful of extremely simple ones. It is very challenging to incorporate proprietary protocols. To mitigate the consequences of the heterogeneity of the enterprise environment, it is recommended to use widely accepted standard technologies such as XML (extended markup language) or web services (Zhao et al., 2015).

1.4. CLIENT/SERVER COMPUTING

Did you Know?

Client/server computing has become ubiquitous in modern computing, enabling efficient and effective communication between clients and servers across various platforms and networks.

Distributing related processing across multiple resources is gaining traction as systems of computing resources become more commonplace. Many different approaches have developed over time to make this dissemination easier. Client/server computing is a common type of distributed architecture [SILV98]. The client/server architecture develops on the modular framework. The goal of modular programming is to separate the development and testing of an application into its constituent parts. A modular program has both a core component and supplementary components. The components of a client/server model are the same as those of a modular programming model: clients and servers. Clients and servers are typically separate computers that communicate with one another over the internet. The component that makes the call is now the server, while the one that receives the call is the client (Sinha, 1992) (Figure 1.7).

In order to get a server to do something, a client app will send it network messages. The client is responsible for managing local resources like I/O devices, disks, and other peripherals. The server application receives requests from clients over the network and processes them as they come in. In response to these requests, servers carry out operations. The client only receives the processed data and results from the server. As a result, less data is transferred between the computer's server and the client. As a result, there is a boost to the network's efficiency (Jing et al., 1999).

The server manages the distribution of data and optimizes the use of available system resources. Whether or not a client discusses directly to the server or if an intermediary process exists in the client and the server is an essential design factor for large client/server systems. One has three levels, while the other has only two (*see* Figure 1.4). Web applications frequently employ N-tier architecture to route requests to additional back-end business services. The two-tier structure is more common in smaller settings due to its simplicity and ease of deployment. Nonetheless, a three-tier architecture offers more scalability than a two-tier one (Lewandowski, 1998).

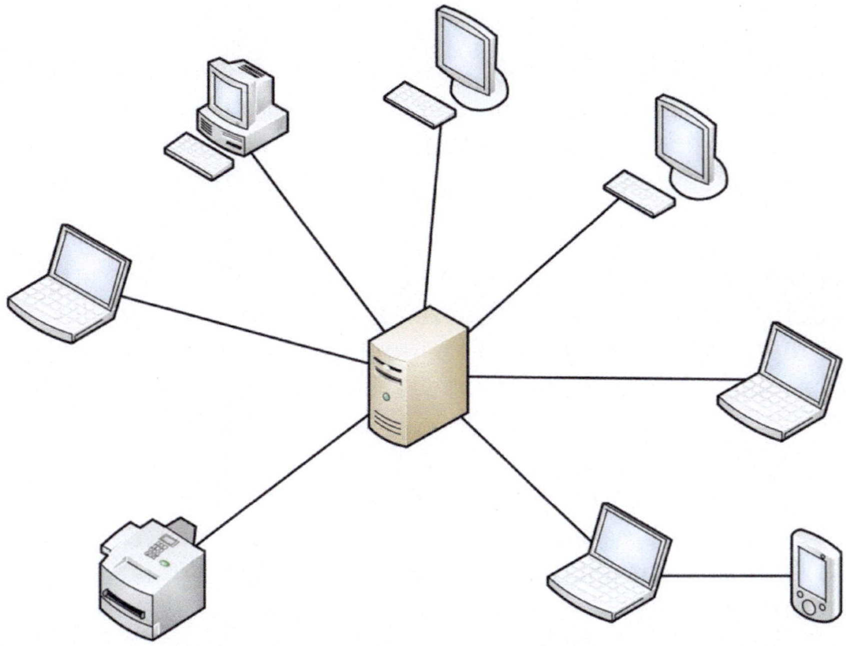

Figure 1.7. Depiction of server/ client computing.

Source: Heavy.ai, Creative Commons License.

Clients and servers are linked by a third process in the structure with three levels shown in Figure 1.5 [CHAN05, JI96]. The intermediary can track which servers are used most often, leading to faster response times and greater scalability. A client machine, an application server, and a database server are the three mainstays of any database-based 3-tier client/server architecture. In this architecture, the business application is hosted on the application server, which is part of the middle tier. The data is fetched by the middle-tier a server from the database server and sent to the client. Creating a client/server application with three distinct layers requires middleware. The database application programming interface (API) is a feature of database-oriented middleware. Applets and servlets can use these classes from the popular Java database connectivity (JDBC) API to connect to any number of databases without knowing or caring about the specifics of each database (Adler, 1995).

Servers also need to solve the issue of authentication for security reasons. Sensitive information stored on a server may be compromised if an unauthorized client gains access in a networked environment. Public key encryption and dedicated authentication servers provide cryptographic client authentication. In order to ensure high levels of availability and fault tolerance, it is sometimes necessary to duplicate critical servers. Clients can continue to access all of the replicas, even if one of the servers hosting the replicas goes down (Oluwatosin, 2014).

Any one layer of a 3-tier architecture can be changed or updated independently of the others. Better load balancing can be achieved by decoupling database and application operations. In addition, the server tiers can be used to implement necessary security guidelines without impacting the clients (Lai & Nieh, 2006).

To boost Internet retrieval performance, many organizations turn to the "proxy server model," a three-tier client/server architecture. The proxy server acts as an intermediary, distributing client requests across multiple servers for simultaneous processing. In order to access a service, such as a web page hosted on a web server, a client must first establish a connection with the proxy server. The request is evaluated by the proxy server against its filtering policies. It may restrict connections based on criteria such as IP address or protocol. If the filter verifies the request's legitimacy, the proxy will make the resource available to the client by making a request to the proper server (Lai & Nieh, 2006). It's possible that a proxy server will handle your request without ever contacting the intended web server. This is made feasible by the proxy server caching the most frequently accessed pages. Proxy servers drastically improve end-user experience by caching frequently requested files on their own servers rather than making repeated requests to the original host. The term "proxy-cache server" is commonly used to refer to a proxy server that can store data for later use. Users can be verified as authorized by a proxy server by having them supply credentials like a username and password. As an added bonus, restricting the utilization of external resources to only those who need it and keeping detailed logs of their usage is a breeze. A reverse proxy can be used to distribute traffic evenly across multiple copies of the same server (Deboosere et al., 2011).

1.4.1. Advantages of Client/Server Model

- Since everything is stored in one place, the server handles the shared components used by all clients. For instance, a centralized database could be used to avoid issues brought on by duplicate and incompatible information.
- As the number of entry points providing the ability to access data is not so crucial, improved security is provided.
- Since clients play a minor function in the client/server architecture, server-level administration is sufficient.

- A scalable network allows for adding or removing clients without negatively impacting performance or necessitating extensive changes to the underlying infrastructure (Esfarjani & Nof, 1998).

1.4.2. Disadvantages of the Client/Server Model

- Costs skyrocketed because of the sophisticated nature of the server technology.
- If the system is not built to handle a server failure, then none of the clients will receive service.
- If the network goes down, it will be impossible to connect to any of the servers.
- If a single user generates a large amount of network traffic, it could cause delays in service for everyone else (Ruffer et al., 1995).

1.5. WORLD WIDE WEB (WWW) – AN IMMENSE DISTRIBUTED SYSTEM

The Internet is a global system of interconnected computer networks that enables any two computers, anywhere in the world, to exchange data and converse. The WWW, often shortened to "Web," is an information retrieval system that operates over the Internet. The WWW is made up of countless millions of pages housed on millions of computers around the globe. It's a system for exchanging data that's designed to work with the Web as its foundation. The computer network hosting websites is probably the most common instance of a distributed system. Words in a hypertext document link to other hypertext documents on the WWW. User-selectable "links" are the highlighted words. Many other documents can be linked to from a single hypertext file (Yan & Chen, 1999).

Pages, or Web pages, are the files that make up the WWW and contain data and links to various resources on the Internet, both textual and visual. The rules established by internet protocols (IPs) govern online data exchange between computers. The HyperText Transfer Protocol (HTTP) is responsible for sending hypertext across the Internet. The Internet operates on this protocol. E-mail messages and any attached files are delivered to one or more inboxes using the Simple Mail Transport Protocol, or SMTP. VoIP (voice over internet protocol) facilitates the transmission of voice calls over IP networks. A web server is a computer that accepts requests made via HTTP from clients and returns those requests, along with any additional data (such as web pages), in the form of an HTTP response (Doan et al., 2011). Hypertext serves as the primary information retrieval mechanism for the WWW. User interactions can generate web pages. Hypertext Markup Language, or HTML, is a document creation language used for the creation of hypertext for the WWW. Document formatting, visual characteristics like font size, italics, and bold, and the generation of hypertext links are all accomplished by inserting tags into the text using HTML. Distributed hypertext and multimedia files are jointly provided by servers implementing the HTTP. Clients use the computer's preexisting web browser to connect to the WWW. A file's URL (uniform resource locator) is its address on the WWW and can be found on any web server. The domain name system (DNS) is responsible for converting URLs into their corresponding IP addresses. The DNS is a network of computers that stores information about website addresses (Baentsch et al., 1997).

The "real" URL is the numeric address, known as the IP address. Once the DNS has completed its translation, the browser can contact the web server and request the requested file. The file is downloaded from the server and displayed in the browser using the URL. The file is then sent to the client, the user's computer, and demonstrated on the attached screen. The web is a client-server network because of this dependency between users and service providers. Every day, millions of people worldwide use the internet to do everything from checking their email and news to listening to music, shopping, and researching topics of interest. While appearing to the user as a single, clickable resource, the web is in reality a massive, decentralized system. Standardization in content creation and distribution is essential for the continued growth and success of the WWW. The World Wide Web (W3C) Consortium is a group at the forefront of efforts to standardize the web (Barabási et al., 2000).

1.5.1. Web Information Retrieval

In order to find the most pertinent results for a user's query, Web retrieval of data [AMI08, AMY04, AMY06, DIRK05, MONI03, VENK97] involves searching the largest and most linked document collection in the world: the WWW. Obtaining data on the web faces many obstacles, including but not limited to: Since: (i) data is dispersed across many computers running different operating systems; (ii) data is volatile (i.e., computers and files are added and removed constantly and are unpredictable); (iii) the volume of data is very large (i.e., growth is exponential); and (iv) data quality is inconsistent (i.e., data may be untrue, error-ridden, invalid, outdated, ambiguous, and so on due to the data's many sources and different interpretations); it can be (v) information that is inherently diverse, including but not limited to different languages, scripts, and media formats. Therefore, it would be physically impossible for one person to examine and sort through all these pages to locate the necessary data. "Search Engine" refers to the software program most people use to look up things online. Input from a user's web browser is analyzed and utilized to query the database for incidents of specific keywords when using a search engine. Google and Yahoo! Search are just two of many available search engines that significantly speed up the process of retrieving information from the web. Centralized and decentralized search architectures are the two most common types of web search architecture (Langville & Meyer, 2005) (Figure 1.8).

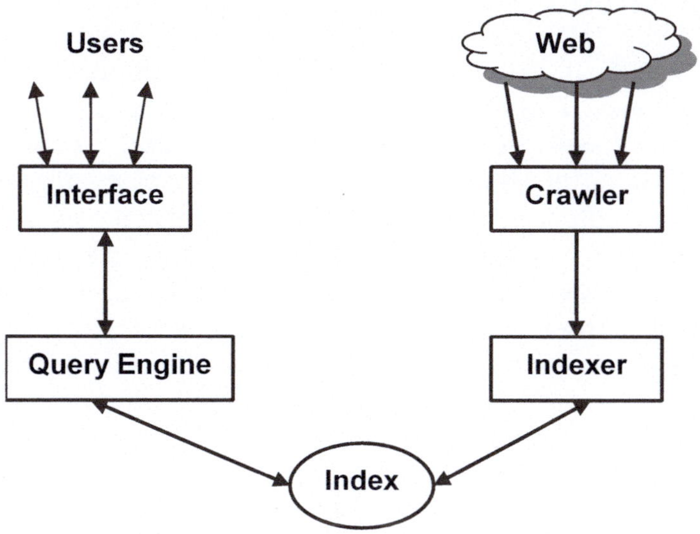

Figure 1.8. Illustration of search engine: Centralized architecture.

Source: Swati Gupta, Creative Commons License.

1.5.2. Centralized Architecture

This centralized method aims to index a substantial portion of the Web without regard to specific topics or domains. Crawlers, indexers, and query handlers are the three main components of a search engine with a centralized architecture. The web pages that are retrieved by the crawler (spider or robot) are then compressed and stored in a database. Crawling (also known as robot spidering, gathering, and harvesting) describes this method. Googlebot, MSNBot, and Yahoo!'s Slurp are three of the most well-known crawlers. A crawler control module specifies a crawler's next destination URLs. The indexer processes the collected web pages, which then constructs the index, the primary data structure utilized by the search engine, which represents the crawled web pages. Each term is represented in the inverted index by a sorted list of couples, including docID and position within the document. The query engine processes user queries and returns relevant results using the index. A ranking algorithm is used to determine the order in which the results are presented to the user. Different search engines use different algorithms to determine which pages in their index contain the most relevant results for a user's query.

In case the target server is down, some search engines keep a local cache copy of many popular pages indexed in their database for speed and redundancy (Singh et al., 2004).

1.5.3. Distributed Planning

Searching is a group effort involving many people who collect and trade data. The information in the documents hosted on any number of web servers is summarized and extracted using Gatherer. It's compatible with numerous documents, including HTML, PDF, Postscript, and more. The broker collects summaries from the collectors, retains them locally, and creates indexes. Data is searchable, data from other agents is fetched, and data is made accessible to user queries and other brokers. Distributed architecture's benefits include less external traffic on the server where the gatherer is running and less work repetition thanks to the gatherer not having to send the same information to multiple brokers (Rau & Wan, 1994).

ACTIVITY 1.1:

How can a company ensure the security and confidentiality of sensitive data stored on a client/server system, while still allowing employees to access the data remotely from different locations?

1.6. ADVANCED DISTRIBUTED SYSTEM MODELS

Distributed systems save money compared to centralized ones. When redundancy is implemented, the system's availability is increased even if some components fail. A distributed system allows for the simultaneous execution of a large number of applications. Distributed systems are scalable, so adding more parts won't slow them down. In distributed computing, many different kinds of computers work together to complete a single task. As a result, distributed systems' response time and throughput are much faster than centralized ones (Dubey et al., 2020). Distributed systems also have the advantage of being very trustworthy. The distributed systems' high availability is a great advantage. These advantages have led to the rapid development and widespread deployment of various dispersed systems and applications. Clusters, grids, P2P networks, dispersed storage systems [ANDR02, BUYY99, IAN99, POUR05], and so on are all examples of well-known distributed computing systems. In addition, distributed systems built on top of mobile computing are taking shape (Chen et al., 2017).

The idea behind clustering is that many smaller machines can be grouped together to create a computing framework that could supply all necessary processing power for much less money. Depending on the needs of the users, a grid is a type of distributed system that enables coordinated expressing and aggregation of dispersed, heterogeneous resources. Grids are typically used to support new e-Science and e-Business application developments. Grid computing typically entails geographically dispersed communities working together to solve significant problems. Sharing resources like computers, data, software, and scientific tools is necessary to accomplish this. P2P networks are distributed, decentralized systems that enable using services like high-performance computing (HPC), instant messaging, internet telephony, and file-sharing. In communities that exchange files, peer-to-peer networking serves its most well-known purpose. P2P technology is also employed in remote storage sharing and the exploitation of idle desktop PC processing power. Users of distributed storage systems are given a unified view of data that is spread across various file systems and computers that may be connected to the same network or different networks (Choi & Kim, 2001).

1.7. SUMMARY

This chapter provides an overview of the concept of distributed systems, its importance, features, and challenges. The chapter begins by highlighting the need for distributed system planning and management due to the increasing demand for more powerful and reliable computing systems. The features of distributed systems, such as scalability, fault tolerance, and transparency, are discussed along with their associated challenges. The chapter also introduces the eight fallacies of distributed computing, which are common misconceptions that can lead to faulty system design and implementation. These fallacies include assumptions about network reliability, latency, and bandwidth, among others. The client/server computing model is explained, and its advantages and disadvantages are discussed. The chapter also highlights the WWW as an immense distributed system, and the challenges associated with managing such a complex system.

Finally, the chapter introduces advanced models of distributed systems, including peer-to-peer systems, grid computing, and cloud computing. The benefits and challenges of each of these models are discussed, providing the reader with a comprehensive overview of the field of distributed systems.

REVIEW QUESTIONS

1. What is a distributed system, and why is it essential to plan for one?
2. What are the primary features of distributed systems, and what are the challenges they present?
3. What are the eight fallacies of distributed computing, and how can they impact the design and operation of distributed systems?
4. What are the advantages and disadvantages of the client/server computing model in a distributed system?
5. How does the World Wide Web represent an immense distributed system, and what are the implications of its design for distributed system development?
6. What are some advanced models of distributed systems, and how do they address the challenges posed by traditional distributed systems.

MULTIPLE CHOICE QUESTIONS

1. What is a distributed system?

a. A system that operates on a single machine
b. A system that operates on multiple machines
c. A system that operates on a network of machines

d. A system that operates on a cloud

2. Why is planning important for distributed systems?

a. To ensure the system is scalable

b. To ensure the system is reliable

c. To ensure the system is secure

d. All of the above

3. Which of the following is a challenge in distributed systems?

a. Network latency

b. Security

c. Data consistency

d. All of the above

4. What are the eight fallacies of distributed computing?

a. Scalability, reliability, security, data consistency, latency, bandwidth, fault tolerance, heterogeneity

b. Security, data consistency, latency, bandwidth, fault tolerance, heterogeneity, scalability, reliability

c. Data consistency, latency, bandwidth, fault tolerance, heterogeneity, scalability, reliability, security

d. Fault tolerance, heterogeneity, scalability, reliability, security, data consistency, latency, bandwidth

5. What are the advantages of the client/server computing model?

a. Scalability

b. Centralized control

c. Reduced network traffic

d. All of the above

6. What are the disadvantages of the client/server computing model?

a. High cost

b. Single point of failure

c. Limited scalability

d. All of the above

7. Which of the following is an example of an immense distributed system?

a. Facebook

b. Amazon

c. Google

d. All of the above

8. What are the advanced models of distributed systems?

a. Peer-to-peer systems

b. Cloud computing

c. Internet of Things (IoT)

d. All of the above

Answers to Multiple Choice Questions

1. (b); 2. (d); 3. (d); 4. (c); 5. (d); 6. (d); 7. (d); 8. (d)

REFERENCES

1. Adler, R. M., (1995). Distributed coordination models for client/server computing. *Computer, 28*(4), 14–22.
2. Al Amri, H., Abolhasan, M., & Wysocki, T., (2010). Scalability of MANET routing protocols for heterogeneous and homogenous networks. *Computers & Electrical Engineering, 36*(4), 752–765.
3. Antamoshkin, O., Kukarcev, V., Pupkov, A., & Tsarev, R., (2014). Intellectual support system of administrative decisions in the big distributed geoinformation systems. In: *14th International Multidisciplinary Scientific Geo Conference SGEM 2014* (pp. 227–232).
4. Babay, A., Wagner, E., Dinitz, M., & Amir, Y., (2017). Timely, reliable, and cost-effective internet transport service using dissemination graphs. In: *2017 IEEE 37th International Conference on Distributed Computing Systems (ICDCS)* (Vol. 1, pp. 1–12). IEEE.
5. Baentsch, M., Baun, L., Molter, G., Rothkugel, S., & Sturn, P., (1997). World wide web caching: The application-level view of the Internet. *IEEE Communications Magazine, 35*(6), 170–178.
6. Barabási, A. L., Albert, R., & Jeong, H., (2000). Scale-free characteristics of random networks: The topology of the world-wide web. *Physica A: Statistical Mechanics and its Applications, 281*(1–4), 69–77.
7. Barker, P. P., & De Mello, R. W., (2000). Determining the impact of distributed generation on power systems. I. Radial distribution systems. In: *2000 Power Engineering Society Summer Meeting (Cat. No. 00CH37134)* (Vol. 3, pp. 1645–1656). IEEE.
8. Batten, S. R., (2001). Topology of interpenetration. *CrystEngComm, 3*(18), 67–72.
9. Beberg, A. L., Ensign, D. L., Jayachandran, G., Khaliq, S., & Pande, V. S., (2009). Folding@ home: Lessons from eight years of volunteer distributed computing. In: *2009 IEEE International Symposium on Parallel & Distributed Processing* (Vol. 1, pp. 1–8). IEEE.

10. Beschastnikh, I., Wang, P., Brun, Y., & Ernst, M. D., (2016). Debugging distributed systems. *Communications of the ACM, 59*(8), 32–37.
11. Bigo, S., (2019). A post-5G network to break the eight fallacies of distributed computing. In: *2019 Asia Communications and Photonics Conference (ACP)* (Vol. 1, pp. 1–3). IEEE.
12. Bredon, G. E., (2013). *Topology and Geometry* (Vol. 139, pp. 1–15). Springer Science & Business Media.
13. Chen, B., Chen, C., Wang, J., & Butler-Purry, K. L., (2017). Multi-time step service restoration for advanced distribution systems and microgrids. *IEEE Transactions on Smart Grid, 9*(6), 6793–6805.
14. Choi, J. H., & Kim, J. C., (2001). Advanced voltage regulation method of power distribution systems interconnected with dispersed storage and generation systems. *IEEE Transactions on Power Delivery, 16*(2), 329–334.
15. Chowdhury, A. A., Agarwal, S. K., & Koval, D. O., (2002). Reliability modeling of distributed generation in conventional distribution systems planning and analysis. In: *Conference Record of the 2002 IEEE Industry Applications Conference; 37th IAS Annual Meeting (Cat. No. 02CH37344)* (Vol. 2, pp. 1089–1094). IEEE.
16. Christofides, P. D., (2001). Control of nonlinear distributed process systems: Recent developments and challenges. *AIChE Journal, 47*(3), 514–518.
17. Deboosere, L., Simoens, P., De Wachter, J., Vankeirsbilck, B., De Turck, F., Dhoedt, B., & Demeester, P., (2011). Grid design for mobile thin client computing. *Future Generation Computer Systems, 27*(6), 681–693.
18. Doan, A., Ramakrishnan, R., & Halevy, A. Y., (2011). Crowdsourcing systems on the world-wide web. *Communications of the ACM, 54*(4), 86–96.
19. Dubey, A., Bose, A., Liu, M., & Ochoa, L. N., (2020). Paving the way for advanced distribution management systems applications: Making the most of models and data. *IEEE Power and Energy Magazine, 18*(1), 63–75.
20. Edwards, D., Simmons, S., & Wilde, N., (2006). An approach to feature location in distributed systems. *Journal of Systems and Software, 79*(1), 57–68.
21. El-Khattam, W., Hegazy, Y. G., & Salama, M. M. A., (2005). An integrated distributed generation optimization model for distribution system planning. *IEEE Transactions on Power Systems, 20*(2), 1158–1165.
22. Esfarjani, K., & Nof, S. Y., (1998). Client-server model of integrated production facilities. *International Journal of Production Research, 36*(12), 3295–3321.
23. Francalanza, A., Pérez, J. A., & Sánchez, C., (2018). *Runtime Verification for Decentralized and Distributed Systems* (Vol. 1, pp. 176–210). Springer International Publishing.
24. Ganguly, S., Sahoo, N. C., & Das, D., (2013). Recent advances on power distribution system planning: A state-of-the-art survey. *Energy Systems, 4*, 165–193.
25. Ghosh, P., Basu, K., & Das, S. K., (2007). A game theory-based pricing strategy to

support single/multiclass job allocation schemes for bandwidth-constrained distributed computing systems. *IEEE Transactions on Parallel and Distributed Systems, 18*(3), 289–306.

26. Gönen, T., & Ramirez-Rosado, I. J., (1986). Review of distribution system planning models: A model for optimal multistage planning. In: *IEE Proceedings C (Generation, Transmission and Distribution)* (Vol. 133, No. 7, pp. 397–408). IET Digital Library.
27. Iwanicki, K., (2018). A distributed systems perspective on industrial IoT. In: *2018 IEEE 38th International Conference on Distributed Computing Systems (ICDCS)* (Vol. 1, pp. 1164–1170). IEEE.
28. Jain, S., Kalambe, S., Agnihotri, G., & Mishra, A., (2017). Distributed generation deployment: State-of-the-art of distribution system planning in sustainable era. *Renewable and Sustainable Energy Reviews, 77*, 363–385.
29. Jing, J., Helal, A. S., & Elmagarmid, A., (1999). Client-server computing in mobile environments. *ACM Computing Surveys (CSUR), 31*(2), 117–157.
30. Kartik, S., & Murthy, C. S. R., (1997). Task allocation algorithms for maximizing reliability of distributed computing systems. *IEEE Transactions on Computers, 46*(6), 719–724.
31. Kim, T. E., & Kim, J. E., (2001). A method for determining the introduction limit of distributed generation system in distribution system. In: *2001 Power Engineering Society Summer Meeting. Conference Proceedings (Cat. No. 01CH37262)* (Vol. 1, pp. 456–461). IEEE.
32. Kumar, A., Jain, S., Naik, U., Raghuraman, A., Kasinadhuni, N., Zermeno, E. C., & Vahdat, A., (2015). BwE: Flexible, hierarchical bandwidth allocation for WAN distributed computing. In: *Proceedings of the 2015 ACM Conference on Special Interest Group on Data Communication* (Vol. 1, pp. 1–14).
33. Lai, A. M., & Nieh, J., (2006). On the performance of wide-area thin-client computing. *ACM Transactions on Computer Systems (TOCS), 24*(2), 175–209.
34. Lamport, L., (2019). Time, clocks, and the ordering of events in a distributed system. In: *Concurrency: The Works of Leslie Lamport* (Vol. 1, pp. 179–196).
35. Langville, A. N., & Meyer, C. D., (2005). A survey of eigenvector methods for web information retrieval. *SIAM Review, 47*(1), 135–161.
36. Lavorato, M., Rider, M. J., Garcia, A. V., & Romero, R., (2010). A constructive heuristic algorithm for distribution system planning. *IEEE Transactions on Power Systems, 25*(3), 1734–1742.
37. Leonini, L., Rivière, É., & Felber, P., (2009). SPLAY: Distributed systems evaluation made simple. In: *Proceedings of the 6th USENIX Symposium on Networked Systems Design and Implementation* (Vol. 1, pp. 185–198).
38. Lewandowski, S. M., (1998). Frameworks for component-based client/server computing. *ACM Computing Surveys (CSUR), 30*(1), 3–27.
39. Liu, J., Gao, H., Ma, Z., & Li, Y., (2015). Review and prospect of active distribution

system planning. *Journal of Modern Power Systems and Clean Energy, 3*(4), 457–467.

40. Lotero, R. C., & Contreras, J., (2011). Distribution system planning with reliability. *IEEE Transactions on Power Delivery, 26*(4), 2552–2562.
41. Naderi, E., Seifi, H., & Sepasian, M. S., (2012). A dynamic approach for distribution system planning considering distributed generation. *IEEE Transactions on Power Delivery, 27*(3), 1313–1322.
42. Oluwatosin, H. S., (2014). Client-server model. *IOSR Journal of Computer Engineering, 16*(1), 67–71.
43. Rau, N. S., & Wan, Y. H., (1994). Optimum location of resources in distributed planning. *IEEE Transactions on Power Systems, 9*(4), 2014–2020.
44. Reisizadeh, A., & Pedarsani, R., (2017). Latency analysis of coded computation schemes over wireless networks. In: *2017 55th Annual Allerton Conference on Communication, Control, and Computing (Allerton)* (Vol. 1, pp. 1256–1263). IEEE.
45. Rodden, T., & Blair, G., (1991). CSCW and distributed systems: The problem of control. In: *ECSCW 1991: Proceedings of the Second European Conference on Computer Supported Cooperative Work* (Vol. 12, pp. 77–85). Kluwer Academic Publishers, Dordrecht, The Netherlands.
46. Ruffer, S. M., Yen, D., & Lee, S., (1995). Client/server computing technology: A framework for feasibility analysis and implementation. *International Journal of Information Management, 15*(2), 135–150.
47. Shi, J. Y., (2016). OSI standards and the top fallacy of distributed computing. In: *2016 45th International Conference on Parallel Processing Workshops (ICPPW)* (Vol. 1, pp. 356–364). IEEE.
48. Shrivastava, S. K., Ezhilchelvan, P. D., Speirs, N. A., Tao, S., & Tully, A., (1991). Principal features of the VOLTAN family of reliable node architectures for distributed systems. *Computing Laboratory Technical Report Series, 1*, 1–12.
49. Shukur, H., Zeebaree, S. R., Ahmed, A. J., Zebari, R. R., Ahmed, O., Tahir, B. S. A., & Sadeeq, M. A., (2020). A state of art survey for concurrent computation and clustering of parallel computing for distributed systems. *Journal of Applied Science and Technology Trends, 1*(4), 148–154.
50. Singh, A., Srivatsa, M., Liu, L., & Miller, T., (2004). Apoidea: A decentralized peer-to-peer architecture for crawling the world wide web. In: *Distributed Multimedia Information Retrieval: SIGIR 2003 Workshop on Distributed Information Retrieval, Toronto, Canada, August 1, 2003. Revised Selected and Invited Papers* (Vol. 1, pp. 126–142). Springer Berlin Heidelberg.
51. Sinha, A., (1992). Client-server computing. *Communications of the ACM, 35*(7), 77–98.
52. Umbrich, J., Gutierrez, C., Hogan, A., Karnstedt, M., & Parreira, J. X., (2013). Eight fallacies when querying the web of data. In: *2013 IEEE 29th International Conference on Data Engineering Workshops (ICDEW)* (Vol.1, pp. 21, 22). IEEE.
53. Wang, G., Yu, J., & Xie, Q., (2012). Security analysis of a single sign-on mechanism

for distributed computer networks. *IEEE Transactions on Industrial Informatics, 9*(1), 294–302.

54. Xue, D., & Xu, Y., (2003). Web-based distributed system and database modeling for concurrent design. *Computer-Aided Design, 35*(5), 433–452.
55. Yan, L., & Chen, C., (1999). Jam: High performance internet computing with massive java applets. In: *Proceedings 19th IEEE International Conference on Distributed Computing Systems; Workshops on Electronic Commerce and Web-based Applications. Middleware* (Vol. 1, pp. 3–8). IEEE.
56. Yang, S. J., Nieh, J., Selsky, M., & Tiwari, N., (2002). The performance of remote display mechanisms for thin-client computing. In: *USENIX Annual Technical Conference, General Track* (Vol. 1, pp. 131–146).
57. Zhao, L., Wang, J., & Huang, R., (2015). Immunization against the spread of rumors in homogenous networks. *PloS One, 10*(5), 124978.

CHAPTER 2

DESIGN PATTERNS OF DISTRIBUTED SYSTEMS

UNIT INTRODUCTION

Introduced in the 1990s, design patterns "provide straightforward and sophisticated answers to precise challenges in OOP design. These patterns document how solutions have changed and advanced over time. Therefore, they are not the first designs that people usually come up with. They result from countless redesign and recoding efforts made by developers as they battled for more software flexibility and reuse. These solutions are succinctly and captured by design patterns" (Babaoglu et al., 2006).

It is a graphical presentation of a common coding issue together with a resolution that has been proven to be efficient and reliable. These patterns are often offered within an OOP framework, despite the fact that the concept is generic and may be applied to a variety of different programming models. A design pattern consists of various components. The three that are more crucial are the pattern's name, a description of the issue it seeks to address, and a description of the remedy. Other things like the pattern's typical application, the results attained by applying it, and the pattern's inspirations are also included (Schmidt, 1996). Therefore, unlike algorithmic skeletons, design patterns themselves are not programming constructs. Instead, they can be thought of as "instructions" that can be followed to solve common programming difficulties effectively.

Standard design patterns include those that are often used in a variety of OO applications, including:

- **Iterator Pattern:** The iterator pattern provides a way to access items in a collection sequentially. It is a commonly used design pattern that simplifies the traversal of data structures. More complex patterns may also be used for this purpose.
- **Mediator Pattern:** The mediator pattern captures interactions between a group of coworker objects. It is a design pattern that defines an object that encapsulates how a set of objects interact. This helps to reduce the coupling between the objects (Uzunov et al., 2012).
- **Proxy Pattern:** The proxy pattern facilitates regional access to far-off services. It is a design pattern that allows for the use of a surrogate object that controls access to another object.
- **Strategy Pattern:** The strategy pattern offers techniques for transparently choosing the optimal service provider while encapsulating a group of related services. It is a design pattern that allows for the encapsulation of algorithms and their selection at runtime.
- **Observer Pattern:** The observer pattern is used to structure asynchronous, event-based applications. It is a design pattern that defines a one-to-many dependency between objects so that when one object changes state, all its dependents are notified and updated automatically.
- **Facade Design:** The Facade design offers a streamlined interface to a complex code/class ensemble. It is a design pattern that provides a simplified interface to a larger body of code or a complex system (Steiner & Rushby, 2011).

In general, a programmer who uses design patterns to organize the application's sequential skeleton will create more reliable and manageable code than a programmer who uses a more conventional, non-design pattern-based OO approach. Only a few patterns are discussed in the initial study mentioned in Gamma's book. The effectiveness of expanding the design pattern collection to include ever-more specialized patterns is up for discussion. This circumstance is very similar to one that was discovered in the bones of the community a few years ago. Some authors asserted that concentrated skeletons should be used to model application-dependent parallelism exploitation patterns. However, skeleton designers acknowledged that just a handful of frameworks might be used to simulate a wide range of parallel applications (Eckert et al., 2012).

Recently, certain problems with design patterns have been raised, but there is still no clear consensus on the matter. For example, should design patterns be turned into coding languages? Should they encourage the adoption of tools that give programmers access to "faster" and more effective OO coding environments? Once more, what happened in the skeleton community is similar to this. Following Cole's work, it was unclear whether skeletons should have been made available as language constructs or if their only purpose should have been to enforce a solid, parallel coding methodology (Pizlo et al., 2004) (Figure 2.1).

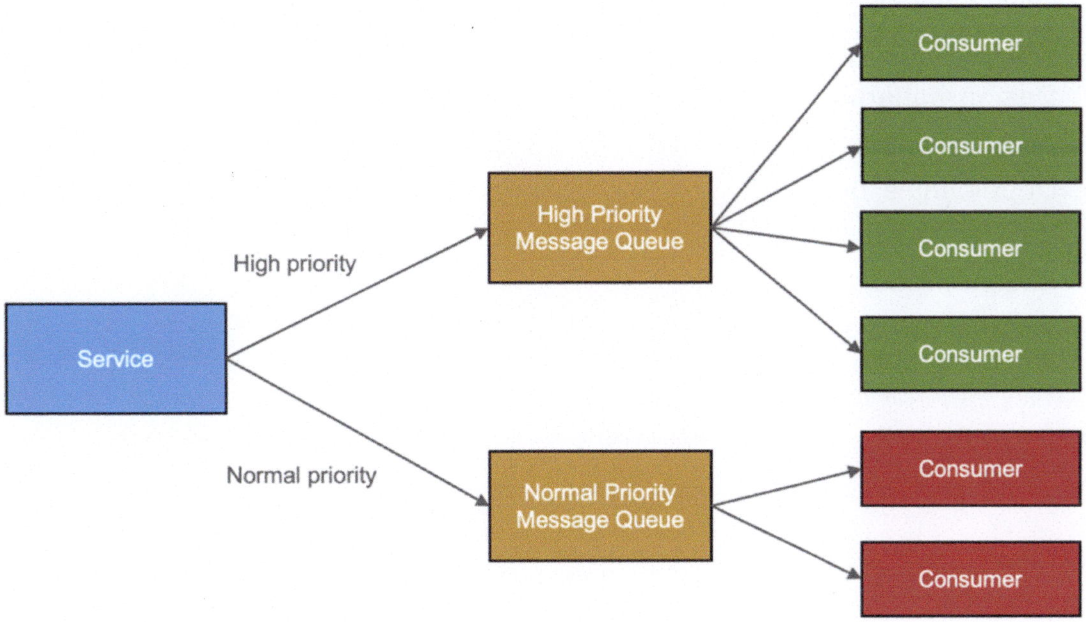

Figure 2.1. Illustration of distributed system design patterns.

Source: Irfan Muhammad, Creative Commons License.

Learning Objectives

At the end of this chapter, the reader will be able to understand:

- The importance of design patterns in distributed systems;
- The concept of parallel design patterns and how to find concurrency design space;
- The algorithm structure design space for parallel design patterns;
- The concept of skeleton design in distributed systems;
- The Cole manifesto principles and their significance in distributed systems design;
- How to propagate a concept with minimal conceptual disruption;
- How to integrate ad-hoc parallelism and accommodate diversity in distributed systems design;
- The importance of showing the payback in distributed systems design;
- Sample template mechanisms such as double/triple buffering, time server, and channel name server.

Key Terms

- Ad-Hoc parallelism
- Channel name server

- Cole manifesto principles
- Cross-skeleton templates
- Design patterns
- Distributed systems
- Double/triple buffering
- Parallel design patterns
- Skeleton design
- Template design

2.1. PARALLEL DESIGN PATTERNS

With the same objectives as design patterns, namely, to define solutions to recurrent issues in the context of interest, parallel design patterns have been presented. Instead of straightforward object-oriented software design, the context relevant in this case is parallel program design (Keutzer & Mattson, 2009).

Similar to how traditional design patterns were presented, a parallel layout pattern is described using a certain set of components, notably:

- **Problem** – what has to be fixed?
- **Context** – the situation in which the pattern would be most appropriate to use.
- **Forces** – the various characteristics affecting the alternating pattern design.
- **Solution** – an explanation of any number of potential answers to the issue the pattern resolves (Adams, 2015).

Examples of parallel design patterns include divide-and-conquer, pipeline, and master-worker, which each address a common issue with parallelism exploitation: how to implement recursive, divide-and-conquer, staged efficiently, and computations split into several distinct tasks.

TIPS

Parallel design patterns can improve the performance of distributed systems by dividing tasks into smaller, independent parts that can be executed simultaneously.

To generate structured parallel coding frameworks that are very similar to algorithmic skeleton ones, parallel design patterns have been used. This has resulted in a significant amount of research activity, which has ultimately led to the realization that parallel patterns may be a key component in the solution of issues about the creation of effective parallel software (Siu et al., 1996).

2.1.1. Design Spaces with Parallel Design Patterns

The division of a parallel application's design space into four distinct but connected design spaces is one of the most intriguing parts of parallel design patterns, as explained in:

- The establishment of the parallelism design space, which comprises parallel design patterns that describe the numerous parallel and simultaneous operation structures that may be effectively deployed in a parallel program.

- The development of a concurrency design space analysis tool.
- The design space for algorithms incorporates parallel design patterns, which are used for designing recurrent parallel algorithm patterns.
- The supporting framework design space incorporates the parallel design pattern, which can be used to apply the algorithmic patterns from the earlier design space. This pattern is included in the preceding design space.
- At some point in the future, the design space for the methods of implementation will include patterns that are representations of the underlying techniques that are used to construct a parallel application (Huda et al., 2015).

The first two design spaces, which they referred to as the "concurrent activity graph" definition and design, correspond to the "implementation" of the synchronized activity graph, according to our algorithmic framework.

The "separation of concerns" implicitly assumed between the developers using the parallel patterns is the basis for the significance of this design space structuring: application developers, who are supposed to be using the parallel patterns to find synchronized and algorithm structure design spaces, will only use their application-specific area expertise to determine the best combination of high-level patterns for modeling parallelism misuse in the application at hand (Danelutto et al., 2021).

Additionally, no understanding of the underlying target architecture is necessary for this process. Then, to properly implement the patterns used at the higher level by the application developers, the system developers—may take advantage of patterns in the supporting structure and operation mechanisms spaces. This is a reflection of the algorithmic framework world, where users of the applications essentially employ pre-defined frameworks that the system developers are responsible for effectively implementing into the target architecture (MacDonald et al., 2000).

2.1.2. Finding Concurrency Design Space

After thinking through the issue that must be handled with the application and identifying the most computationally intensive areas that need parallelization, one can utilize the patterns in the "finding concurrency design space" to begin creating a parallel application (Jahr et al., 2015). In this area, there are three major categories of patterns. One of them, the design evaluation pattern, is related to the fact that the "finding concurrency" space is such that a solution is frequently found iterating with different steps through the decomposition and dependency analysis patterns. The other two are related to how to implement the parallel application (Rajan et al., 2010).

The decomposition patterns involve only two patterns:

- **Task Decomposition Pattern:** These models how a complex application is broken up into some tasks that can be carried out simultaneously (Lu & Ito, 1999).
- **Data Decomposition Pattern:** These simulates how the input data are broken up into subsets that can be individually computed to get the outcome.

These patterns' design is primarily influenced by three factors: adaptability, efficiency, and simplicity. To adjust the application design to various implementation needs, flexibility is required. They are aiming for efficient parallel application development; hence efficiency is required. Not least, simplicity is necessary to encourage app developers to employ patterns in their parallel applications: overly complex patterns lack the appeal necessary to persuade application programmers that they are worthwhile for usage and exploitation (Gursoy, 2004). Three distinct patterns are included in the dependency analysis patterns:

- **Order Tasks:** The pattern of order tasks provides guidelines for arranging tasks or task groups in a manner that meets application constraints related to task execution.
- **Group Tasks Pattern:** The group tasks pattern is intended to represent the grouping of tasks in a way that makes it easier to manage dependencies between them.
- **Data Sharing Pattern:** The data sharing pattern is designed to represent access to a shared data structure.

For example, let's take a closer look at one of these patterns, the order task pattern, which is less clear than the decomposition patterns set. It seeks to identify dependencies within those groups of tasks to establish the order in which the groups of tasks should be completed (Lee & Zomaya, 2006). The final output of the "finding concurrency" design space study is a breakdown of the issue into many design components, including:

- A task decomposition identifying the tasks that can be conducted simultaneously;
- A data decomposition identifying the data local to each of the tasks;
- A method of grouping tasks and ordering the tasks groups in such a way that temporal and data dependencies are satisfied; and
- A study of the tasks' interdependencies (Vogel et al., 2011).

2.1.3. Algorithm Structure Design Space

The results from the "finding concurrency" design space is used in the "algorithm structure design space" to improve our parallel application's design and determine a parallel program structure that is more akin to an actual parallel program and suitable for execution on a parallel target architecture (Rasheed et al., 1997).

A parallel algorithm can be organized in three main ways:

- By task, which considers the tasks as the fundamental units to be computed concurrently or in parallel within the parallel algorithm;
- By data decomposition, which considers the division of data into subsets as the fundamental units to be processed concurrently or in parallel within the parallel algorithm; or
- The flow of data takes the algorithm's defined data to flow into consideration.

There are three different approaches to set up the parallel algorithm. The application developers are expected to walk through each group of patterns in the "finding concurrency" design space. However, in this case, the programmer must select one of the three options and utilize a parallel design pattern from the group (Bergeretti & Carré, 1985) (Figure 2.2).

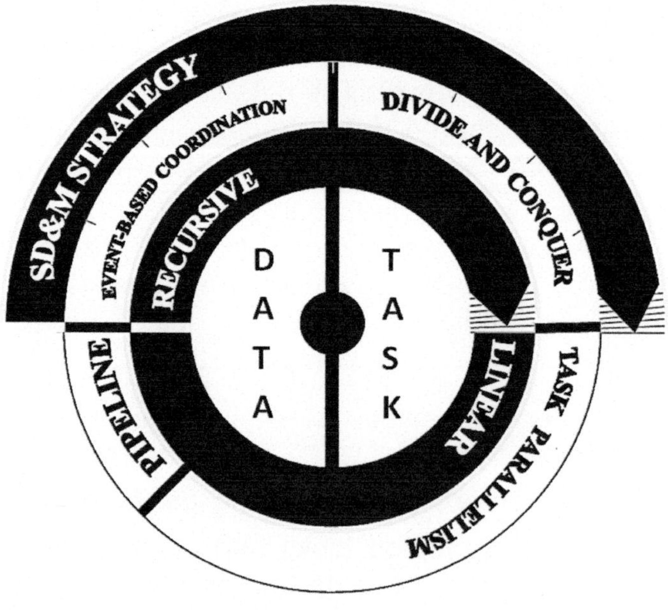

Figure 2.2. Schematic of algorithm structure of design space.

Source: Ramzi Mahmoudi, Creative Commons License.

The organize by Tasks pattern group includes two patterns:

- The task parallelism pattern, which controls the effective execution of groups of tasks. The suggested method for putting the pattern into practice addresses three main issues: the definition of the jobs, their interdependencies, and their scheduling for concurrent execution (Kambadur et al., 2009).

- The well-known split and dominate recursive solution schema use the divide and conquer pattern.

The organize by data decomposition pattern group comprises two patterns:

- **Geometric Decomposition Pattern:** This pattern which models computations that have a specific "geometric shape" of concurrent administrators. This pattern defines the parallel algorithm by identifying the type of computation(s) performed on the shape objects (Dighe & Jakiela, 1995).
- **Recursive Data Pattern:** It is a software design pattern that facilitates the representation of hierarchical or tree-like data structures. It involves defining a data structure in terms of itself, allowing for the creation of nested or recursive data types. This pattern is commonly used in programming languages to create tree-like structures, such as directories or nested lists. The Recursive Data pattern helps to simplify the representation and manipulation of complex data structures (Keim et al., 1995).

The organize by the flow of data pattern group also includes two patterns:

- The pipeline pattern, in which data flows through a sequence of linear stages, each of which represents a function that processes input data from the previous stage and passes it on to the next stage.
- Event-based coordination, which handles irregular interactions between semi-independent concurrent tasks that are caused by the data flow between them.

For example, in order to fix the concepts, let's analyze more in detail the "recursive data" pattern. The **problem** solved by the pattern is the implementation of (efficient and parallel) operations over recursively defined data structures (Ferrari et al., 2008). The context includes any and all situations in which data from a continuously built data structure (such as a tree or list, for example) is handled in its entirety or in segments Tree structured data, as an example, may be processed to obtain a new data tree with all the nodes/leaves substituted by the result of a function *f* applied to the old nodes/leaves. They also have the option of employing a pre-fix method to conduct an iterative search through the data's tree structure in order to locate a particular node. When attempting to describe this pattern, there are a few things that need to be kept in mind that could potentially cause confusion (Fjellheim et al., 2007). The two that stand out the most are the dimensioning of the concurrent activities that are utilized for recurrent data processing, where, for example, the depth of the tree may be unknown and not computable until the end of the computation; and data representation, where typically pointers are used; these are not very portable nor is it practical to use them for parallel processing of all the items in the data structure because, for example, following pointers is typically a fairly sequential process. The design of the pattern is influenced by a variety of different forces. They have to first think about the problem of how the data will be represented. They are required to construct a reliable representation that is capable of being applied in parallel processing. There is a possibility that the representation for the recursive data structure used in sequential programming is different from this one. Even if the addition and deletion of members could need more complicated implementations, for example, a list could be represented as a vector rather than the more usual linked list data structure in order to allow for concurrent item accesses (Dumas et al., 2005). This would allow for concurrent item access to the list's items. Second, they need to make sure that the data representation is easy to understand and keep up to date, in addition to being useful for parallel processing. The pattern can be solved by breaking the computation of the pattern into several stages, the most notable of which are:

- **Data Decomposition:** The data is dissected and restructured to make it more suited for the pattern's processing.
- **Structure:** This determine what sort of "collective"-and-parallel-operation should be applied to the outputs of the data decomposition, perhaps in a loop, to compute the anticipated results.
- **Synchronization:** This determines the type of synchronization required to put the (loop of) group actions leading to the outcome into action (Bengtsson & Lennartson, 2014) (Figure 2.3).

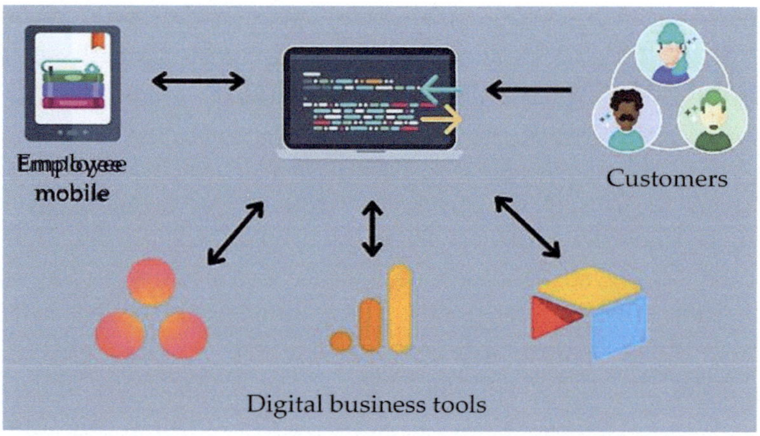

Figure 2.3. Image of data synchronization.

Source: Luna Campas, Creative Commons License.

Take into consideration the challenge of generating a "reduce" using an operator on top of a binary tree. The tree can be broken down into subtrees, each of which is rooted at a certain level l, and then the "reduce" operation can be carried out in parallel on each of the subtrees. This is one way. This process consists of three stages: decomposing the data, applying the structure, and synchronizing the results. During the process of decomposing the data, the sub-tree vector will be extracted from the primary tree. During the phase where the structure is being applied, the reduction is applied concurrently to each of the subtrees. In the final stage of the process, known as the synchrony phase, the processing of the subtree reduces is finished before the computation of the root reduce (Yale et al., 1999).

2.2. SKELETON DESIGN

A parametric, reusable, and portable programming abstraction known as an algorithmic skeleton model a well-known, widespread, and effective parallelism exploitation pattern. They may deduce the guiding principles for the selection and creation of new skeletons from this concept:

- Parallelism misuse patterns should be sought out. This indicates that parallelism is the main topic, that the type of parallelism modeled must be specifically specified and documented, and that the pattern must differ from the patterns already modeled by other previously defined skeletons or by a composite of the previously defined framework.
- It is recommended to make use of a parametric skeleton. If a sufficient set of functional and/or nonfunctional parameters is provided, then it ought to be possible to specialize the framework. In particular, all computations must be able to be expressed using the same framework by merely instantiating it with different parameters, despite the fact that these computations may differ in characteristics that are unrelated to determining the parallelism misuse approach that is being applied (Cole, 1999).
- The framework should be reusable; it should be possible to simulate a range of circumstances, possibly even in application domains other than the one in which it was originally designed to be utilized. If there are only one or two situations in which the framework can be used to model parallelism misuse, then including it in the framework set is not worthwhile unless it turns out to be the only way to model that particular situation, and the limited situations in which it can be used cover very communal app cases. In that case, including it is worthwhile.
- The fundamental category of parallel architectures needs to have implementations, and those implementations need to be effective, despite the fact that effects may be defined differently for each design. The

new skeleton must be easily transportable and productive. Keep in mind that they are describing a new skeleton, which is a word that might be considered rather abstract. However, portability and efficiency are ultimately aspects that pertain to the implementation. The most important thing for them to be able to do here is to visualize how a new framework can be efficiently implemented on a variety of different target architectures. This is done to prevent a scenario in which they have a highly beautiful "instruction set" — the algorithmic framework set (Caromel & Leyton, 2007).

- As a final but essential step, the new framework should encapsulate a typical parallelism exploiting scheme. They have to make some differences in this particular scenario. When making a new skeleton, what they are looking for are common patterns that are parallel to one another. On the other hand, the adverb "common" can be utilized in a number of different contexts and settings. They have the option of defining "common" as "appearing in a wide range of different applications from different application domains," or they can eliminate the requirement for "different application domains" while keeping the remainder of the statement the same (Rieger et al., 2019). They will have genuine algorithmic skeletons if the first scenario plays out. In the latter, they will have extra framework sets that are specific to their domain. In principle, it would be beneficial for research and development to make use of real and domain-specific skeleton sets. They are obligated to call attention to the fact that the aims behind the development of a number of the skeletal frameworks that have been developed in the past (or that are still being maintained) were, at the very least, "domain specific": For example, MALLBA and Skipper have been developed as tools to assist in the process of algorithm construction for optimization purposes (Danelutto et al., 2021).

Remember

A well-designed skeleton is the foundation for a strong and beautiful structure.

2.3. COLE MANIFESTO PRINCIPLES

Cole outlines four ideas that "should guide the design and creation of skeletal programming systems" in his algorithmic skeleton "manifesto" (p. 38). These systems might be interpreted as guiding principles that specify the requirements for the skeletons that must ultimately be present in the skeleton set given to the app programmer. Here, the Cole principles are recalled, and their influence on the skeleton design process is discussed (Cole, 2004).

2.3.1. Propagate the Concept with Minimal Conceptual Disruption

In software design patterns, "Propagate the Concept with Minimal Conceptual Disruption" is often referred to as the "Bridge pattern." The Bridge pattern is used to separate abstraction from its implementation so that both can be modified independently without affecting the other. The goal is to propagate changes to the system with minimal disruption to the existing code. To achieve this, the Bridge pattern uses a "bridge" interface that separates the abstract and concrete parts of the system, allowing them to vary independently. This technique can be used to introduce new features or changes to a system while minimizing the impact on the existing code. The Bridge pattern is commonly used in situations where there are multiple implementations of a system or where changes to the system are expected in the future. By using the Bridge pattern, changes can be propagated with minimal disruption, reducing the likelihood of errors or bugs in the system (Pickett et al., 1989) (Figure 2.4).

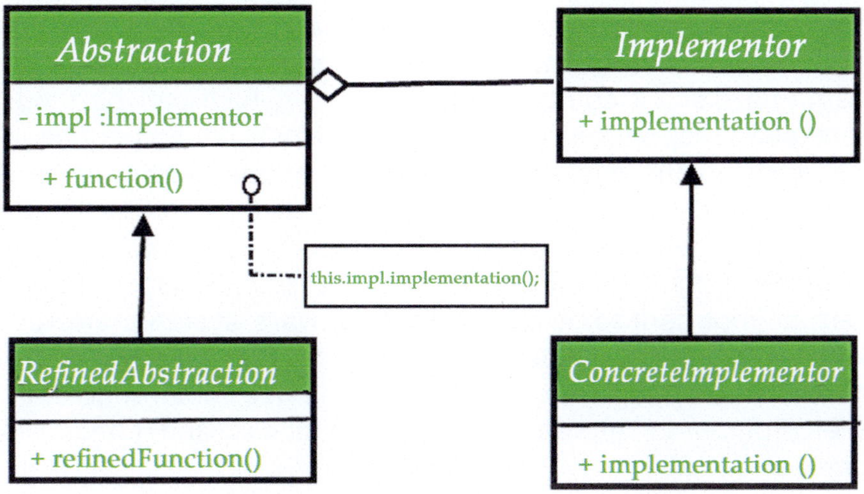

Figure 2.4. Flow diagram of bridge pattern design.

Source: Geeks for Geeks, Creative Commons License.

2.3.2. Integrate Ad-Hoc Parallelism

The "Integrate Ad-Hoc Parallelism" design pattern is used to introduce parallelism into a system or application without requiring a complete redesign. This pattern involves identifying tasks or processes that can be executed in parallel and modifying the system to support parallel execution.

Ad-hoc parallelism can be achieved by dividing the tasks into smaller sub-tasks that can be executed independently, utilizing multi-threading or multi-processing techniques to execute tasks in parallel. The pattern also involves ensuring that the system is able to handle parallel execution, such as by avoiding race conditions, deadlocks, and other synchronization issues. Introducing ad-hoc parallelism can improve the performance and scalability of a system, but it requires careful consideration of the system's architecture and design. When applied correctly, the Integrate Ad-Hoc Parallelism pattern can provide significant benefits, such as reduced processing time, improved resource utilization, and increased system throughput (Karimov et al., 2019).

Did you Know?

The Cole Manifesto Principles have had a profound impact on the development of computer science and the internet, promoting openness, freedom, and the sharing of information for the betterment of society.

2.3.3. Accommodate Diversity

The "Accommodate Diversity" design pattern is used to handle diversity in software systems. Diversity can arise from differences in hardware, software, user preferences, and other factors. The pattern involves designing the system to accommodate these differences and ensure that it works effectively across a range of environments. This can be achieved through a variety of techniques, such as abstraction, modularity, and configuration. Abstraction involves separating the system into distinct components or layers, which can be modified or replaced independently (Burke et al., 1998). Modularity involves breaking down the system into smaller, independent components that can be easily interchanged. Configuration involves designing the system to be easily configurable so that it can adapt to different environments and user preferences. The Accommodate Diversity pattern is important for ensuring that software systems are robust, scalable, and maintainable. By accommodating diversity, software systems can be adapted to meet the needs of a wide range of users and environments, increasing their usefulness and effectiveness (Ferrier et al., 2007).

2.3.4. Show the Payback

This principle has more to do with the overall skeleton set's design. However, to create a skeleton for skeletons that can "show the payback" to the end user, they should only include new skeletons that:

- They must be high-level, which means they should not include implementation-dependent details;
- They must be simpler to use, which implies that they should be integrated with the general coding framework in a way that is not noticeable.
- They must also apply to various well-known situations and application fields (Kist et al., 2015).

2.3.5. Looking for (New) Skeletons

This section takes a look at a method that may be used to both find and create new skeletons. They will differentiate between two different scenarios: the first one will be based on an analysis of currently active programs that are operating in parallel, and the second one will be based on the specific requirements of a user who is developing a particular app. The second version is essentially an adaption of the first, but it uses a different input or beginning point (Angelsky et al., 2014).

2.3.5.1. Analysis

In this instance, the plan is to scour already-running parallel apps for new skeletons. As a result, the process could be described as follows:

- They choose whether to examine applications from many application domains or just one. The process will probably end with individuating new general-purpose skeletons in the first scenario. In contrast, it will probably end with the individuation of domain-specific skeletons in the second scenario. In both situations, they choose many programs whose source code is available and/or whose parallel method is understandable (Delerue et al., 1999).
- They "distill" the parallel patterns utilized to express and model parallelism from the application individuated in the preceding phase. Some form of "reverse engineering" of the code may be necessary for this task. To avoid going through vast volumes of source code, it may occasionally be necessary to receive assistance from the program designers. It must be remembered that in typical parallel apps, the parallel structure of the application is not exposed "per se," so to reconstruct the high-level parallel structure of the app, they must look at the mechanisms used to implement parallelism misuse (Ge & Fitzpatrick, 1996).
- From the frameworks that were distilled in the previous step and do not have a corresponding skeleton in the collection of frameworks that are currently available, they choose the candidate's new framework.
- They conduct a thorough investigation of the potential new skeletons. They focus on determining whether each new candidate skeleton is,

in fact, equal to a composition of other, newer, and simpler skeletons (Torres et al., 2004). If these more basic skeletons model significant parallel patterns, they should be considered for inclusion in the skeleton collection. If the newly individuated frameworks cannot be further decomposed, they examine if the newly individuated framework fits each of the criteria from Cole's manifesto or the algorithmic skeleton definition mentioned at the end of the preceding section. They continue to improve the new skeleton. They create the name, syntax, parameter set, and semantics for the skeleton. They consider both module, non-module, and optional parameters that may be used to distinguish the parallel framework pattern further when designing the framework parameter set. As is customary when defining semantics, they include both functional and parallel semantics (Jang & Chin, 1990).

2.3.5.2. Synthesis

The plan, in this instance, is to move forward with the definition of new skeletons by beginning with the unique requirements of an application developer attempting to implement a particular parallel application. When confirmed that a pattern that is important and beneficial for executing the parallel application under consideration cannot be defined by any of the current skeletons or by a combination of the existing frameworks, the process begins. Then, they carry on as follows:

- They conduct an analytical phase similar to the one described in Procedure Point 4 of the preceding section (Clarke & Emerson, 1982).
- Then, they search for additional scenarios in which such a skeleton might be applied. To identify the parallel application patterns, they, therefore, employ a technique similar to that described in points 1 and 2 of the procedure described in Section 7.2.1. They then search for equal or "similar" patterns. They move on to the new pattern design phase if many scenarios are identified where the new pattern may be employed (as is or significantly changed), but if not, they stop here.
- The next describes the new skeleton name, syntax, arguments, and semantics after further refining the skeleton definition and considering the demands indicated by the additional scenarios in which the new pattern might ultimately be employed (Thummalapenta et al., 2011).

2.4. TEMPLATE DESIGN

An implementation template is a specialized skeleton implemented on a certain target architecture. The "system programmer" is the person who creates an implementation template. Although they will never use the template directly, the application programmer will be its final user. Instead, they will utilize an algorithmic skeleton, which will ultimately be implemented by the compiler tools (and/or the runtime) of the algorithmic skeleton framework through an instantiation of the template (Wu & Tsai, 1992).

A system coder must possess several types of "system" expertise throughout the many stages of template design.

- Alternative template options should first be identified. The system programmer must be aware of the specific semantics of the parallel pattern that the skeleton models to implement the target skeleton effectively using any of these choices. The target architecture's mechanisms and opportunities will ultimately be used by these alternatives; thus, the system programmer should also be an expert programmer of that architecture. Consider the design of a reduced skeleton implementation on a comprehensive interconnection architecture, for instance. Two options may be taken into account:
  - A tree-structured process/thread network in which each node computes a reduction of the results supplied by the children nodes (Figure 2.5).

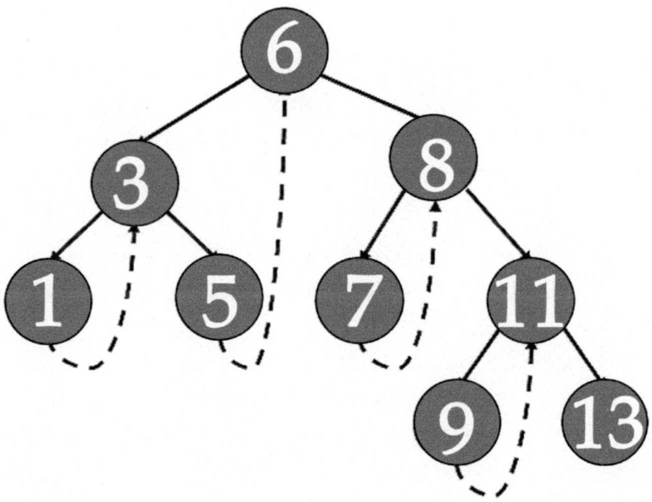

Figure 2.5. Example of threaded binary tree.

Source: Geeks for Geeks, Creative Commons License.

- A series of workers locally information technology the reduction of a portion of the initial information and provide the regional result to one node, and subsequently computing the worldwide result of the reduce (González & Fraguela, 2010).
- Next, a performance model must be created to capture the characteristics of the template that relate to performance before going on to the design of the template implementation. The performance model under

consideration here is abstract because the template's implementation has not yet begun. Nevertheless, it must consider the "kind" of mechanisms employed on the target architecture and their average costs) (Staunton, 1996).

- The options need to be assessed using the performance modeling created in the previous stage. The evaluation process's outcome will determine whether there is only one "better" implementation alternative, in which case it will be the only one taken into consideration for actual implementation, or whether there are several alternatives with comparable performance metrics, in which case they could all be taken into consideration for implementation. The "tree" template is more suited for computationally expensive computations, while the other one is better suited for "light" computations and more reliable communication times, according to these performance models. In light of these findings, they should maintain both options because depending on the volume of the input data, the amount of time required for communications, and reduced operator computation, the first option may be preferable to the second or vice versa (Zhang & Wang, 1996).
- The template interface needs to be created before the actual implementation of the template, i.e., the coding step can begin. The compiling tools will eventually have access to this interface. The template interface helps the skeleton framework compiler tools define the "assembler" target. The interface should therefore be complex enough to offer the compiler tools some latitude in how they use the template while still being straightforward enough to avoid using complicated compiler algorithms. The majority of this phase is concerned with the appropriate design of the template instantiation parameters, keeping in mind that an implementation template is a parametric process (thread) network, e.g., the number of parallel processing elements employed in both scenarios can be specified using parameters in the case of reduction templates. The parameters should also contain the computation (the code) and the data types of processes (the type of the operator alpha, which is:).
- The actual application of the template constitutes the final stage of template design. The target architecture's tools and procedures are best utilized to generate an implementation of the template (Li et al., 2011).

2.4.1. Template Building Blocks

A target architecture implementation template is never created as a single monolithic unit. Typically, they create an implementation template by assembling a few template components. These building blocks for templates include:

- Analyze networks with the specified topologies;
- Thread sets that exhibit a specific behavior (such as producer/consumer configurations);
- Infrastructures for communications;
- Configurations of shared state;
- Infrastructures for synchronization.

The likelihood of implementing effective, accurate, and usable templates is significantly increased by the availability of efficient template building blocks for a specific target architecture that covers all aspects of setting up concurrent activities and synchronization and communication handling (Davis et al., 2001).

In general, existing knowledge about implementing non-structured parallel applications is used as much as possible when developing a template. This allows us to capitalize on already achieved achievements and prevents us from repeatedly trying to achieve the same outcomes. To demonstrate how current results may be utilized in creating an implementation template for skeletons, they will explore three basic template-building pieces in this section. To implement other types of skeletons, these three strategies may be combined with others (McCallien & Sanders, 1995).

2.4.1.1. Client-Server Paradigm

A server offers a variety of services to a group of clients that request them through correctly worded service requests in a client-server paradigm. The client-server paradigm permeates both networking and computer science. To give a few instances, the DNS, NFS, Email, and the entire Web are all constructed using the client-server paradigm.

In general, the queuing theory may be used to model the performance of a client-server system (Sidhu et al., 2003).

According to our viewpoint, the client-server paradigm is beneficial for simulating interactions between parts of a process template. As they have already mentioned, the interactions between some worker processes and a collector process that gathers the workers' output can be seen as a client-server paradigm, with the workers acting as clients and the collection process as the server. In a dual sense, the relationship between a task scheduler and a series of workers doing the planned tasks can be seen as a client-server paradigm, with the scheduler acting as the client concerning a group of workers who stand in for the servers.

In this case, more recent push/pull client-server system variations might also be considered. The pull paradigm is the traditional client-server model. In this scenario, the client messages the server with a service request, and the server replies with the service outcome. Therefore, the server activities are started by the client (Ismail et al., 2000).

Instead, when a push client-server paradigm is used, the server initiates sending service results. The push client-server paradigm can simulate worker interactions with the scheduler when building templates if auto-scheduling is introduced. In this scenario, servers (the workers in the worker string) send "push" messages to the scheduler process (the client, as they previously explained), indicating that the server may start processing a new job. As a result, the client makes a fresh service request to the server.

Templates can use any existing technology used to construct servers for uses other than structured parallel programming. For instance, server multithreading techniques may be utilized to construct workers partially capable of concealing communication latencies even in cases where communications do not entirely overlap with computations (Jain et al., 2000) (Figure 2.6).

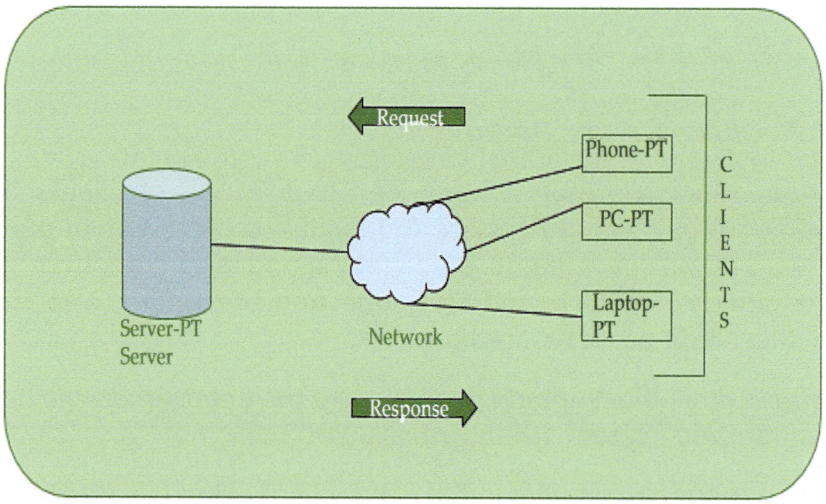

Figure 2.6. Illustration of client server model.

Source: Geeks for Geeks, Creative Commons License.

2.4.1.2. Peer-to-Peer Resource Discovery

They frequently struggle to find people to employ as resources when implementing a specific template. In the appropriate resource databases or resource tables provided by the system, processing resources can be found. More frequently, they want to identify the resources that can be added to their parallel processing. Therefore, some parallel or distributed discovery mechanism is required.

Peer-to-peer technologies form the basis of a widely used discovery mechanism. They begin a process similar to the peer discovery process in peer-to-peer computing while seeking a resource:

- Subsequently, they remain in a waiting state for responses from the processing elements that are executing the skeleton run time and are capable of assisting new computations.
- As another option, they have the ability to query a renowned "service server" to obtain a catalog of the presently accessible peers and resources (Trunfio et al., 2007).

All algorithms created for the traditional peer-to-peer paradigm are applicable in both scenarios. Flooding can therefore be set up so that: (i) flood messages do not survive more hops than the initial time to live; (ii) flood messages are not returned to the sending node; and (iii) the reached peers directly contact the originator of the flood request rather than merely returning a presence message to the host that delivered them the flood discovery request.

If they adopt this discovery strategy, they must, of course, add the appropriate mechanisms to the template run time to respond to discovery flood notifications (Basu et al., 2005).

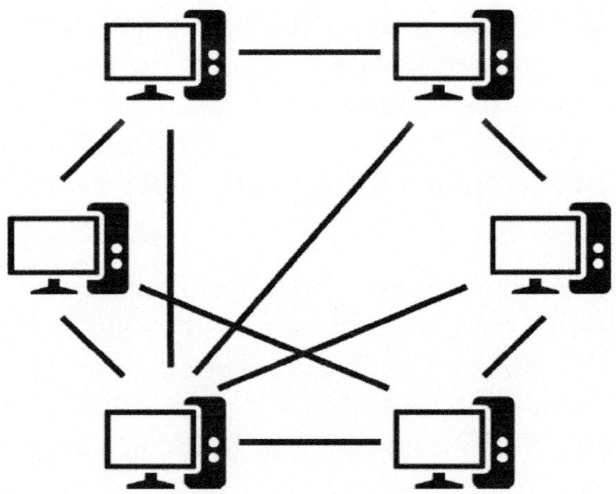

Figure 2.7. Image of peer-to-peer network.

Source: Cope James, Creative Commons License.

Pure peer-to-peer discovery is an option for use in networks like all variants of Ethernet that support broadcasting and multicasting simultaneously. In this particular scenario, the host that is searching for resources to add to the parallel computation may broadcast or, more preferably, multicast a discovery message on a particular port. The resources that are performing the template run time will reply to the discovery message when it is received. The "health" of the answering machine can also be determined by looking at the order in which the responses to the discovery message are received. In most cases, delayed replies point to a resource that is either operating under an excessive load or suffering from poor network connectivity.

Once more, all of the current peer-to-peer findings can be used to create a suitable "resource discovery" template building block (Ranjan et al., 2008) (Figure 2.7).

2.4.1.3. Termination

The task of terminating concurrent programs is not at all simple. It must be the case that multiple parallel, concurrent, or distributed activities interact through messages or some other shared memory to compute the same final results and then synchronize once more through messages or appropriate synchronization primitives. When creating templates, they must be careful to support the termination of all initiated activities, even when errors or atypical terminations occur (Pnueli, 1981).

The procedure will be designed in such a way that, at some time, a tree will be constructed. The tree will have nodes that cover all of the parallel activities that will ultimately be set up in the program, and each node will have leaves that cover all of the activities that will have to end once the node that they belong to has finished. This method is appropriate for finishing up any and all activities when there are no problems with finishing up (normal termination). This tree is able to propagate messages from the root activity to the leaf activities without having to deal with the unpleasant condition of terminating activities before they finished communicating with other concurrent activities and resulting in errors (Hart et al., 1983).

For example, they may implement termination in our stream parallel apps by utilizing the "end-of-stream" mark that flows over the stream channels. This would allow the programs to shut down. The end-of-stream mark is a frequent message that travels over stream channels to indicate that no future actions or data items will travel over that channel. This mark is sent when a stream channel is about to reach its endpoint. Caution is required on their part if they are to "count" the correct number of marks that are coming in and produce the appropriate number of marks that are leaving the system. For example, when a farm emitter has received one EOS as an input, it should continue to emit new EOS marks. Distribute the EOS that was given to you to each of the workers on the farm. It is the responsibility of the collector at the farm to tally any new marks and send only the most recent total (Liang et al., 2014).

It is imperative that it be made abundantly apparent that the channels that are used to support termination messages may, in general, differ from those that are used to transport data (input tasks and outcomes) between activities that use a template. Take into consideration, once more, the conclusion of the farm model stated earlier in the sentence. It is expected that the technique in which the emitter sends the termination signal to the worker processes after receiving requests from the workers for tasks to be computed that are no longer accessible will be a significantly more effective manner of terminating the procedure. The employees resign as soon as they are informed that their employment would be terminated. The emitter then sends a termination message to the final worker, continuing to ask for the tasks to be calculated, and then it sends a termination message to the collector as well. After some time has passed, when the collector finally gets the termination message from the emitter, it turns off (Owicki & Lamport, 1982).

2.5. CROSS-SKELETON TEMPLATES

Implementation templates support a specific target architecture on a specific skeleton. However, some templates are more important and can support various skeletons. The task farm skeleton template provides an example of a typical case. The same template may be used effectively to enable data parallel skeletons like the map one.

When a skeleton is implemented in terms of another (composition of) skeleton(s), that situation is different. Once more, the situation appears when they think of data-parallel skeletons. An input data structure is divided into partitions in a data-parallel skeleton, possibly into single items, and then a computation is run over all of these partitions. The results of the partition computations are collected to create the data parallel skeleton result (Wu et al., 2014).

This parallel pattern can easily be changed into the following stream parallel pattern:

- There is a three-stage pipeline.
- The input data structure is divided into partitions in the first stage. A partition is delivered onto the stage output stream as soon as it is produced.
- A task farm is used in the second step to process a stream of partitions and generate a stream of partition results.
- The 3rd stage, which is once more sequential, "collapses" the results of its input stream into the final product of the parallel data skeleton (Zhou et al., 2022).

By doing so, they effectively employ the parallel stream skeletons as implementation templates when implementing a data parallel construct. For this reason, they refer to this instance as a cross-skeleton template in the chapter on template design. This implementation template technique may be useful in many situations, especially when the target architecture provides facilities that enable stream parallelism well.

Only stream parallel skeletons, such as task farms and pipelines, are offered by Fast-Flow. However, it can also be used to implement data-parallel skeletons because the Fast-Flow task farm template is parametric, and the emitter's scheduling, as well as the collector's data-gathering tactics, can both be user-defined. As a result, the map data parallel skeleton may use the stream parallel skeleton task farm as a cross-skeleton implementation template (Lu et al., 2012).

2.6. SAMPLE TEMPLATE MECHANISMS

Here, they discuss a few methods that might be used to implement templates on multi-core and COW/NOW systems, as well as shared memory and distributed memory architectures. These methods could be employed as mechanisms for the application of templates. Therefore, they are template building blocks like the three in Section 2.4.1. Still, they discuss them separately because they are building blocks that abstract lower-level features compared to the others (Wawryn & Widuliński, 2021).

2.6.1. Double/Triple Buffering

Implementing a triple or double buffering is a useful technique to connect processes (or threads), provided that the hardware allows for at least partial communication and computation overlap. Any process that sends results to other procedures and receives input data from other processes can be implemented using triple buffering. It operates as follows:

- At any one time, one concurrent activity is responsible for receiving the "next" data to be used as an input task, another concurrent activity is responsible for delivering the most recent computation's result, and a third activity is responsible for computing the most recent input job. The tasks use three separate buffers: b1 for data receipt, b2 for data processing, and b3 for results transmission (Toyokura et al., 1994).
- The three concurrent activities switch roles after concurrently completing the three steps—here, logical barrier synchronization is required. The activity I begin acting in the manner of activity (i+1)%3 in the preceding phase. Because of this, the activity that just calculated a result starts

sending it, the activity that just sent a result starts receiving a new task, and the activity that just computed an input task starts computing it. Of course, every task has its buffer for the new responsibility.

The triple buffering acts as an "in-place pipeline" when communication and synchronization fully overlap. The computation time for one step equals the maximum of the latencies of the three activities: computing, receiving a task, and sending a result. By utilizing the buffers again in this fashion, excessive copying and sharing between the three running tasks are also avoided. Simply put, double buffering uses two activities: one for calculations and one for communications (both sends and receives) (Pan et al., 2021).

2.6.2. Time Server

They frequently need to know the wall clock time of some events when performing a parallel calculation. Both troubleshooting and fine-tuning may call for this. The message "the event 'ei' happened at time 'ti'" only makes sense with events generated on the same processing element, which reads the same world clock. On the other hand, events on different processing elements can have access to their own individual clocks (Tassiulas & Ephremides, 1993).

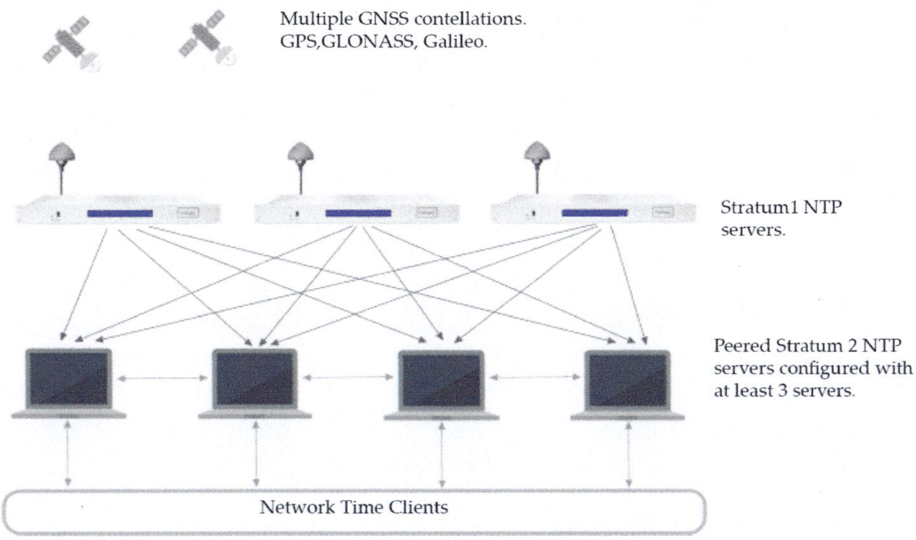

Figure 2.8. Example of network time protocol (NTP).

Source: Timetools, Creative Commons License.

When the importance of the relative ordering of the occurrences is taken into consideration, this is not adequate. In the past, numerous algorithms have been devised in order to either offer a partial ordering of events that are taking place on several workstations or to preserve synchronization between the clocks of networked workstations. Both of these goals have been accomplished. Since 1978, Lampor has held the title of author of one of the most well-known algorithms for the process of producing a partial ordering among events that are taking place in a workstation network. The method uses the local logical clocks of the workstations that are talking with one another in order to compute a partial ordering of the events that are taking place. NTP or the network time protocol, is used by contemporary operating systems such as Linux to synchronize the clocks on all of the workstations connected to a network. Marzullo's approach is the foundation for NTP (Mills, 1991) (Figure 2.8).

On the other hand, there are some circumstances in which people would be interested in learning an estimate of the time that an event will take place. There are circumstances in which having a centralized time server could be helpful. Communication with the centralized time server is accomplished by means of a TCP server socket that is published on a well-known port. This socket is used by processes or threads that want to notify or register an event. The timestamp of the event, which is the precise moment that the event occurred as recorded by the local clock, is included in the messages. The centralized time server is responsible for collecting and storing messages sent by all of the distributed users who are taking part in the parallel computation. These messages are given a local timestamp that corresponds to the moment they were received.

At some point in the process, the events are reported back to the user or the programmer in the order in which they were received. When local and time server time stamps are shown, the user or developer can ultimately determine a rough relative ordering of the scattered events and the amount of time required to carry out a particular action by computing the difference between the starting and ending event timings. This allows for the determination of an estimated relative ordering of the scattered events and the amount of time required to carry out the activity. This makes it possible for the user or the programmer to estimate the approximate proportional order of the events and the amount of time needed to complete the activity. The difference will be established utilizing local time stamps in the event that the action was carried out locally at a single workstation. In that event, it will be decided using the "receive" time stamps that were collected from the time server.

This strategy is generally effective:

- All parallel computation partners have uniformly low communication latency to the time server; and
- The interactions introduced to collect time stamps do not rationally interfere with or disrupt the execution of the communications required to run the parallel program.

As usual, scalability is impacted by the use of a centralized time server. The parallelization of the time server must be considered if a large number of distributed actors are involved. For instance, local time servers that eventually send the collected data to a centralized server could be employed (Franke et al., 2020).

2.6.3. Channel Name Server

Setting up appropriate communication channels is challenging when building an ongoing event matrix on a distributed architecture. To map our concurrent activities, they must first: (i) assign each one to a specific computing resource; and (ii) establish communication channels to link the interacting multiple tasks in the ongoing task graph. The "interconnection network setup" is the name of the second activity, which happens well before parallel computing even begins. Because the bottleneck introduced only affects the time required to set up the parallel computation and not the time required to complete the computation, they can implement it using a central server (Kara et al., 2014).

ACTIVITY 2.1:

How can organizations apply the principles of the Cole Manifesto to ensure that technology development and implementation is ethical and socially responsible, particularly in the context of emerging technologies like artificial intelligence and automation?

A communal method contains the following stages:

- The creation and operation of a central channel server that offers two fundamental services: (i) channel registration; and (ii) channel name lookup. When a channel is registered, its address is recorded, such as an IP address and port number for a TCP socket, the queue id for a SysV message queue, etc., associated with a global and application-specific channel name. If there is no channel registered with that name as of the time the lookup request is executed, a lookup failure message is returned in place of the related address information.
- The input communication channels are initialized and registered with the channel server whenever a synchronized activity is started on one of the distributed processing resources. Before the actual "body" of the concurrent activity begins to execute, there is an initialization/registering phase (Kangasharju & Ross, 2000).

As an illustration, imagine they are generating a synchronized activity graph like the one in Figure 2.9. In this scenario, multiple concurrent activities will be set up and launched on various readily available resources. Assume E, C, and Wi activities are initiated for resources RE, RC, and RWi. Assume they are likewise aiming for a group of workstations connected via TCP sockets. There is an input channel for each activity. The concurrent activity graph 112 establishes the "names" of these channels. Consequently, if "farm3" is the template name:

- *E* will create a server socket named "farm3-tasks-E-in" and inform the channel server of its IP address and port.
- *C* initializes a server socket named "farm3-results-C-in" and notifies the channel server of its IP address and port.
- Each Wi initializes a server socket named "farm3-task-Wi-in" and notifies the channel server of its IP address and port.
- *E* will query the channel server for "farm3-task-W1-in," "farm3-task-W2-in,"..., "farm3-task-Wnw-in."
- Each Wi will search for "farm3-results-C-in" on the channel server (e).
- *C* will perform an address lookup for the channel that will be used to convey results (for example, "pipe4-tasking").

And at this time, every activity running concurrently will have every required channel address (You et al., 2007) (Figure 2.9).

Figure 2.9. Example of channel name server.

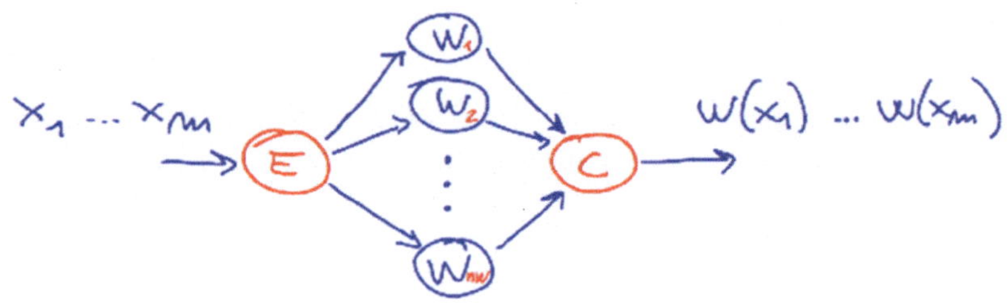

Source: Time Tool, Creative Commons License.

2.7. SUMMARY

The chapter "Design Patterns of Distributed Systems" discusses the importance of design patterns in distributed systems and how they can help in achieving better system performance, scalability, and fault tolerance. The chapter explains the concept of parallel design patterns and the algorithm structure design space for parallel design patterns. It also describes the skeleton design approach to distributed systems, which helps in designing distributed systems that are flexible, adaptable, and easy to maintain. The chapter further discusses the Cole manifesto principles and their significance in distributed systems design, and how to propagate a concept with minimal conceptual disruption. It also emphasizes the importance of accommodating diversity and integrating ad-hoc parallelism in distributed systems design. Finally, the chapter provides sample template mechanisms such as double/triple buffering, time server, and channel name server that can be used to improve the design of distributed systems and shows the payback in distributed systems design.

REVIEW QUESTIONS

1. What is the significance of design patterns in the context of distributed systems?
2. How do parallel design patterns differ from concurrency design patterns?
3. How can we explore the algorithm structure design space for parallel design patterns?
4. What is skeleton design, and how can it be useful in distributed systems?
5. What are the Cole manifesto principles, and how are they relevant to distributed systems design?
6. What are some strategies for propagating a concept with minimal conceptual disruption in distributed systems design?
7. How can we integrate ad-hoc parallelism and accommodate diversity in distributed systems design?
8. Why is it important to demonstrate the payback of design decisions in distributed systems?
9. What are some sample template mechanisms that can be used in distributed systems design, such as double/triple buffering, time server, and channel name server?

MULTIPLE CHOICE QUESTIONS

1. What is the importance of design patterns in distributed systems?

a. They allow for more efficient communication between components

b. They provide a standardized solution to common design problems

c. They reduce the complexity of distributed systems
d. All of the above

2. **What are parallel design patterns?**
   a. Patterns that allow for parallel processing in distributed systems
   b. Patterns that use multiple threads to execute a single task
   c. Patterns that optimize network communication in distributed systems
   d. Patterns that use distributed caches to improve performance
3. **What is the algorithm structure design space for parallel design patterns?**
   a. The set of algorithms used to implement parallel patterns
   b. The set of constraints that determine the feasibility of parallel patterns
   c. The set of data structures used in parallel patterns
   d. The set of parallelization techniques used in distributed systems
4. **What is skeleton design in distributed systems?**
   a. A design pattern that provides a framework for building distributed systems
   b. A design pattern that defines the communication protocol between distributed components
   c. A design pattern that provides a centralized control mechanism for distributed systems
   d. A design pattern that improves fault tolerance in distributed systems
5. **What are the Cole manifesto principles in distributed systems design?**
   a. Principles that promote simplicity, modularity, and scalability in distributed systems
   b. Principles that emphasize the importance of fault tolerance in distributed systems
   c. Principles that prioritize security and privacy in distributed systems
   d. Principles that encourage the use of open standards and interoperability in distributed systems
6. **How can a concept be propagated with minimal conceptual disruption?**
   a. By using a standard communication protocol between components
   b. By using a design pattern that is already familiar to developers
   c. By providing clear documentation and examples of the concept
   d. All of the above
7. **How can ad-hoc parallelism be integrated, and diversity accommodated in distributed systems design?**
   a. By using design patterns that allow for flexible configurations of components
   b. By using a distributed cache to store and retrieve data
   c. By using a centralized control mechanism for all components

d. By using a single-threaded architecture for all components

8. **Why is it important to show the payback in distributed systems design?**
   a. To justify the investment in distributed systems
   b. To demonstrate the scalability and modularity of the design
   c. To show that the design is fault tolerant and can handle failures
   d. All of the above
9. **What are some sample template mechanisms used in distributed systems design?**
   a. Double/triple buffering, time server, and channel name server
   b. Load balancing, caching, and replication
   c. Encryption, authentication, and authorization
   d. Queuing, messaging, and event-driven architecture

Answers to Multiple Choice Questions

1. (b); 2. (a); 3. (d); 4. (a); 5. (a); 6. (d); 7. (a); 8. (a); 9. (a)

REFERENCES

1. Adams, J. C., (2015). Patternlets: A teaching tool for introducing students to parallel design patterns. In: *2015 IEEE International Parallel and Distributed Processing Symposium Workshop* (Vol.2, pp. 752–759). IEEE.
2. Angelsky, O. V., Gorsky, M. P., Hanson, S. G., Lukin, V. P., Mokhun, I. I., Polyanskii, P. V., & Ryabiy, P. A., (2014). Optical correlation algorithm for reconstructing phase skeleton of complex optical fields for solving the phase problem. *Optics Express, 22*(5), 6186–6193.
3. Babaoglu, O., Canright, G., Deutsch, A., Caro, G. A. D., Ducatelle, F., Gambardella, L. M., & Urnes, T., (2006). Design patterns from biology for distributed computing. *ACM Transactions on Autonomous and Adaptive Systems (TAAS), 1*(1), 26–66.
4. Basu, S., Banerjee, S., Sharma, P., & Lee, S. J., (2005). Nodewiz: Peer-to-peer resource discovery for grids. In: *CCGrid 2005: IEEE International Symposium on Cluster Computing and the Grid, 2005* (Vol. 1, pp. 213–220). IEEE.
5. Bengtsson, K., & Lennartson, B., (2014). Patient coordination in emergency departments using an event-based information architecture. In: *Proceedings of the 2014 IEEE Emerging Technology and Factory Automation (ETFA)* (Vol. 1, pp. 1–6). IEEE.
6. Bergeretti, J. F., & Carré, B. A., (1985). Information-flow and data-flow analysis of while-programs. *ACM Transactions on Programming Languages and Systems (TOPLAS), 7*(1), 37–61.
7. Burke, M. D., Hagan, S. L., & Grossen, B., (1998). What curricular designs and

strategies accommodate diverse learners? *Teaching Exceptional Children, 31*(1), 34–38.

8. Caromel, D., & Leyton, M., (2007). Fine tuning algorithmic skeletons. In: *Euro-Par 2007 Parallel Processing: 13th International Euro-Par Conference, Rennes, France, August 28–31, 2007. Proceedings 13* (Vol. 3, pp. 72–81). Springer Berlin Heidelberg.
9. Clarke, E. M., & Emerson, E. A., (1982). Design and synthesis of synchronization skeletons using branching time temporal logic. In: *Logics of Programs: Workshop, Yorktown Heights, New York, May 1981* (Vol. 1, pp. 52–71). Springer Berlin Heidelberg.
10. Cole, M., (1999). Algorithmic skeletons. *Research Directions in Parallel Functional Programming, 4*, 289–303.
11. Cole, M., (2004). Bringing skeletons out of the closet: A pragmatic manifesto for skeletal parallel programming. *Parallel Computing, 30*(3), 389–406.
12. Danelutto, M., & Di Cosmo, R., (2012). A "minimal disruption" skeleton experiment: Seamless map & reduce embedding in OCaml. *Procedia Computer Science, 9*, 1837–1846.
13. Danelutto, M., Mencagli, G., Torquati, M., González-Vélez, H., & Kilpatrick, P., (2021). Algorithmic skeletons and parallel design patterns in mainstream parallel programming. *International Journal of Parallel Programming, 49*, 177–198.
14. Davis, S. A., Breulmann, M., Rhodes, K. H., Zhang, B., & Mann, S., (2001). Template-directed assembly using nanoparticle building blocks: A nanotectonic approach to organized materials. *Chemistry of Materials, 13*(10), 3218–3226.
15. Delerue, J. F., Perrier, E., Yu, Z. Y., & Velde, B., (1999). New algorithms in 3D image analysis and their application to the measurement of a spatialized pore size distribution in soils. *Physics and Chemistry of the Earth, Part A: Solid Earth and Geodesy, 24*(7), 639–644.
16. Dighe, R., & Jakiela, M. J., (1995). Solving pattern nesting problems with genetic algorithms employing task decomposition and contact detection. *Evolutionary Computation, 3*(3), 239–266.
17. Dumas, M., Fjellheim, T., Milliner, S., & Vayssiere, J., (2005). Event-based coordination of process-oriented composite applications. In: *Business Process Management: 3rd International Conference, BPM 2005, Nancy, France, September 5–8, 2005; Proceedings 3* (Vol. 1, pp. 236–251). Springer Berlin Heidelberg.
18. Eckert, K., Fay, A., Hadlich, T., Diedrich, C., Frank, T., & Vogel-Heuser, B., (2012). Design patterns for distributed automation systems with consideration of non-functional requirements. In: *Proceedings of 2012 IEEE 17th International Conference on Emerging Technologies & Factory Automation (ETFA 2012)* (Vol. 1, pp. 1–9). IEEE.
19. Ferrari, G. L., Guanciale, R., Strollo, D., & Tuosto, E., (2008). Event-based service coordination. *Concurrency, Graphs and Models: Essays Dedicated to Ugo Montanari on the Occasion of His 65th Birthday, 12*(1), 312–329.
20. Ferrier, S., Manion, G., Elith, J., & Richardson, K., (2007). Using generalized dissimilarity modelling to analyze and predict patterns of beta diversity in regional

biodiversity assessment. *Diversity and Distributions, 13*(3), 252–264.

21. Fjellheim, T., Milliner, S., Dumas, M., & Vayssiere, J., (2007). A process-based methodology for designing event-based mobile composite applications. *Data & Knowledge Engineering, 61*(1), 6–22.
22. Franke, D., Sibold, D., Teichel, K., Dansarie, M., & Sundblad, R., (2020). *Network Time Security for the Network Time Protocol. RFC 8915*, 258–358.
23. Ge, Y., & Fitzpatrick, J. M., (1996). On the generation of skeletons from discrete Euclidean distance maps. *IEEE Transactions on Pattern Analysis and Machine Intelligence, 18*(11), 1055–1066.
24. González, C. H., & Fraguela, B. B., (2010). A generic algorithm template for divide-and-conquer in multicore systems. In: *2010 IEEE 12th International Conference on High Performance Computing and Communications (HPCC)* (Vol. 1, pp. 79–88). IEEE.
25. Gursoy, A., (2004). Data decomposition for parallel k-means clustering. In: *Parallel Processing and Applied Mathematics: 5th International Conference, PPAM 2003, Czestochowa, Poland, September 7–10, 2003. Revised Papers 5* (Vol. 1, pp. 241–248). Springer Berlin Heidelberg.
26. Hart, S., Sharir, M., & Pnueli, A., (1983). Termination of probabilistic concurrent program. *ACM Transactions on Programming Languages and Systems (TOPLAS), 5*(3), 356–380.
27. Huda, Z. U., Jannesari, A., & Wolf, F., (2015). Using template matching to infer parallel design patterns. *ACM Transactions on Architecture and Code Optimization (TACO), 11*(4), 1–21.
28. Ismail, L., Hagimont, D., & Mossiere, J., (2000). Evaluation of the mobile agents technology: Comparison with the client/server paradigm. *Information Science and Technology (IST), 19*, 123.
29. Jahr, R., Calborean, H., Vintan, L., & Ungerer, T., (2015). Finding near□perfect parameters for hardware and code optimizations with automatic multi□objective design space explorations. *Concurrency and Computation: Practice and Experience, 27*(9), 2196–2214.
30. Jain, R., Anjum, F., & Umar, A., (2000). A comparison of mobile agent and client-server paradigms for information retrieval tasks in virtual enterprises. In: *Proceedings Academia/Industry Working Conference on Research Challenges' 00; Next Generation Enterprises: Virtual Organizations and Mobile/Pervasive Technologies; AIWORC' 00 (Cat. No. PR00628)* (Vol. 1, pp. 209–213). IEEE.
31. Jang, B. K., & Chin, R. T., (1990). Analysis of thinning algorithms using mathematical morphology. *IEEE Transactions on Pattern Analysis and Machine Intelligence, 12*(6), 541–551.
32. Kambadur, P., Gupta, A., Ghoting, A., Avron, H., & Lumsdaine, A., (2009). PFunc: Modern task parallelism for modern high-performance computing. In: *Proceedings of the Conference on High Performance Computing Networking, Storage and Analysis* (Vol. 1, pp. 1–11).

33. Kangasharju, J., & Ross, K. W., (2000). A replicated architecture for the domain name system. In: *Proceedings IEEE INFOCOM 2000; Conference on Computer Communications. Nineteenth Annual Joint Conference of the IEEE Computer and Communications Societies (Cat. No. 00CH37064)* (Vol. 2, pp. 660–669). IEEE.
34. Kara, A. M., Binsalleeh, H., Mannan, M., Youssef, A., & Debbabi, M., (2014). Detection of malicious payload distribution channels in DNS. In: *2014 IEEE International Conference on Communications (ICC)* (Vol. 1, pp. 853–858). IEEE.
35. Karimov, J., Rabl, T., & Markl, V., (2019). AStream: Ad-hoc shared stream processing. In: *Proceedings of the 2019 International Conference on Management of Data* (Vol. 1, pp. 607–622).
36. Keim, D. A., Kriegel, H. P., & Ankerst, M., (1995). Recursive pattern: A technique for visualizing very large amounts of data. In: *Proceedings Visualization'95* (Vol. 1, pp. 279–286). IEEE.
37. Keutzer, K., & Mattson, T., (2009). Our pattern language (OPL): A design pattern language for engineering (parallel) software. In: *ParaPLoP Workshop on Parallel Programming Patterns* (Vol. 14, pp. 10–1145).
38. Kist, D., Pinto, B., Bazo, R., Du Bois, A. R., & Cavalheiro, G. G. H., (2015). Kanga: A skeleton-based generic interface for parallel programming. In: *2015 International Symposium on Computer Architecture and High Performance Computing Workshop (SBAC-PADW)* (Vol. 1, pp. 68–72). IEEE.
39. Lee, Y. C., & Zomaya, A. Y., (2006). Data sharing pattern aware scheduling on grids. In: *2006 International Conference on Parallel Processing (ICPP'06)* (Vol. 1, pp. 365–372). IEEE.
40. Li, X., Yin, Z., Wei, L., Wan, S., Yu, W., & Li, M., (2011). Symmetry and template guided completion of damaged skulls. *Computers & Graphics, 35*(4), 885–893.
41. Liang, H., Feng, X., & Shao, Z., (2014). Compositional verification of termination-preserving refinement of concurrent programs. In: *Proceedings of the Joint Meeting of the Twenty-Third EACSL Annual Conference on Computer Science Logic (CSL) and the Twenty-Ninth Annual ACM/IEEE Symposium on Logic in Computer Science (LICS)* (Vol.1, pp. 1–10).
42. Lu, B. L., & Ito, M., (1999). Task decomposition and module combination based on class relations: A modular neural network for pattern classification. *IEEE Transactions on Neural Networks, 10*(5), 1244–1256.
43. Lu, J., Shi, K., Min, D., Lin, L., & Do, M. N., (2012). Cross-based local multipoint filtering. In: *2012 IEEE Conference on Computer Vision and Pattern Recognition* (Vol. 1, pp. 430–437). IEEE.
44. MacDonald, S., Szafron, D., Schaeffer, J., & Bromling, S., (2000). Generating parallel program frameworks from parallel design patterns. In: *Euro-Par 2000 Parallel Processing: 6th International Euro-Par Conference Munich, Germany, August 29–September 1, 2000 Proceedings 6* (Vol. 2, pp. 95–104). Springer Berlin Heidelberg.
45. McCallien, D. W., & Sanders, J. K., (1995). Dioxoporphyrins as supramolecular

building blocks: Oligomer synthesis via preassembly on a ligand template. *Journal of the American Chemical Society, 117*(24), 6611, 6612.

46. Mills, D. L., (1991). Internet time synchronization: The network time protocol. *IEEE Transactions on Communications, 39*(10), 1482–1493.
47. Owicki, S., & Lamport, L., (1982). Proving liveness properties of concurrent programs. *ACM Transactions on Programming Languages and Systems (TOPLAS), 4*(3), 455–495.
48. Pan, L., Xia, H., Yang, J., Niu, W., Wang, R., Song, H., & Qin, Y., (2021). Mapping cropping intensity in Huaihe basin using phenology algorithm, all sentinel-2 and Landsat images in Google Earth engine. *International Journal of Applied Earth Observation and Geoinformation, 102*, 102376.
49. Pickett, S. T. A., Kolasa, J., Armesto, J. J., & Collins, S. L., (1989). The ecological concept of disturbance and its expression at various hierarchical levels. *Oikos, 1*, 129–136.
50. Pizlo, F., Fox, J. M., Holmes, D., & Vitek, J., (2004). Real-time java scoped memory: Design patterns and semantics. In: *Seventh IEEE International Symposium on Object-Oriented Real-Time Distributed Computing, 2004; Proceedings.* (Vol. 1, pp. 101–110). IEEE.
51. Pnueli, A., (1981). The temporal semantics of concurrent programs. *Theoretical Computer Science, 13*(1), 45–60.
52. Rajan, H., Kautz, S. M., & Rowcliffe, W., (2010). Concurrency by modularity: Design patterns, a case in point. *ACM Sigplan Notices, 45*(10), 790–805.
53. Ranjan, R., Harwood, A., & Buyya, R., (2008). Peer-to-peer-based resource discovery in global grids: A tutorial. *IEEE Communications Surveys & Tutorials, 10*(2), 6–33.
54. Rasheed, K., Hirsh, H., & Gelsey, A., (1997). A genetic algorithm for continuous design space search. *Artificial Intelligence in Engineering, 11*(3), 295–305.
55. Rieger, C., Wrede, F., & Kuchen, H., (2019). Musket: A domain-specific language for high-level parallel programming with algorithmic skeletons. In: *Proceedings of the 34th ACM/SIGAPP Symposium on Applied Computing* (Vol. 1, pp. 1534–1543).
56. Schmidt, D. C., (1996). A family of design patterns for flexibly configuring network services in distributed systems. In: *Proceedings of International Conference on Configurable Distributed Systems* (Vol. 1, pp. 124–135). IEEE.
57. Sidhu, T. S., Selvy, M. T., & Das, A., (2003). A client-server paradigm for protection studies. In: *2003 IEEE PES Transmission and Distribution Conference and Exposition (IEEE Cat. No. 03CH37495)* (Vol. 1, pp. 303–308). IEEE.
58. Siu, S., De Simone, M., Goswami, D., & Singh, A., (1996). Design patterns for parallel programming. In: *PDPTA* (Vol. 96, pp. 230–240).
59. Staunton, R. C., (1996). An analysis of hexagonal thinning algorithms and skeletal shape representation. *Pattern Recognition, 29*(7), 1131–1146.
60. Steiner, W., & Rushby, J., (2011). TTA and PALS: Formally verified design patterns for distributed cyber-physical systems. In: *2011 IEEE/AIAA 30th Digital Avionics Systems Conference* (Vol. 1, pp. 75–81). IEEE.

61. Tassiulas, L., & Ephremides, A., (1993). Dynamic server allocation to parallel queues with randomly varying connectivity. *IEEE Transactions on Information Theory, 39*(2), 466–478.
62. Thummalapenta, S., Xie, T., Tillmann, N., De Halleux, J., & Su, Z., (2011). Synthesizing method sequences for high-coverage testing. *ACM SIGPLAN Notices, 46*(10), 189–206.
63. Torres, R. D. S., Falcão, A. X., & Costa, L. D. F., (2004). A graph-based approach for multiscale shape analysis. *Pattern Recognition, 37*(6), 1163–1174.
64. Toyokura, M., Kodama, H., Miyagoshi, E., Okamoto, K., Gion, M., Minemaru, T., & Aono, K., (1994). A video DSP with a macroblock-level-pipeline and a SIMD type vector-pipeline architecture for MPEG2 CODEC. *IEEE journal of Solid-State Circuits, 29*(12), 1474–1481.
65. Trunfio, P., Talia, D., Papadakis, H., Fragopoulou, P., Mordacchini, M., Pennanen, M., & Haridi, S., (2007). Peer-to-peer resource discovery in grids: Models and systems. *Future Generation Computer Systems, 23*(7), 864–878.
66. Uzunov, A. V., Fernandez, E. B., & Falkner, K., (2012). Securing distributed systems using patterns: A survey. *Computers & Security, 31*(5), 681–703.
67. Vogel, P., Greiser, T., & Mattfeld, D. C., (2011). Understanding bike-sharing systems using data mining: Exploring activity patterns. *Procedia-Social and Behavioral Sciences, 20*, 514–523.
68. Wawryn, K., & Widuliński, P., (2021). Detection of anomalies in compiled computer program files inspired by immune mechanisms using a template method. *Journal of Computer Virology and Hacking Techniques, 17*, 47–59.
69. Wu, Q., Zhao, X., & Li, X., (2014). Stereo matching algorithm of color image based on weber's law and census. In: *2014 Tenth International Conference on Intelligent Information Hiding and Multimedia Signal Processing* (pp. 199–202). IEEE.
70. Wu, R. Y., & Tsai, W. H., (1992). A new one-pass parallel thinning algorithm for binary images. *Pattern Recognition Letters, 13*(10), 715–723.
71. Yale, M. E., Messinger, D. S., Cobo-Lewis, A. B., Oller, D. K., & Eilers, R. E., (1999). An event-based analysis of the coordination of early infant vocalizations and facial actions. *Developmental Psychology, 35*(2), 505.
72. You, Y. K., Han, S., Song, S. K., & Youn, H. Y., (2007). Context-based dynamic channel management for efficient event service in pervasive computing. In: *2007 International Conference on Computational Science and its Applications (ICCSA 2007)* (Vol. 3, pp. 24–32). IEEE.
73. Zhang, Y. Y., & Wang, P. S. P., (1996). A parallel thinning algorithm with two-subiteration that generates one-pixel-wide skeletons. In: *Proceedings of 13th International Conference on Pattern Recognition* (Vol. 4, pp. 457–461). IEEE.
74. Zhou, F., Yang, X., Chen, F., Chen, L., Jiang, Z., Zhu, H., & Zhou, H., (2022). *Cross-Skeleton Interaction Graph Aggregation Network for Representation Learning of Mouse Social Behavior* (pp. 18, 19). arXiv preprint arXiv:2208.

CHAPTER 3

DATA COMMUNICATION AND COMPUTER NETWORKS

UNIT INTRODUCTION

In today's digital age, data communication and computer networks are essential components of modern communication systems. They enable the exchange of information and resources between computers, devices, and users across different locations and networks. Data communication refers to the transfer of data between devices or computers, while computer networks are the interconnected systems that allow these devices to communicate with each other.

These networks can be local or global, wired or wireless, and can support various applications and services such as email, web browsing, and file sharing. This chapter will provide a comprehensive introduction to data communication and computer networks. It will cover the basic concepts and principles of data communication. It will also discuss different types of computer networks, and their topologies.

In conclusion, this chapter aims to provide a foundation for understanding the concepts and technologies involved in data communication and computer networks. It will be useful for students, professionals, and anyone interested in gaining a deeper understanding of the communication systems that enable our modern digital world.

Learning Objectives

At the end of this chapter, the reader will be able to understand:

- The basics of data communication and its importance in computer networks;
- Different data transmission modes including simplex, half-duplex, and full duplex;
- Difference between parallel and serial transmission;
- The differences between asynchronous and synchronous transmission;
- The seven layers of the OSI model;
- The criteria for designing a network and the different physical structures;
- Different types of networks including LAN, MAN, and WAN;
- Different connecting devices used in computer networks;
- The differences between analog and digital data, periodic and nonperiodic signals, and characteristics of signals such as amplitude, frequency, and phase.

Key Terms

- Analog data
- Asynchronous transmission
- Data communication
- Digital data
- FTP
- Full duplex
- Half-duplex
- HTTP
- IMAP
- Local area networks
- Metropolitan area network
- OSI model
- Parallel transmission
- Periodic Signals
- POP_3
- Serial transmission
- Simplex
- Sine wave
- Synchronous transmission
- TELNET
- Web-based mail
- Wide area networks

3.1. DATA COMMUNICATIONS

The process of transferring data between two devices through any transmission medium is called data communications. For there to be data communications, devices that are doing the talking have to be a part of a communication system that's comprised of both software (actual computer programs) and hardware (the actual physical equipment). Jitter, delivery, accuracy, and timeliness are the four primary factors that determine how successful a data communications system will be (Pahlavan & Levesque, 1994):

- **Delivery:** It is necessary for the system to transmit the data to the appropriate location. The data can only be received by device or user for which it was intended, and only by that user or device (Zhao et al., 2004).
- **Accuracy:** Data have to be sent in a correct manner by the system. It is impossible to make use of data that has been corrupted during transmission and has not been rectified.
- **Timeliness:** The data must be sent by the system in timely fashion. Data given late are meaningless. When referring to the distribution of audio and video data, "timely delivery" refers to the delivery of said data as it's being created, in same order that it's being produced, and without considerable delay. This type of distribution is known as real-time transmission (Oh & Ngo, 2018).
- **Jitter:** This term "jitter" means arrival times of packet's variation. The term "jitter" refers to fluctuation in the times at which packets arrive (Stephens, 2004).

3.1.1. Components

A data transmission system consists of five parts (Figure 3.1).

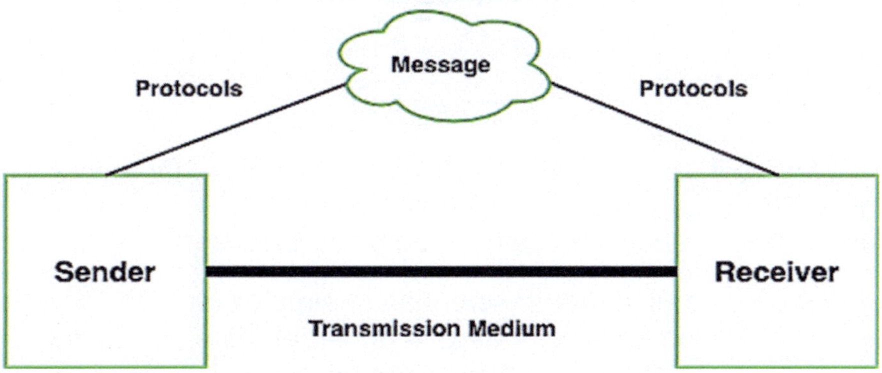

Figure 3.1. Illustration of components of data transmission system.

Source: Geeksforgeeks, Creative Commons License.

- **Message:** An information (data) that has to be communicated is message. Information in popular formats of numbers, images, text, audio, and video.
- **Sender:** A data message's sender is a sending device. It could be a workstation, computer, phone, video camera, and other devices (Giri et al., 2017).
- **Receiver:** The component which's responsible for receiving the message is known as receiver. It could be a workstation, television, telephone handset, computer, or any number of other electronic devices (Qureshi & Newhall, 1973).
- **Transmission Medium:** It is the actual route a message takes to get from source to receiver. Fiber-optic cable, coaxial cable, radio waves and twisted-pair wire are some types of transmission media (Handa et al., 1997).
- **Protocol:** Set of guidelines which controls how data is communicated is a protocol. It means that the communication devices will comprehend one another (Liu et al., 2017).

3.2. DATA TRANSMISSION MODES

Few of the modes of data transmission are as in subsections.

3.2.1. Simplex

Similar to a one-way street, simplex mode communication is unidirectional. When two devices are linked together, one of them can send data while other can only receive it.

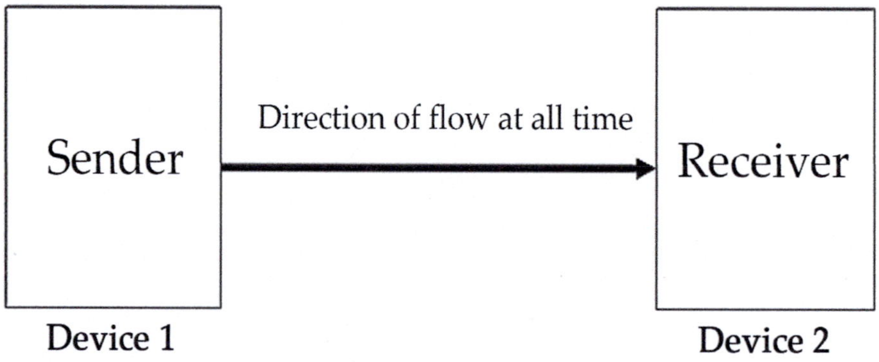

Figure 3.2. Schematic of simplex mode.

Source: After Academy, Creative Commons License.

Keyboards and standard screens are simplex devices examples. The only function of a keyboard is to enter data, while the only function of a monitor is to display output. A simplex mode is able to convey data in only one direction while utilizing full capacity of channel (Burdin et al., 2020) (Figure 3.2).

3.2.2. Half-Duplex

In the half-duplex mode, every station is able to send and receive information, but not simultaneously. One device can only receive data when other is broadcasting, and vice versa. During transmission using a half-duplex scheme, channel's entire capacity is utilized by whichever of two devices is delivering data at any given time. CB (citizens band) and Walkie-talkies radios are examples of communication devices that use half-duplex technology. When it is not necessary to communicate in both directions at once, half-duplex mode is employed. This allows channel capacity to be utilized in its entirety by each direction (Tang & Wang, 2015) (Figure 3.3).

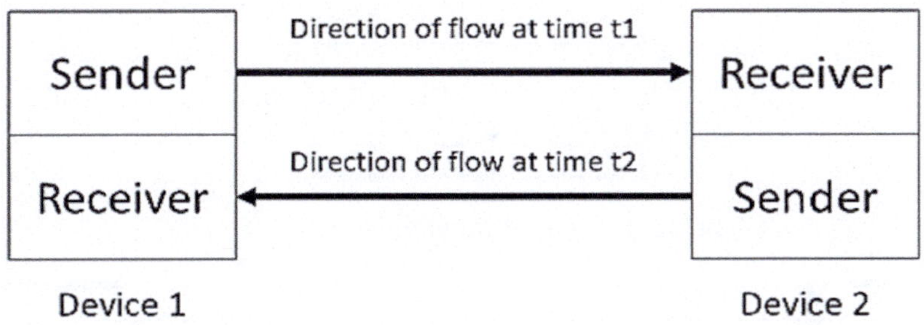

Figure 3.3. Schematic of half duplex.

Source: After Academy, Creative Commons License.

3.2.3. Full-Duplex

The simultaneous broadcast and receipt from both stations is possible with full-duplex communication. A full-duplex mode operates in a manner analogous to that of a road that can accommodate traffic traveling in both directions at the same time. When a link is operating in full-duplex mode, it allows signals moving in both directions to potentially share link's capacity. Full-duplex communication is typically demonstrated via telephone network. Both sides can listen and talk at same time when speaking on phone. A full-duplex mode is utilized if there's a requirement for ongoing communication in both directions. However, canal's capacity needs to be split into two directions (Bartlett et al., 1969).

3.2.4. Parallel Transmission

> **TIPS**
>
> In half-duplex communication, each participant can either send or receive information at a given time, which can lead to delays and reduced efficiency.

n-bit groups of binary data, which consists only of 1s and 0s, can be created. In a manner similar to how people think about and utilize spoken language, computers create and consume data in groups of bits rather than individual letters. Data can be sent n bits at a time rather than 1 by grouping. Parallel transmission is the term used for this. The parallel transmission technique is essentially straightforward: Send n bits at once using *n* wires. With each clock tick, all *n* bits of one group can be sent from one device to another because each bit has its own cable in this arrangement. Figure 3.4 demonstrates parallel transmission for $n = 8$ in action. Usually, a cable with connectors on both ends is made up of eight wires. Speed is a benefit of parallel transmission. When everything else is equal, parallel transmission can outperform serial transmission in terms of transfer speed by a factor of *n*.

Cost, however, is a serious drawback. *N* communication lines are needed for parallel transmission merely to send the data stream. Parallel transmission is typically only used for short distances due to its high cost (Saltzberg, 1967).

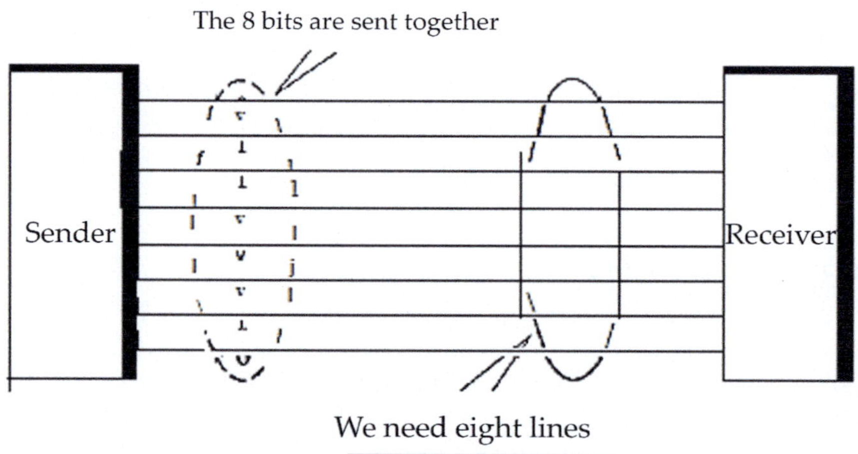

Figure 3.4. Image of parallel transmission.

Source: Network Encyclopedia, Creative Commons License.

3.2.5. Serial Transmission

One bit follows another when data is transmitted serially between two communicating devices, therefore we only need one communication channel instead of *n* (Figure 3.5).

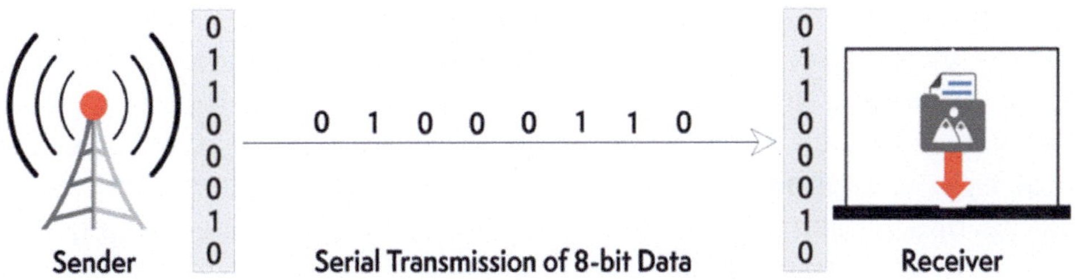

Figure 3.5. Picture of serial transmission.

Source: Quantil, Creative Commons License.

Serial transmission, which has an advantage over parallel transmission, lowers transmission's cost by roughly factor of n with only one communication channel. Interface between transmitter and line (parallel-to-serial) as well as between line and receiver (serial-to-parallel) both require conversion devices since communication between devices is parallel.

There're 3 different ways that serial transmission can happen: asynchronous, synchronous, and isochronous (Walker, 2003) (Figure 3.6).

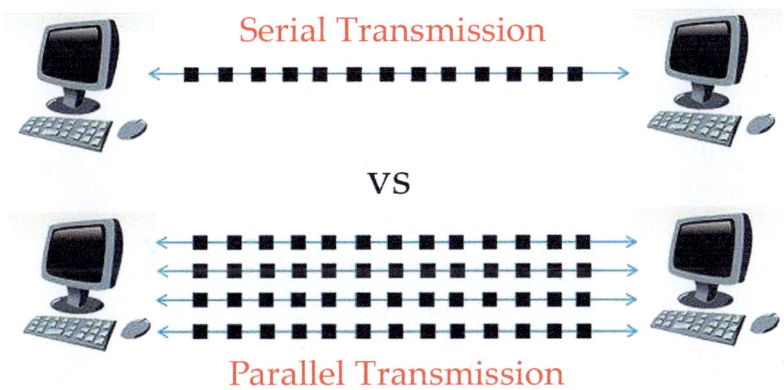

Figure 3.6. Depiction of difference between parallel and serial transmission modes.

Source: Tech Differences, Creative Commons License.

3.2.6. Asynchronous Transmission

Asynchronous transmission gets its name from fact that signal timing isn't crucial. Instead, predetermined patterns are used to interpret and receive information. The information can be retrieved by the receiving device without regard to the rhythm in which it is supplied if those patterns are followed. Basis of patterns is the division of bit stream into bytes. A link transmits each group, which typically consists of 8 bits, individually. Without respect to a timer, the transmitting system manages each group independently and relays it to the connection when it is ready. The receiver cannot utilize time to anticipate when following group will arrive without synchronization. Therefore, a bit is added to beginning of every byte to notify receiver of arrival of new group. The start bit is this bit, which is often a 0. One or more extra bits are added to end of byte to signal to the receiver that the byte is complete. Stop bits refer to these bits, which are typically Is (Lin et al., 2011). By using this technique, each byte is expanded to a minimum of 10 bits, where 8 bits are used for information and 2 bits or more for signals to receiver. Transmission of each byte may subsequently be followed by gap that lasts for various amounts of time. This gap can be represented by either an empty channel or a stream of extra stop bits. A receiver is made aware of the beginning and end of each byte by start and stop bits, as well as by the gap, which also helps it synchronize with the data stream. Because the transmitter and receiver do not need to be in sync at the byte level, this method is referred to as *asynchronous*. However, receiver must still be synced with incoming bit stream within each byte. In other words, some synchronization is necessary, but only for a single byte. At beginning of every new byte, receiving device resynchronizes. The receiver starts a timer and starts counting bits when it notices a start bit. The receiver searches for a stop bit n bit later. It waits until it finds following start bit after detecting stop bit. As opposed to additional stop bits, an idle line is used to represent the gap in this example's start and stop bits (Gheng & Chee, 2019).

Due to the need for control information and the insertion of gaps into the bit stream, asynchronous transmission is less efficient than other kinds of transmission. However, it is inexpensive and efficient, two features that make it a desirable option in circumstances like low-speed communication. An obvious application for asynchronous transmission is the connection of a keyboard to a computer. In terms of data proçessing, the user types slowly and randomly space out the characters (Tassiulas & Papavassiliou, 1995).

3.2.7. Synchronous Transmission

A bit stream is merged into longer "frames," that may include several bytes, during synchronous transmission. But there is no pause between one byte and the next as they are all inserted simultaneously onto the transmission network. It's up to receiver to divide bit stream into its component bytes for decoding. To put it another way, information is transmitted as an uninterrupted string of 1s and 0s, and the recipient breaks that string down into the bytes, or characters, which are required to reconstruct the data. The distinctions between bytes have been depicted (Luo & Südhof, 2017). These distinctions are fictitious; the sender just sends its data as one single string across the line. The spaces between bursts must be filled with a particular sequence of Os & Is that stands for idle if sender wants to deliver data in discrete bursts. As the bits come in, the receiver counts them and divides them into 8-bit chunks. Without gaps and start and stop bits, there is no built-in mechanism to help the receiving device adjust its bit synchronization midstream. Timing becomes crucial since the precision of the information received is entirely dependent on the receiver's capacity to maintain an accurate count of the bits as they arrive. Synchronous transmission has benefit of speed. Synchronous transmission is quicker than asynchronous transmission because there aren't any extra bits or gaps to add at sending end and remove at receiving end, and consequently, since there are less bits to transmit across the link. This makes it more advantageous for high-speed applications like data transmission between computers. Data link layer byte synchronization is completed (Oostvogels et al., 2020) (Figure 3.7).

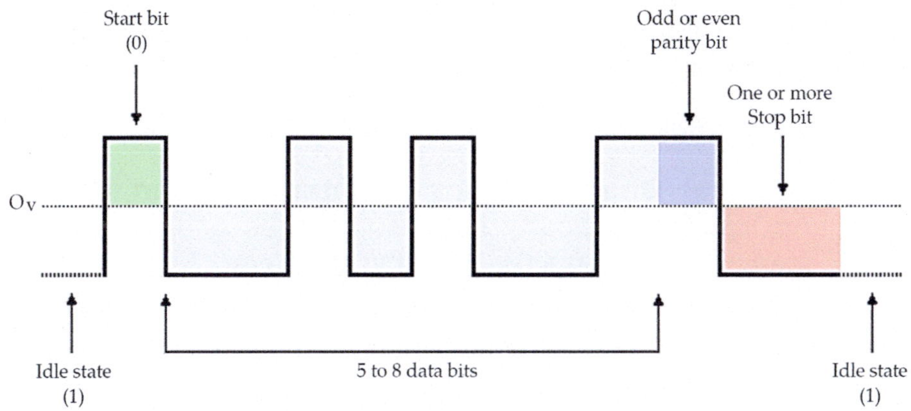

Figure 3.7. Illustration of difference between asynchronous and synchronous transmission.

Source: Technology UK, Creative Commons License.

3.3. LAYERS IN THE OSI MODEL

When music and video are played back in real-time, the frame delays can be unequal. The OSI model is based on a suggestion made by the International Standards Organization (ISO) as a preliminary step toward global standardization of the protocols used in the various layers (Day & Zimmermann, 1983). . Because it deals with integrating open systems—that is, systems that are accessible for communication with other systems—the model is known as the ISO-OSI (open systems interconnection). The OSI model, which is a layered framework for network system design, enables communication across all types of computer systems. It consists of seven different but linked layers, each of which describes stage in transmission of data over network (Saha et al., 2017).

Physical (layer 1), data connection (layer 2), network (layer 3), transport (layer 4), session (layer 5), presentation (layer 6), and application (layer 7) are the seven layers that make up OSI model. The diagram below shows the layers involved in transmitting a message from device A to device B. The message may go from point A to point B via a large number of intermediate nodes. Only first three OSI model layers are typically involved in these intermediary nodes.

Remember

The layers in the OSI model are like a language that network devices use to communicate with each other.

3.3.1. Physical Layer

The steps necessary to transport a bit stream through a physical medium are coordinated by the physical layer. The mechanical and electrical requirements of transmission medium interface are covered. It also describes actions and responsibilities that physical equipment and interfaces must take in order for transmission to occur (Soni et al., 2017).

The following issues are likewise of relevance to the physical layer:

- **Physical Characteristics of Interfaces and Medium:** An interface property between devices and transmission media are determined by physical layer. Furthermore, it specifies kind of transmission media (Sinha et al., 2017).
- **Representation of Bits:** A data in physical layer is just a stream of bits (a series of Os or 1s) without any meaning. Before being delivered, bits must first be encoded into electrical or optical signals. The physical layer determines type of encoding (Kim et al., 2020).
- **Data Rate:** Additionally, transmission rate, or number of bits that are transferred per second, is established at physical layer. In other words, duration of a bit, or how long it lasts, is defined by physical layer.
- **Synchronization of Bits:** In addition to using the same bit rate, the transmitter and receiver both need to be in sync at the bit level. To put it another way, the clocks of the sender and the recipient must match (Tang et al., 2009).
- **Line Configuration:** The physical layer deals with how devices are connected to media. Two devices are connected point-to-point using dedicated link. A multipoint configuration has multiple devices sharing a link (Guan et al., 2006).
- **Physical Topology:** It describes connections between network components. A mesh topology connects every device to every other device, and a hybrid topology, which mixes two or more topologies, connects every device to

every other device. Each device is connected to the next to form a ring in a bus topology.

- **Transmission Mode:** Simplex, half-duplex, or full-duplex transmission between two devices are all defined by the physical layer. In simplex mode, only one device can send, while the other can only receive. A one-way communication technique is simplex. In half-duplex mode, two devices can send and receive, but not simultaneously. Two devices can send and receive simultaneously while operating in full-duplex (or just duplex) mode (Mabrouk et al., 2016) (Figure 3.8).

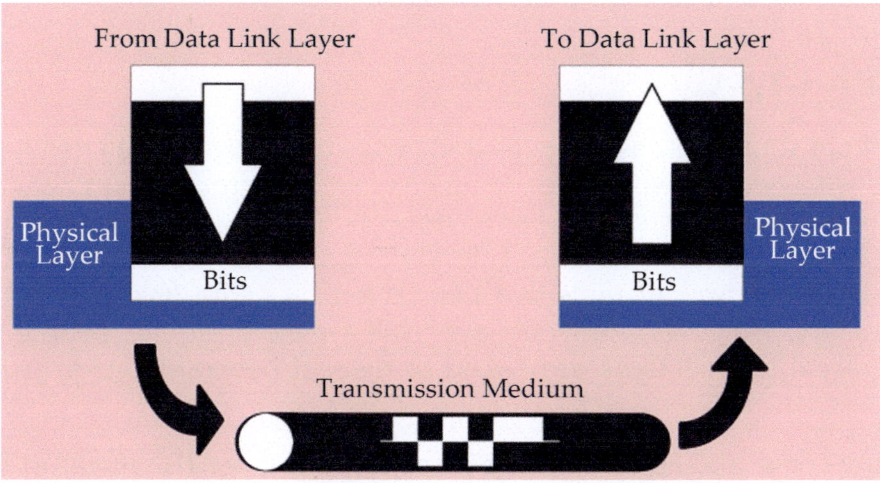

Figure 3.8. Illustration of physical layer of OSI model.

Source: Study Opedia, Creative Commons License.

3.3.2. Data Link Layer

The data link layer converts the physical layer, a fundamental transmission facility, into a reliable link. It creates an illusion that physical layer is error-free at upper layer (network layer). A data link layer also performs following extra tasks:

- **Framing:** Data link layer receives a stream of bits from network layer and converts them into frames, which are small, manageable data units (Lynch et al., 1988)
- **Physical Addressing:** If frames must be dispersed among numerous computers on the network, to identify sender and/ or recipient of frame, data link layer adds header to frame. Address of device which connects network of sender to system for which frame is intended is known as receiver address of frame (Njoh, 2010).

- **Flow Control:** If the rate at which data are produced in the sender is lower than the rate at which data are absorbed by the receiver, a data connection layer applies flow control to prevent overloading the receiver.
- **Error Control:** A data link layer improves physical layer dependability by introducing methods to detect and retransmit corrupted or missing frames. It also makes use of technique to find duplicate frames. To achieve error control, a trailer is often introduced at end of frame (AfiqahAzahari et al., 2013).
- **Access Control:** When multiple devices are sharing the same link, data link layer protocols are required to determine which device is in charge at any one time (OConnor, 2010).

3.3.3. Network Layer

Sending packet from source to destination—and occasionally over many networks (links)—is responsibility of network layer. Data link layer controls packet delivery between two systems connected by same network (links), whereas network layer ensures every packet arrives at its intended destination from the point of origin. In most cases, if two systems are connected by same link, a network layer isn't necessary. However, network layer will typically require source-to-destination delivery if two systems are linked to distinct networks (links) using devices.

Following are some additional duties of the network layer (Bhagwat et al., 1996):

- **Logical Addressing:** The data link layer's physical addressing solution addresses the addressing issue locally. When a packet crosses a network boundary, a different addressing scheme is needed to help identify source and destination systems. The network layer adds a header, among other things, logical addresses of sender and receiver, to the packet originating from the top layer (Larkins & Dinan, 2016).
- **Routing:** When two separate links or networks are connected to create a larger network or a network of networks, the connecting devices, which are known as routers or switches, are responsible for directing data packets to the appropriate destination. It is one of the network layer's duties to offer this mechanism (Maihofer, 2004).

3.3.4. Transport Layer

From one operation to another, the complete message must be transmitted over the transport layer. A process is a running application program on a host. Although network layer regulates packet delivery from source to destination, it has no knowledge of how the packets are related. It treats each element independently, regardless of whether it is part of another message. Assuring that complete message arrives intact and in right order is responsibility of transport layer, which also controls flow from source to destination (Iren et al., 1999).

The transport layer also has the following obligations:

- **Service-Point Addressing:** Nowadays, computers typically have several programs active at once. As a result, transmission of data between two computers is referred to as source-to-destination delivery, as well as between one specific process (running program) on one computer and another specific process (running program) on another computer. Therefore, a service-point address (sometimes called a port address) must be included in transport layer header. Following delivery of each packet by network layer to appropriate computer, transport layer transfers full message to that computer's relevant process (LaMagna et al., 2016).
- **Segmentation and Reassembly:** A message is separated into sendable sections, each with its own sequence number. When message arrives at its destination, transport layer may accurately rebuild it by utilizing these numbers to identify and replace any missing packets during transmission (Gruen & Woods, 1983).
- **Connection Control:** A transport layer might be either connection-oriented or connection-free. A connectionless transport layer is used to transfer each segment to the target machine's transport layer, which interprets each one as a single packet. A connection-oriented transport layer connects to transport layer at destination computer before sending packets. Once all of data has been sent, the connection is terminated (Varvarigos & Sharma, 1998).
- **Flow Control:** It is handled by transport layer, which is also responsible for data connection layer. But at this layer, flow regulation takes place over multiple links rather than just one (Bewley, 2001).
- **Error Control:** It is handled by transport layer, as well as the data connection layer. However, at this layer, error handling is done process-to-process rather than across a single link. While being sent to receiving transport layer, sending transport layer ensures that no part of the message is lost, duplicated, or destroyed. Retransmission is frequently used to correct errors (Moon & Kim, 2007) (Figure 3.9).

KEYWORD

Error control is basically process in data link layer of detecting or identifying and re-transmitting data frames that might be lost or corrupted during transmission.

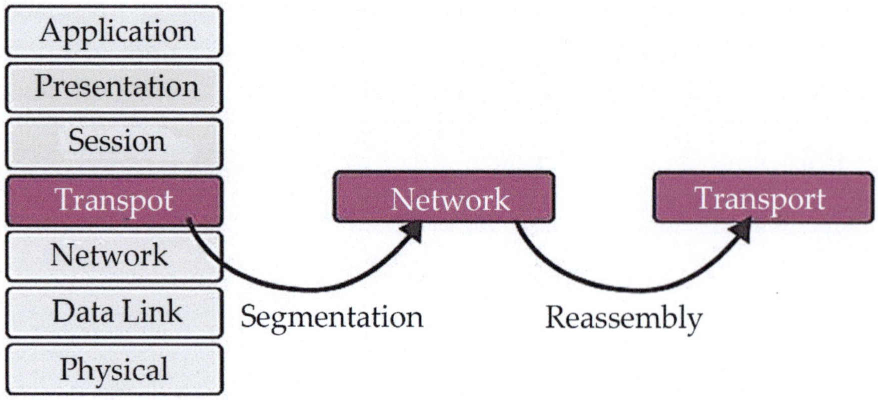

Figure 3.9. Schematic of transport layer.

Source: Fiberbit, Creative Commons License.

3.3.5. Session Layer

There are some tasks that need for greater assistance than what first 3 layers (physical, data link, and network) can provide. Network dialog controller is located at session layer. It's responsible for establishing, maintaining, and synchronizing system communication (Landfeldt et al., 1999).

The session layer is required to perform the following specialized duties:

- **Dialog Control:** Two separate systems are able to communicate with one another in session layer. It allows two processes to communicate either in half-duplex (only one direction at a time) or full duplex (both ways at once) (Bottoni et al., 1999).
- **Synchronization:** A process can use the session layer to insert synchronization and checkpoint points into a data stream (Ehley et al., 1994).

3.3.6. Presentation Layer

Between two systems, the presentation layer controls syntax and semantics of the information communicated.

The following are some specific responsibilities for the presentation layer (Fiala et al., 2004):

- **Translation:** Character strings, integers, and other data types are widely used to communicate between two processes (running programs). The information must be transformed into bit streams before it can be transmitted. In light of the fact that diverse computers employ distinct encoding schemes, it falls on the presentation layer to guarantee compatibility. At sender, the presentation layer converts the data from the format that is unique to the sender to a more universal one. A receiving device's presentation layer converts common format into the receiver-specific format (Śmiałek et al., 2012).

- **Encryption:** When dealing with sensitive information, a system needs to be able to maintain users' privacy. Encryption is used by sender to convert the original data into a new format before sending the new message through network. Decryption reverses first procedure of returning message's original format (Guangyong & Ruolan, 2021).
- **Compression:** Data compression reduces an amount of bits required to hold data. When transmitting multimedia elements such as music, text, and video, data compression is critical.

KEYWORD

Encryption is the process of encoding information. This process converts the original representation of the information, known as plaintext, into an alternative form known as ciphertext. Ideally, only authorized parties can decipher a ciphertext back to plaintext and access the original information.

3.3.7. Application Layer

The application layer provides network connectivity to both software and human users. Email, shared database administration, remote file access and transfer and variety of other distributed information services are available, as are user interfaces and support (Bhattacharjee et al., 1997).

The application layer provides the services listed below:

- **Network Virtual Terminal (NVT):** Users can connect to far-off hosts using NVT, software that replicates genuine terminal.
- **File Transfer, Access, and Management:** A user can download files to their local workstation using this program, manage or control those files locally, and access files on a remote host (to make changes or read data) all at same time (Engler et al., 1995).
- **Mail Services:** This application is basis for email archiving and forwarding.
- **Directory Services:** This program provides information about numerous items and services, as well as worldwide access to external database sources (Bujas et al., 2015) (Figure 3.10).

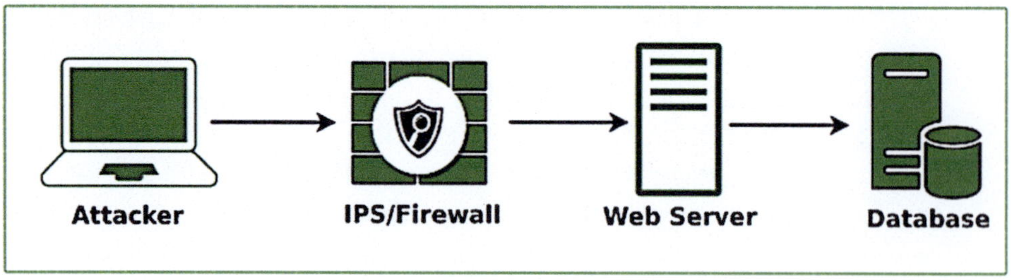

Figure 3.10. Schematic of application layers attacks.

Source: Geeks for Geeks, Creative Commons License.

3.4. NETWORKS

Nodes are the individual components that make up a network. They are connected to one another through communication lines. Any machine, like a computer or printer, which can send or receive data created by other nodes on network is referred to as a node (Wilkov, 1972).

3.4.1. Network Criteria

Network needs to be able to fulfill variety of needs. Performance, dependability, and security are the three that are most important.

3.4.1.1. Performance

You can measure performance in different ways, such as reaction and transit times. Transit time is amount of time it takes for message to travel between two devices. Response time is period of time between request and a response. Network performance is determined by multitude of elements, some of which are number of users, transmission channel's kind, linked equipment's capabilities, and software effectiveness (Stoilova et al., 2020).

3.4.1.2. Reliability

Network dependability can be assessed using frequency of failure, time it takes for link to recover from failure, and network's resilience in case of disaster (Seemkooei, 2001).

3.4.1.3. Security

Examples of network security problems are protecting data from unauthorized access, preventing data loss and development, and creating guidelines and methods for recovering from breaches and data loss (Ling & Masao, 2011) (Figure 3.11).

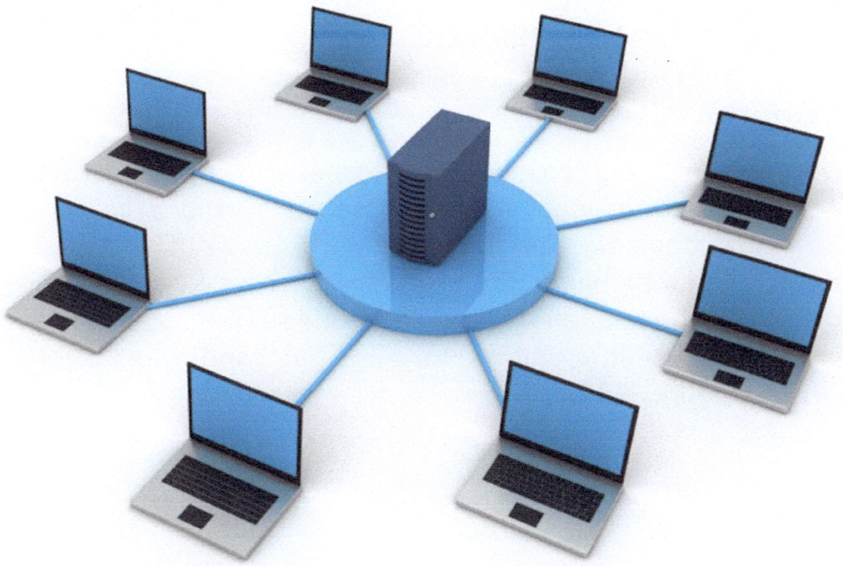

Figure 3.11. Image of computer networking.

Source: Bourneto Code, Creative Commons License.

3.4.2. Physical Structures

3.4.2.1. Types of Connections

Network is made up of two or more devices connected by connections. Connection enables data flow between two devices, which is a communications channel. Connections that are both point-to-point and multipoint are possible:

- **Point-to-Point:** This connection establishes direct link between two devices. Only these two gadgets are permitted to use the link's maximum transmission speed. Point-to-point connections frequently include a physical wire or cable going between two ends, although alternative options, such satellite connectivity or as microwave, are also possible. To change channel on a television, use an infrared remote control, which establishes point-to-point connection with television's control system (Modarressi et al., 2010).
- **Multipoint:** More than two devices can be linked together through a single connection in a multipoint setup. In a multipoint setting, channel capacity is split between multiple

users over either space or time. If several different devices are able to use same connection at same time, then we call that a *spatially shared* connection. When users must alternate using a connection, it's deemed *timeshared* (Bubenik et al., 1991).

3.4.2.2. Physical Topology

This term "physical topology" refers to network's physical topology. A topology is made up of two or more links, and a link connects one or more devices. The topology of a network is represented geometrically to highlight the relationships between each of the connections and links, also known as nodes. There are four primary topologies that could exist: mesh, ring, bus, and star (Bejerano et al., 2003) (Figure 3.12):

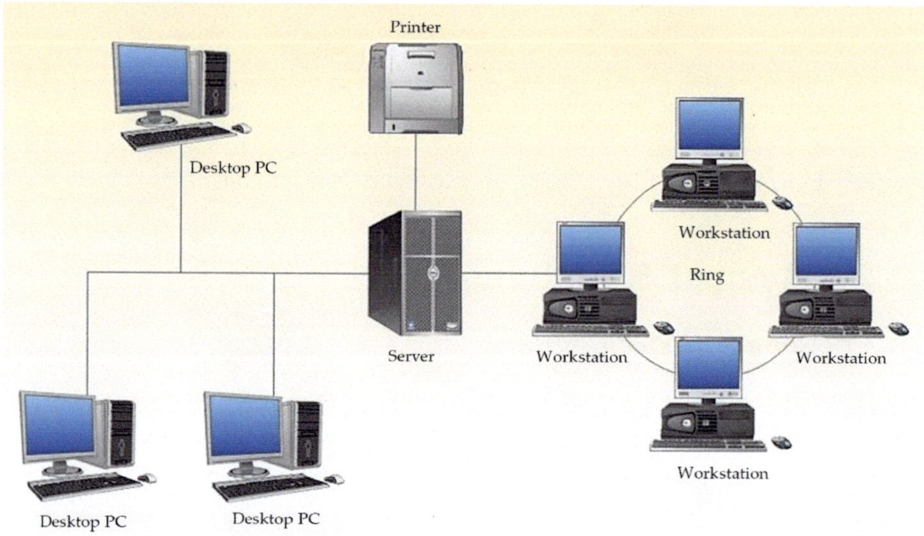

Figure 3.12. Diagram of physical topology.

Source: IT Release, Creative Commons License.

- **Mesh:** Each device has distinct point-to-point connection with other device, in mesh toplogy. According to definition of the phrase, a dedicated link only sends data between two devices it connects. In order to determine mesh network with n node's total number of physical links, we first address requirement that every node should be connected to every other node. Nodes in n-l group should be connected to node 1, nodes in the n-l group must be connected to node 2, and nodes in the n-l group must be connected to node n. There should be n(n–1) physical connections. On the other hand, if each physical link supports two-way communication (duplex mode), number of links can be divided by two. In other words, a mesh topology requires n(n–1)/2 duplex-mode links. To support those many links, each network device should've n–1 input/output ports in order to communicate with other n–1 station (Mubeen & Kumar, 2010).

Advantages

- Since each connection can support its own data load when using dedicated links, traffic issues which arise when links are shared by many devices are avoided.
- Mesh topology is trustworthy. One broken link does not render the system useless.
- The advantages of security or privacy exist. When a message is sent over a dedicated line, only intended recipient can see it. Other users are prevented from viewing messages by physical obstacles.
- Identification and isolation of faults are made simple by point-to-point connections. Traffic can be rerouted to avoid links that might have issues. This feature helps the network manager to locate fault precisely and assists in determining its source and resolution (Bianchi et al., 2003).

Disadvantages:

- A mesh's drawbacks are linked quantity of cabling required for each device to communicate with each other.
- Installation and reconnecting might be challenging.
- There may not be enough room (in the form of ceilings, floors or walls) to accommodate sheer weight of the wiring.
- The cost of the cable and I/O ports required to connect each link may be unaffordable (Maxemchuk, 1985).
- **Star Topology:** In star topology, the hub, which serves as the central controller, is the sole dedicated point-to-point link that each device has. Devices are not connected to one another directly. A star topology, on the other hand, does not provide direct traffic between devices, in contrast to a mesh topology. The controller performs the role of a market: A device must transfer data to controller before controller may pass data to other connected device in order for the two devices to communicate (Zhu et al., 2019).

Advantages:

- The cost of star topology is lower than that of mesh topology. For any device in a star to connect to any number of other devices, only one connection and one I/O port are needed.
- Simple to install and modify.

- The amount of wiring required is significantly reduced, and adding, moving, or removing devices only requires one connection: that between the device and hub.
- Strongness is another benefit. If only one of the links is broken, only that connection will be disrupted. The remaining connections are active. This element also makes fault isolation and fault identification simple. As long as hub is operational, it can be used to track link issues and avoid broken links (Barranco et al., 2009).
- **Disadvantages:** The dependence of star topology on a single point, hub, is one of its major drawbacks. If the hub breaks, the system is useless. When compared to mesh, a star requires a far lower number of wires; nonetheless, each node must still be connected to the central hub. Because of this, a star topology frequently requires more cabling than certain other topologies (such as bus or ring) (Balabanov et al., 2016) (Figure 3.13).

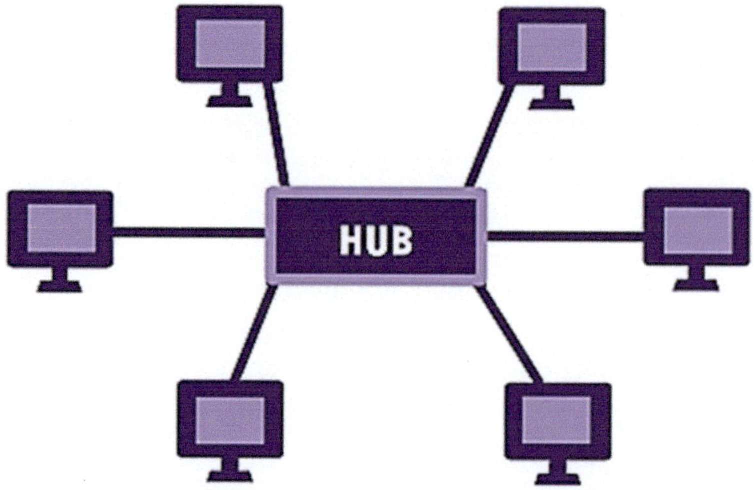

Figure 3.13. Depiction of star topology.

Source: Java T Point, Creative Commons License.

- **Bus:** The topology of bus is multipoint. The backbone of a network is the main connection between all of the nodes. To connect nodes to bus cable, drop lines and taps are used. Drop lines are connections between devices and main cables. A tap is connector which makes a connection with the metallic core of a cable by either splicing into main cable or cutting through cable's wrapping. Some of an energy of a signal is converted into heat as it moves along the backbone. As a result, as it moves farther and farther, it gets weaker and weaker. As a result, there are restrictions on the amount of taps and the spacing between them that a bus can sustain (Lafata & Vodrazka, 2011).

- **Advantages:** A bus topology has the benefit of being simple to implement. The most effective route for laying backbone cable can be chosen and drop lines of various lengths can be used to connect it to the nodes. In this regard, the cabling demands of a bus topology are lower than those of a mesh or star topology. For instance, four lengths of cable that reach the hub are needed if there are four network devices configured in a star pattern in the same room. This redundancy is removed in a bus. Only the backbone wire traverses entire construction. Each drop line simply needs to extend as far as closest bone point (Cerutti et al., 2016).
- **Disadvantages:** Inconvenient reconnecting and fault separation are two drawbacks. Typically, a bus is built to be installed as efficiently as possible. Therefore, adding more devices may be challenging. Quality reduction may result from signal reflection at the taps. This deterioration can be avoided by limiting number and closeness of devices connected to particular cable length. The backbone might consequently need to be changed or replaced to accommodate additional devices. Additionally, even communication between devices on same side of the issue is halted by failure or break in bus cable. Noise is produced in both directions as a result of damaged area reflecting signals in direction of origin (Pavel, 2015).

• **Ring:** The only other two devices are on either side of each point-to-point link that each device in ring topology has. Until it reaches its destination, signal is delivered along a ring in a single direction from one device to the next. Each component of ring contains a repeater. A device's repeater regenerates bits and sends them on when it receives a signal meant for another device (Yoon et al., 2006).

- **Advantages:** Installing and rearranging a ring is not that difficult. Only the immediate neighbors of each device are connected, either physically or logically. Adding or removing device simply requires two connections to be changed. The only limitations are those related to media and traffic (such as the number of devices and the maximum ring length). Fault isolation is also made simpler. In a ring, a signal typically circulates constantly. One device can sound an alarm if it doesn't get a signal within a predetermined time frame. Alarm notifies network operator of issue and where it is (Ross, 1987).
- **Disadvantages:** Traffic that is only going one way can be problematic. The entire network might go down in one ring if

there is break in ring (e.g., station that is disabled). Using a secondary ring or a switch that can turn the break off can remedy this problem. Ring topologies were widespread when IBM debuted their local-area network Token Ring. Today, this topology is less common due to the demand for faster LANs (Jebamalai et al., 2022).

3.5. NETWORK CATEGORIES

3.5.1. Local Area Networks (LAN)

Local area networks (LANs), commonly known as LANs, are privately owned networks that can cover huge areas on a campus or in a building. In corporate offices and manufacturing facilities, personal computers and workstations are frequently connected in order to share resources (such printers) and transmit information. LANs differ from other networks in three ways:

> **Did you Know?**
>
> Local area networks (LANs) are essential components of modern workplaces, facilitating fast and reliable communication and data transfer between connected devices.

- Their transmission technology;
- Their size; and
- Their topology.

Due to LAN size limitations, the worst-case transmission time is constrained and known ahead. It is possible to use specific types of designs that would not be feasible without knowledge of this bond. It also makes network administration simpler. LANs may employ a transmission technique similar to the party lines historically employed by telephone companies in rural regions, which consists of a cable to which all the devices are connected. Traditional LANs feature rates between 10 and 100 Mbps, a delay of a few microseconds or nanoseconds, and a low error rate.

Modern LANs can reach speeds of 10 Gbps (Clark et al., 1978) (Figure 3.14).

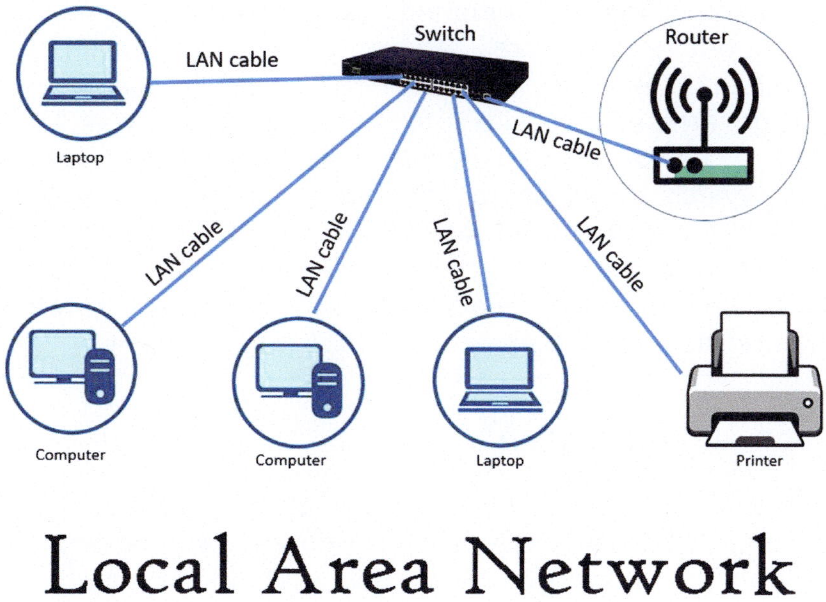

Figure 3.14. Illustration of local network area (LAN).

Source: Heavy.ai, Creative Commons License.

3.5.2. Metropolitan Area Network (MAN)

The city is surrounded by a MAN, or metropolitan area network. The most well-known MAN is the cable television network, which may be found in many different locations. Communities without sufficient over-the-air television coverage formerly relied on communal antenna installations.

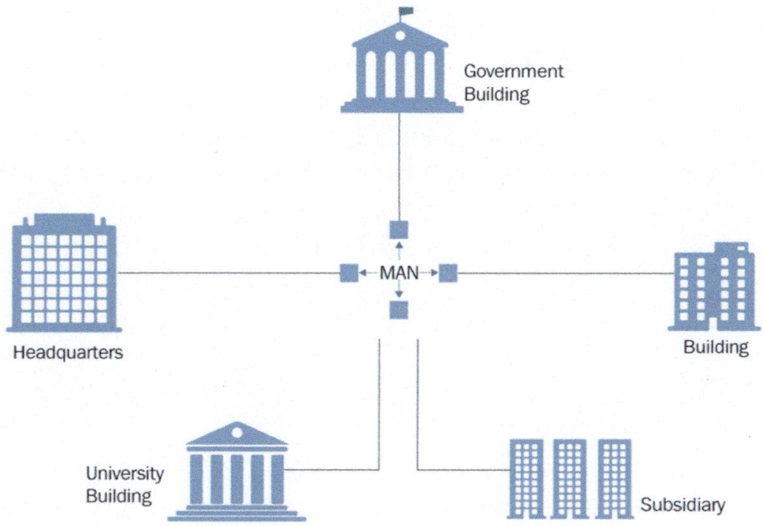

Figure 3.15. Image of metropolitan area network (MAN).

Source: CyberHoot, Creative Commons License.

In these early systems, massive antenna was installed on a nearby hill, and signal was then sent to clients' residences. These were initially ad hoc, locally developed systems. Then businesses started to enter the market, winning contracts from local governments to wire a full city. Next phase was television content, including entire channels made only for cable. These channels frequently have a narrow focus, such as all sports, all cuisine, all gardening, etc. But from the time they were developed until late 1990s, they were solely made for receiving television. The MAN is not limited to cable television. Another MAN, known as IEEE 802.16, has been developed recently in connection with high-speed wireless Internet access (Green et al., 1993) (Figure 3.15).

3.5.3. Wide Area Network (WAN)

Wide area networks or WANs, typically cover whole continent or country. It has a number of computers designed to run user (or application) programs. These devices are referred to as hosts. A communication subnet, or simply subnet, connects the hosts. Hosts, such as people's personal computers, are owned and controlled by the consumers, as opposed to communication subnets, which are frequently operated and owned by telephone companies or Internet service providers. Similar to how the telephone system transmits speech from speaker to listener, the function of subnet is to transport messages from host to host. An entire network design is significantly simplified by separating the network's purely communication-related components—the subnet—from its application-related components—the hosts (Yang et al., 2019). Transmission lines and switching equipment make up the subnet in the majority of WANs. Between machines, bits are moved using transmission lines. Optical fiber, copper wire, or even radio links can be used to construct them. In the majority of WANs, the network has a large number of transmission lines, each of which connects two routers. Without a common transmission line, two routers can only talk to one another via going through a third router. For a packet to be transmitted from one router to another, it must first be received by all of the intermediate routers along the path, stored until the appropriate output line becomes available, and then forwarded. A store-and-forward or packet-switched subnet is one that is set up using this technique (Kandula et al., 2014). Store-and-forward subnets are present in almost all WANs, with the exception of satellite-based ones. Cells are frequently used to describe small, uniformly sized packets. The idea behind a packet-switched WAN is crucial. In most cases, when a process on one host has to transmit a message to a process on another computer, sending host first divides message into packets, each of which bears its own sequential number. A network is then rapidly bombarded with these packets, one at a time. The packets are transmitted to the receiving host individually through the network, where they're combined back into original message and sent to receiving process. Not all WANs use packet switching. Satellite network is an additional option. Every router has an antenna that it uses to transmit and receive data. Every router can hear the satellite's output, and in some situations, they may also hear each other's upward transmissions to the satellite. When just some of the routers have a satellite antenna, they may be connected to a sizable point-to-point subnet. Satellite networks are broadcast by nature and perform best when that characteristic is significant (Wang et al., 1998) (Figure 3.16).

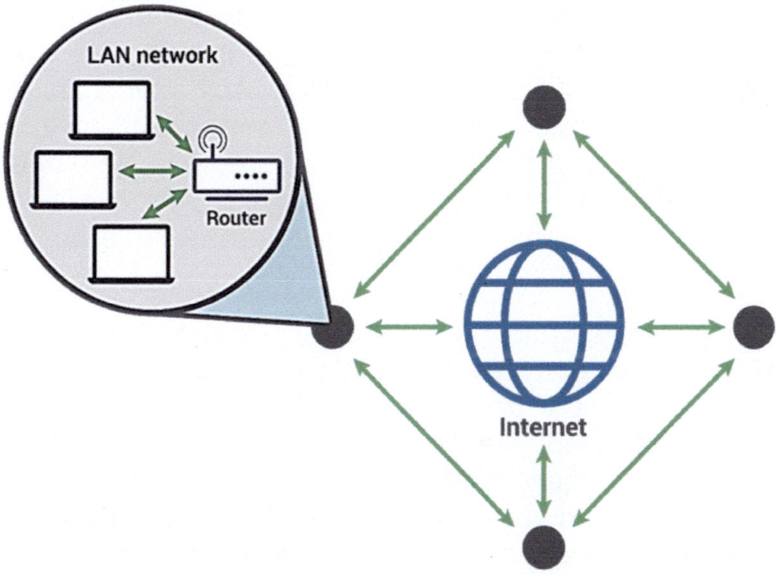

Figure 3.16. Schematic of wide area network (WAN).

Source: Cloudflare, Creative Commons License.

3.6. CONNECTING DEVICES

3.6.1. Repeaters

A device that solely functions at physical layer is called a repeater. Within a network, signals that contain information can only travel so far before attenuation compromises integrity of data. Before the signal deteriorates or becomes corrupted, a repeater receives it and recreates the original bit pattern. A signal is then sent by the repeater. A repeater joins two segments of the same LAN, not two separate LANs. The connected segments continue to be a part of a single LAN. A repeater cannot connect two LANs that use different protocols. Although it's tempting, it is incorrect to equate repeater to an amplifier. An amplifier amplifies anything that is supplied into it without being able to distinguish between intended signal and background noise. A repeater regenerates the signal rather than amplifying it. It makes a copy, bit for bit, at original strength of signal that's weak or corrupted (Lucamarini et al., 2018).

3.6.2. Bridges or Link Layer Switches

Both physical layer and data connection layer are utilized by bridge or link layer switch (also known as a switch). As a component of the physical layer, it is responsible for regenerating the signal that it is given. Due to fact that the bridge operates at data link layer, it's possible for it to investigate physical (MAC) addresses that are contained within frame. A bridge has the ability to filter. It has the ability to examine a frame's destination address and determine whether it should be forwarded or dropped. The decision must state the port if the frame is to be forwarded. A table on a bridge links addresses to ports.

Let's use an illustration. In Figure 3.17, a bridge links two LANs together. A bridge analyzes its table to determine departure port when a frame with the destination station 712B13456142 arrives at port 1. Its table indicates that since frames for 7I2B13456142 depart from port 1, there is no requirement for forwarding and the frame can be deleted. On other hand, if a frame for the address 712B13456141 arrives at port 2, frame is forwarded, and the departure port is port 1. In the first scenario, LAN 2 is left without any traffic; in second scenario, both LANs are active. In our illustration, two-port bridge is shown; in practice, bridge typically includes more ports (Ortiz et al., 2012).

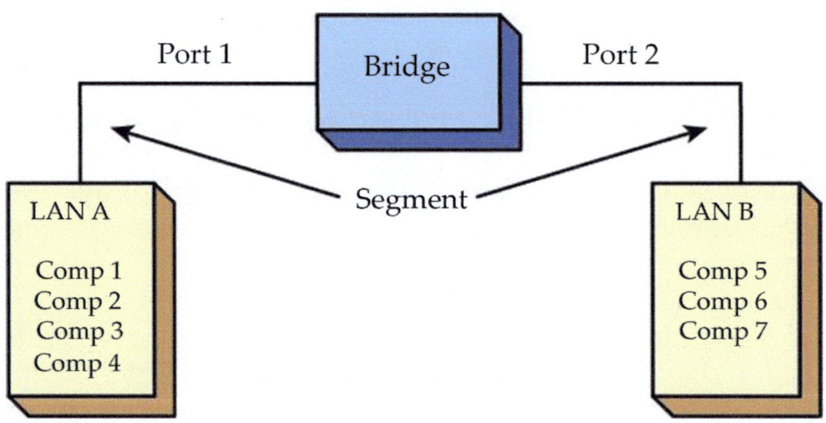

Figure 3.17. Illustration of bridge that links two LANs together.

Source: Pearson Education, Creative Commons License.

3.6.3. Hubs

A hub is a piece of equipment which only works at physical layer. Within a network, signals which contain information can only travel so far before attenuation compromises integrity of data. When a signal is received, a repeater regenerates and retimes original bit pattern before it is too weak or corrupted. After then, the signal will be sent via the repeater. A repeater is a multiport device, frequently referred to as a hub, which may act as both a repeater and a connecting point in a star architecture. Upon arrival at the hub, a packet from station A to station B has its frame's signal regenerated to eliminate any potential corrupting noise. However, the hub forwards packets from all outgoing terminals except one that received signal. In other words, frame is broadcasted. Every station in LAN receives it, but only station B saves it and other station discard it. A physical layer device is a hub. They lack a link layer address and don't look at the receiving frame's link layer address. They just regenerate damaged bits and release them through every port (Goldenberg et al., 2009).

3.6.4. Routers

Using host-to-host addressing, router is 3-layer device which routes packets according to their logical addresses. When linking LANs and WANs to internet, a router will consult its routing table to determine the best route to take. To update routing tables routing protocols are used, which are usually dynamic in nature. A three-layer device is a router. It functions at the network, data connection, and physical layers. As a device operating at the physical layer, it recreates signal that it receives. The router examines packet's physical addresses as link layer device. A router examines network layer addresses in its capacity as network layer device. Networks can be linked through a router. To put it another way, a router is an internetworking tool that joins separate networks to create an internetwork.

A router differs significantly from a repeater or switch in three ways.

- Each interface on a router is assigned both physical and logical address;
- A router only responds to packets whose link layer destination address coincides with interface's address at which packet arrives; and
- When a router forwards a packet, it modifies the link layer address of the packet (Chao, 2002).

3.6.5. Gateways

Gateway is often a computer which performs operations on all seven OSI model layers or all five Internet layers. An application message is received, read, and evaluated by a gateway. As a consequence of this, it is possible to utilize it in the role of a connecting device between two distinct forms of internetworks. For example, a network built using the OSI model can be linked to another network built using the Internet model. A frame received from first system may be moved up to OSI application layer and deleted by gateway bridging the two systems (Gong, 2001).

3.7. ANALOG AND DIGITAL

3.7.1. Analog Data

Continuous information is referred to as "analog data." For example, a continuous type of information is provided by an analog clock with minute, second, and hour hands. Analog data, such as sounds produced by a human voice, can use continuous values. An analog wave is generated in air whenever someone speaks. A microphone may record this, and the analog signal it produces can then be transformed to a digital signal by sampling (Lguensat et al., 2017).

3.7.2. Digital Data

Information with discrete states is referred to as digital data. For instance, a digital clock that displays the minutes and hours will abruptly shift from 8:05 to 8:06. Discrete values can be found in digital data. As an illustration, data are stored in computer memory as 0s and 1s. For transmission via a media, they can be modulated into an analog signal or turned into digital signal (Selwyn, 2015).

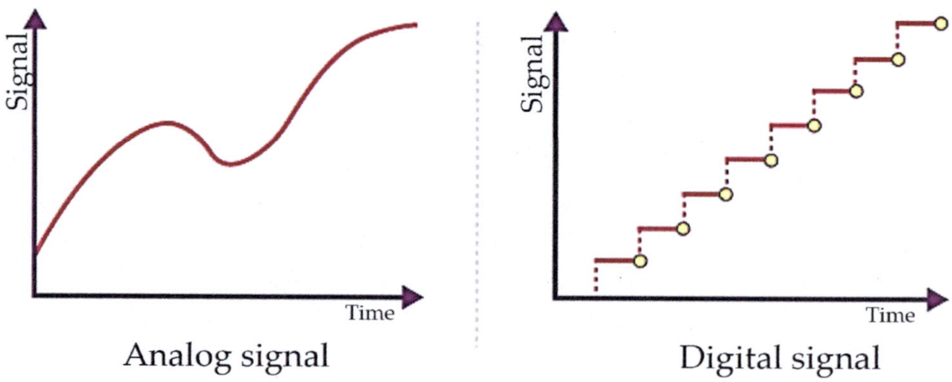

Figure 3.18. Graphical representation of analog and digital signals.

Source: Byju's, Creative Commons License.

Signals can be digital or/and analog, much like data they represent. An analog signal can have an infinite number of levels of intensity over time. There are an endless number of values along the wave's path as it travels from value A to value B. On other hand, there are finite number of defined values for a digital signal. While each value might be any integer, it's frequently as straightforward as 1 & O. Plotting signals on two perpendicular axes is the most basic technique to display them. Strength or value of a signal is shown on vertical axis. Time is represented via horizontal axis. A digital signal and analog signal are shown in Figure 3.18. There is infinity of points that the curve that represents the analog signal travels through. However, the digital signal's vertical lines show how the signal abruptly switches from one value to another (Petrova et al., 2010).

3.7.3. Periodic and Nonperiodic Signals

In a defined amount of time, known as a period, a periodic signal completes a pattern and then repeats that pattern across consecutive similar periods. A cycle is result of one whole pattern being completed. Nonperiodic signal swings without showing a pattern or cycle that repeats over time (Gregory & Loredo, 1993).

KEYWORD

analog signal is a voltage, current, or physical quantity that continuously and infinitely varies in accordance with some time-varying parameter.

3.7.4. Periodic Analog Signals

There are 2 types of periodic analog signals: basic and composite. Sine waves and other similarly simple periodic analog signals cannot be decomposed into their component parts. The sine waves that make up a composite periodic analog signal are individually identifiable.

3.8. SINE WAVE

Most basic type of periodic analog signal is the sine wave. The change that takes place over the course of a cycle is consistent and unchanging, taking the form of a continuous, rolling flow when we think of it as simple oscillating curve. You can see the sine wave in Figure 3.19. A single arc above time axis and single arc below it make up each cycle (Dorman et al., 1997).

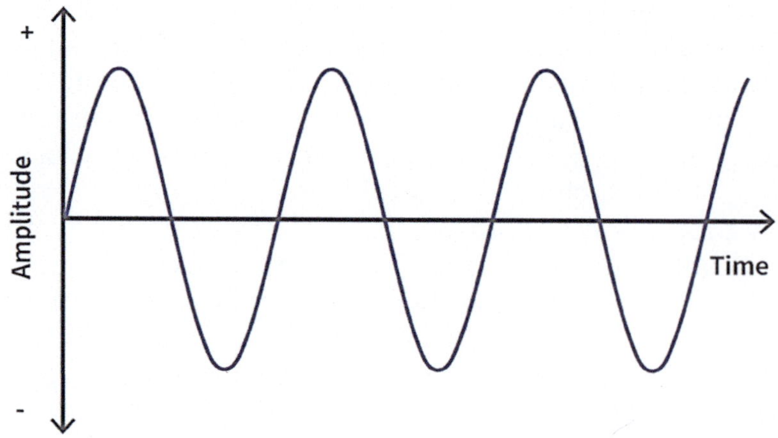

Figure 3.19. *Image of sine wave.*

Source: Investopedia, Creative Commons License.

3.8.1. Characteristics of Signals

3.8.1.1. Peak Amplitude

Absolute value of signal's peak intensity is its peak amplitude, which is proportional to energy it contains. Electric signal peak amplitude is frequently expressed in volts (Hartmann, 1978).

3.8.1.2. Period and Frequency

The term "period" describes how many seconds it takes for a signal to go through one cycle. The quantity of periods in I s is referred to as frequency. Remember that period and frequency are just two different ways to define the same thing. The calculations below demonstrate that period is inverse of frequency and frequency is inverse of period.

$$f = 1/T \text{ and } T = 1/f$$

Duration is formally measured in seconds. The official frequency measurement unit is Hertz (Hz), or cycle per second (Jha et al., 2014).

3.8.1.3. Phase

The waveform's location in relation to time O is indicated by the word phase. Phase specifies the amount of the movement if we consider the wave to be something that may move either backward or forward along time axis. It shows situation of the first cycle right now. Degrees or radians are used to express phase [1° is 2n/360 rad, and 1 rad is 360/(2n)]. A phase shift of 360° is equivalent to shift of full period, phase shift of 180° is equivalent to change of half period, and phase shift of 90° is equivalent to shift of a quarter period:

- A sine wave with phase of 0° and zero amplitude starts at time 0. The size is expanding.
- A sine wave with a 90° phase has its maximum amplitude at time 0. Less amplitude is being seen.
- A sine wave having zero amplitude and phase of 0° starts at 0 time. The magnitude is increasing (Haider et al., 2012).

3.8.1.4. Wavelength

Another feature of signal passing across transmission medium is its wavelength. The wavelength of a fundamental sine wave links its period or frequency to the medium's transmission speed.

The wavelength of a signal depends on both medium and frequency, whereas signal frequency is independent of medium. Every signal has a characteristic called a wavelength. The term wavelength is frequently used in data communications to describe how light travels through an optical cable. A simple signal can reach a maximum distance in one wavelength. If one knows the signal's duration and propagation speed (speed of light), one may compute wavelength. However, because period and frequency are connected to one another, if we express – wavelength by 'λ,' frequency by 'f,' and propagation speed by 'c' (speed of light), we get:

Wavelength = Propagation speed * Period = propagation speed/frequency

$\lambda = c/f$

Typically, wavelength is measured in micrometers (microns) rather than meters (Roy et al., 2009).

3.8.1.5. Bandwidth

The bandwidth of a composite signal is the range of frequencies that it contains. In most cases, bandwidth simply the difference between two numbers. A composite signal's bandwidth, for instance, is 5,000–1,000, or 4,000, if its frequencies range from 1,000 to 5,000. All integer frequencies between 1,000 and 5,000 are included in the periodic signal's bandwidth (for example, 1,000, 1001, 1,002,). The nonperiodic signals' bandwidth is similar to that of periodic signals, but their frequencies are continuous (Lai & Baker, 1999).

3.9. COMMON NETWORK APPLICATIONS

3.9.1. TELNET

TErminaL NETwork is referred to by the acronym TELNET. It follows International Organization for Standards' (ISO) recommended standard TCP/IP protocol for virtual terminal service. Through use of TELNET, it is possible to connect to a remote system so that local terminal seems to be one at remote system. When TELNET was developed, timesharing was the norm for most operating systems, including UNIX. Multiple users can access a huge computer in this setting. A terminal, which typically consists of a keyboard, monitor, and mouse, is how a user interacts with a computer. With the aid of a terminal emulator, even a microcomputer may emulate a terminal (Marx et al., 2022).

3.9.1.1. Logging

Users who participate in timesharing have some access rights to certain resources. Every authorized user has a username and, most likely, a password. The user is identified as a system component by the user identification. With a user ID or log-in name, user logs into system to gain access. To stop unauthorized users from accessing the resources, the system also has password checking.

Local log-in is the process of logging into a local timesharing system. The terminal driver accepts the keystrokes entered by the user at terminal or on computer running terminal emulator. An operating system receives the characters from terminal driver. Following the operating system's interpretation of character combination, desired application program or utility is called. A user logs in remotely when she wishes to use an application software or utility that is hosted on another computer. TELNET client and server programs are utilized here. The user's keystrokes are acknowledged by the local operating system but are not translated by the terminal driver. TELNET client receives characters and transforms them into the international character set known as network virtual terminal (NVT) characters before sending them to the local TCP/IP protocol stack. Instructions or text, in NVT format, are transmitted over the Internet and reach the remote machine's TCP/IP stack. Here, the operating system receives the characters and sends them along to TELNET server, which converts them into equivalent characters that the distant computer can comprehend. The remote operating system, however, isn't made to accept characters from TELNET server; rather, it's made to receive characters from terminal driver, thus characters cannot be delivered directly to an operating system. Answer is to include software known as a *pseudoterminal* driver that makes it appear as though characters are coming from a terminal. An appropriate application program is then sent the characters by the operating system (Pallen, 1995).

3.9.2. Electronic Mail

Email is one of a most widely used Internet services. The success of this application program was probably never anticipated by the Internet's creators. Early electronic mail messages were brief and text-only; they allowed users to communicate quickly, such as exchanging memoranda. Electronic mail is significantly more complicated now. It permits the use of text, audio, and video in messages. Additionally, it permits sending a single message to one or more receivers (Markus, 1994).

3.9.2.1. User Agent

First element of an electronic mail system is a user agent. It offers assistance to user to make sending as well as receiving messages simpler.

- **Services Provided by User Agent:** A software application (user agent) composes, reads, responds to, and forwards messages. Moreover, this manages mailboxes.

3.9.2.2. Composing Messages

The user is assisted in writing the email message that will be sent by a user agent. The majority of user agents display a template for the user to fill out on the screen. Some even have an editor that can perform duties like grammar and spell checking as well as other advanced word processing functions. Of course, a user might also construct the message in their own text editor or word processor and import it, or paste or cut it, into user agent template (Malone et al., 1987).

3.9.2.3. Reading Messages

Reading incoming messages is the user agent's second responsibility. When a user activates it, a user agent first confirms mail in an incoming inbox. Most user agents display a one-line summary of each piece of mail they have received. Here are the fields included in each email:

- A flag field which displays mail's state, such as whether it's new, already read but unanswered, or read and responded to;
- A number field;
- The message's size;
- A sender;
- An optional subject field.

3.9.2.4. Replying to Messages

User can respond to a message using user agent after reading it. User agent often enables user to reply to message's original sender or to every recipient. Original message and revised message could both be included in the reply message.

3.9.2.5. Forwarding Messages

It's called "replying" when you send a message back to original sender or to people who received the copy. Sending a communication to a third party is referred to as forwarding. A user agent enables the recipient to transmit message to a third party with or without additional comments:

- **Handling Mailboxes:** An inbox and outbox are the two mailboxes that a user agent typically produces. Each box is file with unique format which only user agent can handle. All received emails are kept in the inbox until user deletes them. All sent emails are stored in outbox until user deletes them. Today's user agents can usually create personalized mailboxes (Khare et al., 2022).
- **User Agent Types:** There are two types of user agents: command-driven & GUI-based.
- **Command-Driven:** These user agents have existed since early days of electronic mail. They continue to exist in servers as an underlying user agent. In order to do its duty, a keyboard command of one character is often accepted by a command-driven user agent. For instance, at the command prompt, a user can write letter R to reply to message's sender or letter R to reply to all recipients and sender. *Pine, Elm & Mail,* are command-driven user agents' examples.
- **GUI-Based:** These user agents are common today. They have graphical user interface (GUI) elements which let user utilize keyboard and mouse to interact with the software. They feature visual elements like menu bars, panels, and icons that make it simple to access the services. User agents with GUIs include Microsoft Outlook, Eudora & Netscape (Levi & Güder, 2009).

3.9.2.6. Addresses

In order to distribute mail a mail handling system should use a unique addressing system. An @ symbol separates the local element of the address from domain name on the Internet:

- **Local Part:** All mail received for a user is saved in the user mailbox, a distinct file defined in the local part, for subsequent retrieval by message access agent.

- **Domain Name:** It is 2nd component of address. A company often chooses one or more hosts, also known as *mail servers or exchangers*, to receive and deliver email. Each mail exchanger's allocated domain name either originates from DNS database or is a logical name (company's name).

3.9.2.7. SMTP

Message transfer agents handle the actual mail transfer. A system needs a server MTA in order to receive mail, and a client MTA in order to send mail. A simple mail transfer protocol (SMTP) is an official protocol which describes MTA client and server on Internet.

The sender and mail server of sender, as well as two mail servers, both use SMTP. SMTP only outlines the requirements for sending commands and responses back and forth (Moore, 2003).

3.9.2.8. Commands and Responses

SMTP transfers messages between an MTA server and an MTA client using commands and responses:

- **Commands:** The client sends commands to server. It is made up of a keyword and one to many arguments. Around 14 commands are included in SMTP. Every implementation must support the first five instructions, which are requirements. The following three are quite useful and advised. The latter six are rarely used (Bazydło et al., 2017).
- **Responses:** The server sends responses to client. A three-digit code which represents a response maybe followed by more textual data.

3.9.2.9. Mail Transfer Phases

There are three steps involved in moving a mail message: connection formation, mail transfer, and connection termination.

3.9.3. POP_3

POP_3 is a straightforward protocol with constrained functionality. The receiver computer has client POP_3 software installed, while mail server has server POP_3 software. When a user needs to download email from a mailbox hosted on a mail server, the client is the first step in the mail access process. On TCP port 110, the client and server create a connection. Then, in order to access the mailbox, it submits its username and password. Following that, a user can list and get each individual mail message. The delete mode and keep mode are POP_3's 2 operating modes. After each retrieval in delete mode, mail is removed from mailbox. After recovery, mail stays in mailbox when in keep mode. When a user is seated at her desk-based computer and able to store and organize incoming mail after reading or responding, delete mode is typically employed. When a user accesses her email from a device other than her primary computer (such a laptop, for example), user will frequently switch to retain mode. Message is read, but it's preserved in system so you can find it and organize it later (Tzerefos et al., 1997).

3.9.4. IMAP

Internet mail access protocol, version 4 (IMAP4) is another mail access protocol. POP_3 and IMAP4 are comparable, however IMAP4 offers additional functions and is more capable and sophisticated.

POP_3 has a number of deficiencies. It prevents the user from organizing her mail on server and prevents user from having several folders on server. Additionally, POP_3 does not permit the user to scan a portion of mail before downloading it. IMAP4 offers the following additional features:

- Before downloading, a user can examine email header;
- Before downloading, a user can scan email's contents for a certain string of characters;
- Email can be partially downloaded by the user. This is especially helpful if the email has multimedia that requires a lot of bandwidth, and your bandwidth is constrained;
- On the mail server, a user has the option to create, delete, or rename mailboxes;
- A user's folder for storing emails can have a hierarchy of mailboxes (Crispin, 1996).

3.9.5. Web-Based Mail

Since email is used so often these days, several websites offer this function to all visitors. *Hotmail* and *Yahoo* are two popular web pages. The concept is extremely basic. Through HTTP, mail is transferred from Alice's browser to her mail server. SMTP is still used for message transfer from originating mail server to receiving mail server. Finally, message is sent from transmitting server (Web server) to Bob's browser using HTTP. The final stage is quite fascinating. The most common protocol used is HTTP, not POP_3 or IMAP4. Bob sends a message to website (such as Hotmail) asking for ability to recover his emails. The website sends Bob form to complete, along with the login name and password. The email is transmitted in HTML format from Web server to Bob's browser if login name and password match (Cobanoglu et al., 2001).

3.9.6. FTP

The TCP/IP standard mechanism for moving file from one host to another is called file transfer protocol (FTP). Although this may seem easy and uncomplicated to transfer information between systems, there are a few issues that must be resolved beforehand. For instance, two systems might employ various file naming standards. Text and data may be represented by two distinct systems in two different ways.

On two separate computers, distinct directory structures could occur. FTP has provided an incredibly straightforward and elegant solution to all of these issues.

FTP creates two connections between the hosts, which sets it apart from other client/server programs. Data transfer occurs over one link, while control information (commands and responses) occurs over the other. FTP is more effective when commands and data transport are separated. Simple communication protocols are used by control connection. Only one line of command or one line of response has to be transferred at a time. On the other hand, the data connection requires more complicated regulations because it transfers a wide variety of data kinds. However, rather than TCP, FTP has a higher level of sophistication. Both connections are handled equally by TCP. FTP uses the well-known TCP ports 20 and 21 for control and data connections, respectively.

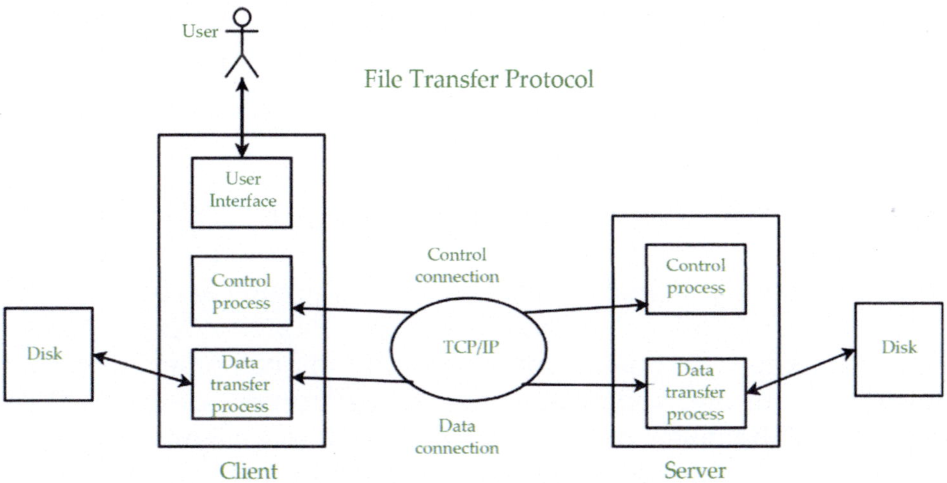

Figure 3.20. Illustration of fundamental model of file transfer protocol.

Source: Geeks for Geeks, Creative Commons License.

The fundamental model of FTP is shown in Figure 3.20. Client control process, user interface, and client data transmission process are the three parts of the client. The server's control process and data transfer procedure are its two main parts. The means of control connect the control processes. And data is connected to processes of data transfer.

The control connection is active, throughout whole interactive FTP session. Each file transmission involves opening and closing the data connection. It opens each time a command involving file transfers is executed and shuts once the file has been transmitted. In other words, control connection opens when user initiates an FTP session. Data connection may close and open several times if many files are transferred while control connection is active.

3.9.6.1. Transmission Mode

Block mode, Stream mode, and compressed mode are three transmission modes that FTP might use to send a file through data connection. A default mode is stream mode. A steady stream of bytes is sent from FTP to TCP carrying data. Data is divided into segments of the correct size by TCP. There is no requirement for an end-of-file (EOF) if data are only a stream of bytes (file structure). In this instance, the sender's termination of data connection signifies the end of the file. A 1-byte end-of-record (EOR) character and 1-byte EOF character are both present at the end of a file if data are broken up into records (record structure). While in block mode, data can be sent from FTP to TCP in blocks. Each block in this example has a 3-byte header before it. The *block descriptor* is the first byte, and the next two bytes specify the block's size in bytes. If file is large, data can be compressed in the compressed mode. Runlength encoding is the often-employed compression technique. This approach replaces a data unit's repeated appearances with a single occurrence and the number of repetitions. This typically consists of blank spaces in text files. Null characters are typically compressed in binary files (Circiumarescu et al., 2015).

3.9.7. HTTP

The World Wide Web's (WWW) hypertext transfer protocol (HTTP) is a protocol mostly used to access data there. FTP and SMTP are combined to form HTTP. Because it transports files and makes use of TCP, it's comparable to FTP. However, because it only makes use of one TCP connection, it is easier to use than FTP. There is no separate connection for control; all communication that takes place between client and server is limited to the transfer of data. HTTP is comparable to SMTP because data transmitted between client and server looks like SMTP messages. Additionally, MIME-like headers are used to govern how the messages are formatted. In contrast to SMTP, HTTP communications are understood and read by HTTP server & HTTP client (browser), not by humans. HTTP messages are delivered instantly, whereas SMTP messages are archived and forwarded. The request message contains commands that client sends to server. A response message includes contents of downloaded file or other data. TCP services are used by HTTP on the well-known port 80 (Jestratjew & Kwiecien, 2012).

3.9.7.1. HTTP Transaction

HTTP is a stateless protocol, despite the fact that it makes use of TCP's services. The transaction is started by the client sending request message. A server responds by sending the response:

- **Messages:** Request lines, headers, and occasionally bodies make up a request message. There are three parts to a response message: status line, header, and occasionally body (Naik, 2017).
- **Request and Status Lines:** First line of request message is known as the request line, while first line of a response message is known as status line. One common field is present (Hadi & Ali, 2019).
    - **Request Type:** In the request message, this field is utilized. There are various defined request types in HTTP version 1.1. Request type is divided into categories called methods.
    - **URL:** URL means uniform resource locator.
    - **Version:** A current version of HTTP.
    - **Status Code:** In response message, it's utilized. Similar fields exist in SMTP & FTP protocols as well as the status code field. There are three digits in it. The values in 200 range signify successful request, as opposed to codes in 100 range, which are only informative. A client site error is indicated by codes in the 400 range and a client site redirection code in the 300 range. The codes in the 500 range, lastly, denote a server-side problem.
    - **Status Phrase:** It functions as a reply signal. Status phrase provides a text explanation of the status code (Kockelman, 2007).

ACTIVITY 3.1:

In what ways can the implementation of a local area network (LAN) in a small business improve productivity and collaboration among employees, while also potentially introducing new security risks and management challenges?

3.10. SUMMARY

The chapter "Data Communication and Computer Networks" provides an overview of the basics of data communication and computer networks. It covers the different modes of data transmission, including simplex, half-duplex, and full duplex, as well as the differences between parallel and serial transmission and asynchronous and synchronous transmission. The chapter also explains the seven layers of the OSI model and their functions in network communication. It discusses the criteria for designing a network and the different physical structures that can be used to build a network. Additionally, the chapter covers different types of networks such as LAN, MAN, and WAN, and the connecting devices used in computer networks. Furthermore, the chapter explains the differences between analog and digital data, periodic and non-periodic signals, and the characteristics of signals such as amplitude, frequency, and phase. This information is important in understanding how data is transmitted across a network.

Overall, the chapter provides a foundational understanding of data communication and computer networks, which is essential for anyone interested in working in the field of information technology.

REVIEW QUESTIONS

1. What is the importance of data communication in computer networks and why is it essential?
2. What are the different modes of data transmission, and how do they differ from each other? Give examples of scenarios where each mode is useful.
3. What is the difference between parallel and serial transmission, and what are the advantages and disadvantages of each?
4. Explain the difference between asynchronous and synchronous transmission and provide examples of when each would be used.
5. What are the seven layers of the OSI model, and how do they relate to data communication and computer networks?
6. What are the criteria for designing a network, and what are the different physical structures that can be used to implement a network?
7. Describe the different types of networks, including LAN, MAN, and WAN, and how they differ from each other.
8. What are some examples of connecting devices used in computer networks, and what are their roles in network communication?
9. Explain the differences between analog and digital data, periodic and non-periodic signals, and the characteristics of signals such as amplitude, frequency, and phase. How are these concepts related to data communication and computer networks?

MULTIPLE CHOICE QUESTIONS

1. **What is the importance of data communication in computer networks?**
   a. To save data
   b. To transmit data
   c. To delete data
   d. To encrypt data
2. **What is simplex transmission?**
   a. Communication in both directions simultaneously
   b. Communication in one direction only
   c. Communication in both directions but not simultaneously
   d. Communication through a single medium
3. **What is the difference between parallel and serial transmission?**
   a. Parallel transmission uses multiple channels while serial transmission uses a single channel.
   b. Parallel transmission is faster than serial transmission.
   c. Parallel transmission is used for short distances while serial transmission is used for long distances.
   d. Parallel transmission sends multiple bits at once while serial transmission sends one bit at a time.
4. **What is synchronous transmission?**
   a. Data transmission without a clock signal
   b. Data transmission with a clock signal
   c. Data transmission in both directions simultaneously
   d. Data transmission through multiple channels
5. **How many layers are there in the OSI model?**
   a. 5
   b. 6
   c. 7
   d. 8

Answers to Multiple Choice Questions

1. (b); 2. (b); 3. (d); 4. (b); 5. (c)

REFERENCES

1. AfiqahAzahari, R. A., Al-Hubaishi, M., & Uddin, M., (2013). Review of error detection of data link layer in computer network. *Middle-East Journal of Scientific Research, 18*(7), 968–973.
2. Amphawan, A., Chaudhary, S., & Chan, V. W. S., (2014). 2 x 20 Gbps-40 GHz OFDM Ro-FSO transmission with mode division multiplexing. *Journal of the European Optical Society-Rapid Publications, 9*, 28–35.
3. Balabanov, T., Zankinski, I., & Barova, M., (2016). Strategy for individuals distribution by incident nodes participation in star topology of distributed evolutionary algorithms. *Cybernetics and Information Technologies, 16*(1), 80–88.
4. Barranco, M., Proenza, J., & Almeida, L., (2009). Quantitative comparison of the error-containment capabilities of a bus and a star topology in CAN networks. *IEEE Transactions on Industrial Electronics, 58*(3), 802–813.
5. Bartlett, K. A., Scantlebury, R. A., & Wilkinson, P. T., (1969). A note on reliable full-duplex transmission over half-duplex links. *Communications of the ACM, 12*(5), 260–261.
6. Bazydło, P., Lasota, K., & Kozakiewicz, A., (2017). Botnet fingerprinting: Anomaly detection in SMTP conversations. *IEEE Security & Privacy, 15*(6), 25–32.
7. Bejerano, Y., Breitbart, Y., Garofalakis, M., & Rastogi, R., (2003). Physical topology discovery for large multisubnet networks. In: *IEEE INFOCOM 2003. Twenty-second Annual Joint Conference of the IEEE Computer and Communications Societies (IEEE Cat. No. 03CH37428)* (Vol. 1, pp. 342–352). IEEE.
8. Bewley, T. R., (2001). Flow control: New challenges for a new renaissance. *Progress in Aerospace Sciences, 37*(1), 21–58.
9. Bhagwat, P., Perkins, C., & Tripathi, S., (1996). Network layer mobility: An architecture and survey. *IEEE Personal Communications, 3*(3), 54–64.
10. Bhattacharjee, S., Ammar, M. H., Zegura, E. W., Shah, V., & Fei, Z., (1997). Application-layer any casting. In: *Proceedings of INFOCOM'97* (Vol. 3, pp. 1388–1396). IEEE.
11. Bianchi, G., Harders, M., & Székely, G., (2003). Mesh topology identification for mass-spring models. In: *Medical Image Computing and Computer-Assisted Intervention-MICCAI 2003: 6th International Conference, Montréal, Canada, November 15–18, 2003; Proceedings 6* (Vol. 1, pp. 50–58). Springer Berlin Heidelberg.
12. Bottoni, P., Costabile, M. F., & Mussio, P., (1999). Specification and dialogue control of visual interaction through visual rewriting systems. *ACM Transactions on Programming Languages and Systems (TOPLAS), 21*(6), 1077–1136.
13. Bubenik, R., DeHart, J., & Gaddis, M., (1991). Multipoint connection management in high speed networks. In: *IEEE INFCOM'91-Communications Societies Proceedings* (Vol. 3, pp. 59–60). IEEE Computer Society.
14. Bujas, G., Vuković, M., Vasić, V., & Mikuc, M., (2015). Smart detection and classification of application-layer intrusions in web directories. *SmartCR, 5*(6), 510–519.

15. Burdin, V., Gubareva, O., Gureev, V., & Masyuk, S., (2020). Simulation of data transmission in a simplex acousto-optical channel on dual-mode optical fiber. In: *2020 International Conference on Information Technology and Nanotechnology (ITNT)* (Vol.1, pp. 1–4). IEEE.

16. Cerutti, I., Behredin, A. M., Andriolli, N., Ladouceur, O. L., & Castoldi, P., (2016). Ring versus bus topology: A network performance comparison of photonic integrated NoC. In: *2016 18th International Conference on Transparent Optical Networks (ICTON)* (Vol.1, pp. 1–4). IEEE.

17. Chao, H. J., (2002). Next generation routers. *Proceedings of the IEEE, 90*(9), 1518–1558.

18. Circiumarescu, L. D., Predusca, G., Angelescu, N., & Puchianu, D., (2015). Comparative analysis of protocol RIP, OSPF, RIGRP and IGRP for service video conferencing, E-mail, FTP, HTTP. In: *2015 20th International Conference on Control Systems and Computer Science* (Vol. 1, pp. 584–589). IEEE.

19. Clark, D. D., Pogran, K. T., & Reed, D. P., (1978). An introduction to local area networks. *Proceedings of the IEEE, 66*(11), 1497–1517.

20. Cobanoglu, C., Moreo, P. J., & Warde, B., (2001). A comparison of mail, fax and web-based survey methods. *International Journal of Market Research, 43*(4), 1–15.

21. Crispin, M., (1996). *RFC2060: Internet Message Access Protocol-Version 4rev1, 1*(2), 213.

22. Crochiere, R. E., & Rabiner, L. R., (1981). Interpolation and decimation of digital signals—A tutorial review. *Proceedings of the IEEE, 69*(3), 300–331.

23. Dorman, M. F., Loizou, P. C., & Rainey, D., (1997). Speech intelligibility as a function of the number of channels of stimulation for signal processors using sine-wave and noise-band outputs. *The Journal of the Acoustical Society of America, 102*(4), 2403–2411.

24. Ehley, L., Furht, B., & Ilyas, M., (1994). Evaluation of multimedia synchronization techniques. In: *ICMCS* (Vol. 94, pp. 514–519).

25. Engler, D. R., Kaashoek, M. F., & O'Toole, Jr. J., (1995). Exokernel: An operating system architecture for application-level resource management. *ACM SIGOPS Operating Systems Review, 29*(5), 251–266.

26. Fiala, Z., Frasincar, F., Hinz, M., Houben, G. J., Barna, P., & Meissner, K., (2004). Engineering the presentation layer of adaptable web information systems. In: *Web Engineering: 4th International Conference, ICWE 2004, Munich, Germany, July 26–30, 2004; Proceedings 4* (Vol. 1, pp. 459–472). Springer Berlin Heidelberg.

27. Gheng, T. Y., & Chee, Y. L., (2019). Low cost light fidelity (Li-Fi) system employing on-off keying data modulation in half-duplex asynchronous transmission mode. In: *IOP Conference Series: Earth and Environmental Science* (Vol. 268, pp. 12015).

28. Giri, D., Obaidat, M. S., & Maitra, T., (2017). Sechealth: An efficient fog based sender initiated secure data transmission of healthcare sensors for e-medical system. In:

GLOBECOM 2017–2017 IEEE Global Communications Conference (Vol.1, pp. 1–6). IEEE.

29. Goldenberg, J., Han, S., Lehmann, D. R., & Hong, J. W., (2009). The role of hubs in the adoption process. *Journal of Marketing, 73*(2), 1–13.
30. Gong, L., (2001). A software architecture for open service gateways. *IEEE Internet Computing, 5*(1), 64–70.
31. Green, P. E., Coldren, L. A., Johnson, K. M., Lewis, J. G., Miller, C. M., Morrison, J. F., & Smithand, E. H., (1993). All-optical packet-switched metropolitan-area network proposal. *Journal of Lightwave Technology, 11*(5, 6), 754–763.
32. Gregory, P. C., & Loredo, T. J., (1993). A Bayesian method for the detection of unknown periodic and nonperiodic signals in binned time series. *Maximum Entropy and Bayesian Methods: Paris, France, 1992*, 225–232.
33. Gruen, L. C., & Woods, E. F., (1983). Structural studies on the microfibrillar proteins of wool. Interaction between α-helical segments and reassembly of a four-chain structure. *Biochemical Journal, 209*(3), 587–595.
34. Guan, J. F., Yang, H., & Wirasinghe, S. C., (2006). Simultaneous optimization of transit line configuration and passenger line assignment. *Transportation Research Part B: Methodological, 40*(10), 885–902.
35. Guangyong, L., & Ruolan, L., (2021). Analysis and design of graduation design management system based on des encryption algorithm. In: *2021 4th International Conference on Advanced Electronic Materials, Computers and Software Engineering (AEMCSE)* (Vol. 1, pp. 682–685). IEEE.
36. Hadi, A. S., & Ali, S. H., (2019). Resource description framework representation for transaction log file. *Journal of Computational and Theoretical Nanoscience, 16*(3), 1093–1099.
37. Haider, R., Alam, R., Yousuf, N. B., & Salim, K. M., (2012). Design and construction of single phase pure sine wave inverter for photovoltaic application. In: *2012 International Conference on Informatics, Electronics & Vision (ICIEV)* (Vol.1, pp. 190–194). IEEE.
38. Handa, T., Shoji, S., Ike, S., Takeda, S., & Sekiguchi, T., (1997). A very low-power consumption wireless ECG monitoring system using body as a signal transmission medium. In: *Proceedings of International Solid State Sensors and Actuators Conference (Transducers' 97)* (Vol. 2, pp. 1003–1006). IEEE.
39. Hartmann, W. M., (1978). The effect of amplitude envelope on the pitch of sine wave tones. *The Journal of the Acoustical Society of America, 63*(4), 1105–1113.
40. Iren, S., Amer, P. D., & Conrad, P. T., (1999). The transport layer: Tutorial and survey. *ACM Computing Surveys (CSUR), 31*(4), 360–404.
41. Jebamalai, J. M., Marlein, K., & Laverge, J., (2022). Design and cost comparison of district heating and cooling (DHC) network configurations using ring topology: A case study. *Energy, 258*, 124777.
42. Jestratjew, A., & Kwiecien, A., (2012). Performance of HTTP protocol in networked

control systems. *IEEE Transactions on Industrial Informatics, 9*(1), 271–276.

43. Jha, K., Mishra, S., & Joshi, A., (2014). High-quality sine wave generation using a differential boost inverter at higher operating frequency. *IEEE Transactions on Industry Applications, 51*(1), 373–384.
44. Kandula, S., Menache, I., Schwartz, R., & Babbula, S. R., (2014). Calendaring for wide area networks. In: *Proceedings of the 2014 ACM Conference on SIGCOMM* (Vol. 1, pp. 515–526).
45. Khare, A., Singh, S., Mishra, R., Prakash, S., & Dixit, P., (2022). E-mail assistant–automation of E-mail handling and management using robotic process automation. In: *2022 International Conference on Decision Aid Sciences and Applications (DASA)* (Vol. 1, pp. 511–516). IEEE.
46. Kim, H., Oh, S., & Viswanath, P., (2020). Physical layer communication via deep learning. *IEEE Journal on Selected Areas in Information Theory, 1*(1), 5–18.
47. Kockelman, P., (2007). From status to contract revisited: Value, temporality, circulation and subjectivity. *Anthropological Theory, 7*(2), 151–176.
48. Lafata, P., & Vodrazka, J., (2011). Application of passive optical network with optimized bus topology for local backbone data network. *Microwave and Optical Technology Letters, 53*(10), 2351–2355.
49. Lai, K., & Baker, M., (1999). Measuring bandwidth. In: *IEEE INFOCOM'99. Conference on Computer Communications. Proceedings. Eighteenth Annual Joint Conference of the IEEE Computer and Communications Societies. The Future is Now (Cat. No. 99CH36320)*. (Vol. 1, pp. 235–245). IEEE.
50. LaMagna, M., Hartman-Caverly, S., & Marchetti, L., (2016). Redefining roles and responsibilities: Implementing a triage reference model at a single service point. *Journal of Access Services, 13*(2), 53–65.
51. Landfeldt, B., Larsson, T., Ismailov, Y., & Seneviratne, A., (1999). SLM, a framework for session layer mobility management. In: *Proceedings Eight International Conference on Computer Communications and Networks (Cat. No. 99EX370)* (Vol. 1, pp. 452–456). IEEE.
52. Larkins, D. B., & Dinan, J., (2016). Extending a message passing runtime to support partitioned, global logical address spaces. In: *2016 First International Workshop on Communication Optimizations in HPC (COMHPC)* (Vol.1, pp. 11–16). IEEE.
53. Levi, A., & Güder, C. B., (2009). Understanding the limitations of S/MIME digital signatures for e-mails: A GUI based approach. *Computers & Security, 28*(3, 4), 105–120.
54. Lguensat, R., Tandeo, P., Ailliot, P., Pulido, M., & Fablet, R., (2017). The analog data assimilation. *Monthly Weather Review, 145*(10), 4093–4107.
55. Lin, H., Tang, Y., Guan, L., & Shao, S., (2011). Ordered successive interference cancellation (OSIC) in V-BLAST systems with asynchronous transmission mode. *Wireless Personal Communications, 60*(2), 263–275.

56. Lin, L. J., & Ortega, A., (1998). Bit-rate control using piecewise approximated rate-distortion characteristics. *IEEE Transactions on Circuits and Systems for Video Technology, 8*(4), 446–459.
57. Ling, A. P. A., & Masao, M., (2011). Selection of model in developing information security criteria on smart grid security system. In: *2011 IEEE Ninth International Symposium on Parallel and Distributed Processing with Applications Workshops* (Vol. 1, pp. 91–98). IEEE.
58. Liu, Y., Liu, A., Li, Y., Li, Z., Choi, Y. J., Sekiya, H., & Li, J., (2017). APMD: A fast data transmission protocol with reliability guarantee for pervasive sensing data communication. *Pervasive and Mobile Computing, 41*, 413–435.
59. Lucamarini, M., Yuan, Z. L., Dynes, J. F., & Shields, A. J., (2018). Overcoming the rate–distance limit of quantum key distribution without quantum repeaters. *Nature, 557*(7705), 400–403.
60. Luo, F., & Südhof, T. C., (2017). Synaptotagmin-7-mediated asynchronous release boosts high-fidelity synchronous transmission at a central synapse. *Neuron, 94*(4), 826–839.
61. Lynch, N. A., Mansour, Y., & Fekete, A., (1988). Data link layer: Two impossibility results. In: *Proceedings of the Seventh Annual ACM Symposium on Principles of Distributed Computing* (Vol.1, pp. 149–170).
62. Mabrouk, A., Tourki, K., & Hamdi, N., (2016). Transmission mode selection scheme for physical layer security in multi-user multi-relay systems. In: *2016 IEEE 27th Annual International Symposium on Personal, Indoor, and Mobile Radio Communications (PIMRC)* (Vol.1, pp. 1–6). IEEE.
63. Maihofer, C., (2004). A survey of geocast routing protocols. *IEEE Communications Surveys & Tutorials, 6*(2), 32–42.
64. Malone, T. W., Grant, K. R., Lai, K. Y., Rao, R., & Rosenblitt, D., (1987). Semistructured messages are surprisingly useful for computer-supported coordination. *ACM Transactions on Information Systems (TOIS), 5*(2), 115–131.
65. Markus, M. L., (1994). Electronic mail as the medium of managerial choice. *Organization Science, 5*(4), 502–527.
66. Marx, G., Greiner, W., Juhra, C., Elkenkamp, S., Gensorowsky, D., Lemmen, S., & Deisz, R., (2022). An innovative telemedical network to improve infectious disease management in critically ill patients and outpatients (TELnet@ NRW): Stepped-wedge cluster randomized controlled trial. *Journal of Medical Internet Research, 24*(3), 34098.
67. Maxemchuk, N. F., (1985). Regular mesh topologies in local and metropolitan area networks. *AT&T Technical Journal, 64*(7), 1659–1685.
68. Modarressi, M., Tavakkol, A., & Sarbazi-Azad, H., (2010). Virtual point-to-point connections for NoCs. *IEEE Transactions on Computer-Aided Design of Integrated Circuits and Systems, 29*(6), 855–868.
69. Moon, S., & Kim, J., (2007). Network-adaptive selection of transport error control

(NASTE) for video streaming over WLAN. *IEEE Transactions on Consumer Electronics, 53*(4), 1440–1448.

70. Moore, K., (2003). *Simple Mail Transfer Protocol (SMTP) Service Extension for Delivery Status Notifications (DSNs)* (Vol. 1, pp. 3461).
71. Mubeen, S., & Kumar, S., (2010). Designing efficient source routing for mesh topology network on chip platforms. In: *2010 13th Euromicro Conference on Digital System Design: Architectures, Methods and Tools* (Vol.1, pp. 181–188). IEEE.
72. Naik, N., (2017). Choice of effective messaging protocols for IoT systems: MQTT, CoAP, AMQP and HTTP. In: *2017 IEEE International Systems Engineering Symposium (ISSE)* (Vol. 1, pp. 1–7). IEEE.
73. Njoh, A. J., (2010). Toponymic inscription, physical addressing and the challenge of urban management in an era of globalization in Cameroon. *Habitat International, 34*(4), 427–435.
74. OConnor, T. J., (2010). Detecting and responding to data link layer attacks. *SANS Institute InfoSec Reading Room, 13*, 125.
75. Oh, H., & Ngo, C. T., (2018). A slotted sense multiple access protocol for timely and reliable data transmission in dynamic wireless sensor networks. *IEEE Sensors Journal, 18*(5), 2184–2194.
76. Oostvogels, J., Yang, F., Michiels, S., & Hughes, D., (2020). Zero-wire: A deterministic and low-latency wireless bus through symbol-synchronous transmission of optical signals. In: *Proceedings of the 18th Conference on Embedded Networked Sensor Systems* (Vol. 1, pp. 164–178).
77. Ortiz, G., Uemura, H., Bortis, D., Kolar, J. W., & Apeldoorn, O., (2012). Modeling of soft-switching losses of IGBTs in high-power high-efficiency dual-active-bridge DC/DC converters. *IEEE Transactions on Electron Devices, 60*(2), 587–597.
78. Pahlavan, K., & Levesque, A. H., (1994). Wireless data communications. *Proceedings of the IEEE, 82*(9), 1398–1430.
79. Pallen, M., (1995). Guide to the Internet: Logging in, fetching files, reading news. *BMJ, 311*(7020), 1626–1630.
80. Pavel, L., (2015). Novel protection strategies for passive optical networks based on ring and bus topologies. *Transactions on Emerging Telecommunications Technologies, 26*(9), 1131–1153.
81. Petrova, M., Mähönen, P., & Osuna, A., (2010). Multi-class classification of analog and digital signals in cognitive radios using support vector machines. In: *2010 7th International Symposium on Wireless Communication Systems* (Vol.1, pp. 986–990). IEEE.
82. Qureshi, S. U. H. H., & Newhall, E., (1973). Adaptive receiver for data transmission over time-dispersive channels. *IEEE Transactions on Information Theory, 19*(4), 448–457.
83. Ross, F. E., (1987). Rings are' round for good! *IEEE Network, 1*(1), 31–39.

84. Roy, S., Jayakumar, J., Martin, P. R., Dreher, B., Saalmann, Y. B., Hu, D., & Vidyasagar, T. R., (2009). Segregation of short□wavelength□sensitive (S) cone signals in the macaque dorsal lateral geniculate nucleus. *European Journal of Neuroscience, 30*(8), 1517–1526.

85. Saha, S., Landsiedel, O., & Chan, M. C., (2017). Efficient many-to-many data sharing using synchronous transmission and TDMA. In: *2017 13th International Conference on Distributed Computing in Sensor Systems (DCOSS)* (Vol. 1, pp. 19–26). IEEE.

86. Saltzberg, B., (1967). Performance of an efficient parallel data transmission system. *IEEE Transactions on Communication Technology, 15*(6), 805–811.

87. Seemkooei, A. A., (2001). Comparison of reliability and geometrical strength criteria in geodetic networks. *Journal of Geodesy, 75*, 227–233.

88. Selwyn, N., (2015). Data entry: Towards the critical study of digital data and education. *Learning, Media and Technology, 40*(1), 64–82.

89. Sinha, P., Jha, V. K., Rai, A. K., & Bhushan, B., (2017). Security vulnerabilities, attacks and countermeasures in wireless sensor networks at various layers of OSI reference model: A survey. In: *2017 International Conference on Signal Processing and Communication (ICSPC).* (Vol. 1, pp. 288–293). IEEE.

90. Śmiałek, M., Jarzębowski, N., & Nowakowski, W., (2012). Translation of use case scenarios to java code. *Computer Science, 13*, 35–52.

91. Soni, A., Upadhyay, R., & Jain, A., (2017). Internet of Things and wireless physical layer security: A survey. In: *Computer Communication, Networking and Internet Security: Proceedings of IC3T 2016* (Vol. 3, pp. 115–123). Springer Singapore.

92. Stephens, R., (2004). Analyzing jitter at high data rates. *IEEE Communications Magazine, 42*(2), S6–10.

93. Stoilova, S., Munier, N., Kendra, M., & Skrúcaný, T., (2020). Multi-criteria evaluation of railway network performance in countries of the TEN-T orient–east med corridor. *Sustainability, 12*(4), 1482.

94. Tang, A., & Wang, X., (2015). A-duplex: Medium access control for efficient coexistence between full-duplex and half-duplex communications. *IEEE Transactions on Wireless Communications, 14*(10), 5871–5885.

95. Tang, Y., Moon, K., & Lee, H. J., (2009). Write synchronization in bit-patterned media. *IEEE Transactions on Magnetics, 45*(2), 822–827.

96. Tassiulas, L., & Papavassiliou, S., (1995). Optimal anticipative scheduling with asynchronous transmission opportunities. *IEEE Transactions on Automatic Control, 40*(12), 2052–2062.

97. Tzerefos, P., Smythe, C., Stergiou, I., & Cvetkovic, S., (1997). A comparative study of simple mail transfer protocol (SMTP), post office protocol (POP) and X. 400 electronic mail protocols. In: *Proceedings of 22nd Annual Conference on Local Computer Networks* (Vol. 1, pp. 545–554). IEEE.

98. Varvarigos, E. A., & Sharma, V., (1998). An efficient reservation connection control protocol for gigabit networks. *Computer Networks and ISDN Systems, 30*(12), 1135–1156.

99. Walker, R. C., (2003). Designing bang-bang PLLs for clock and data recovery in serial data transmission systems. *Phase-Locking in High-Performance Systems, 2*, 34–45.

100. Wang, Y., Zhang, Z. L., Du, D. H. C., & Su, D., (1998). A network-conscious approach to end-to-end video delivery over wide area networks using proxy servers. In: *Proceedings; IEEE INFOCOM'98, the Conference on Computer Communications. Seventeenth Annual Joint Conference of the IEEE Computer and Communications Societies. Gateway to the 21st Century (Cat. No. 98)* (Vol. 2, pp. 660–667). IEEE.

101. Wilkov, R., (1972). Analysis and design of reliable computer networks. *IEEE Transactions on Communications, 20*(3), 660–678.

102. Yang, Z., Cui, Y., Li, B., Liu, Y., & Xu, Y., (2019). Software-defined wide area network (SD-WAN): Architecture, advances and opportunities. In: *2019 28th International Conference on Computer Communication and Networks (ICCCN)* (Vol. 1, pp. 1–9). IEEE.

103. Yoon, G., Kwon, D. H., Kwon, S. C., Park, Y. O., & Lee, Y. J., (2006). Ring topology-based redundancy ethernet for industrial network. In: *2006 SICE-ICASE International Joint Conference* (Vol. 1, pp. 1404–1407). IEEE.

104. Zhao, W., Ammar, M., & Zegura, E., (2004). A message ferrying approach for data delivery in sparse mobile ad hoc networks. In: *Proceedings of the 5th ACM International Symposium on Mobile ad Hoc Networking and Computing* (Vol. 1, pp. 187–198).

105. Zhu, Y., Qian, D., Ren, D., & Xia, H., (2019). Starnet: Pedestrian trajectory prediction using deep neural network in star topology. In: *2019 IEEE/RSJ International Conference on Intelligent Robots and Systems (IROS)* (Vol.1, pp. 8075–8080). IEEE.

CHAPTER 4

CONSISTENCY AND REPLICATION

UNIT INTRODUCTION

To achieve scalable, available, and transparent data distribution in distributed databases, partitioning and replication are two frequently used techniques. Different parts of the total data set are contained in each partition that makes up the data space. Replicas, or multiple copies, are made for these partitions. The cluster members are all given access to partition replicas. Each member can only be assigned to one replica for the partition. Different replication methods can be applied in this situation to get to the data and maintain the replicas up to date with changes. Because distributed data stores must adhere to the CAP (consistency, availability, and partition tolerance) principle, the method being used directly impacts the guarantees and qualities offered (Wu, 1998).

One aspect of replication techniques is where a replicated data set is accessed and updated. To access the data, for example, primary-copy systems first choose a replica—which may be referred to as primary, master, etc., and use that replica. Data modifications made to the primary replica propagate to the secondary replicas. Different names for this strategy include primary copy, single-master, and passive replication (Baumann et al., 2009). The primary-copy technique is an effective model because it avoids disputes and deadlocks between the replicas. Primary replicas might, however, develop bottlenecks. On the contrary hand, by doing away with the primary copy and treating every replica equally, we can have a distinct strategy. Because any replica can access and update a data entry, these systems may attain higher availability. However, maintaining the replicas' synchronization can get more challenging (Van Steen & Tanenbaum, 2002) (Figure 4.1).

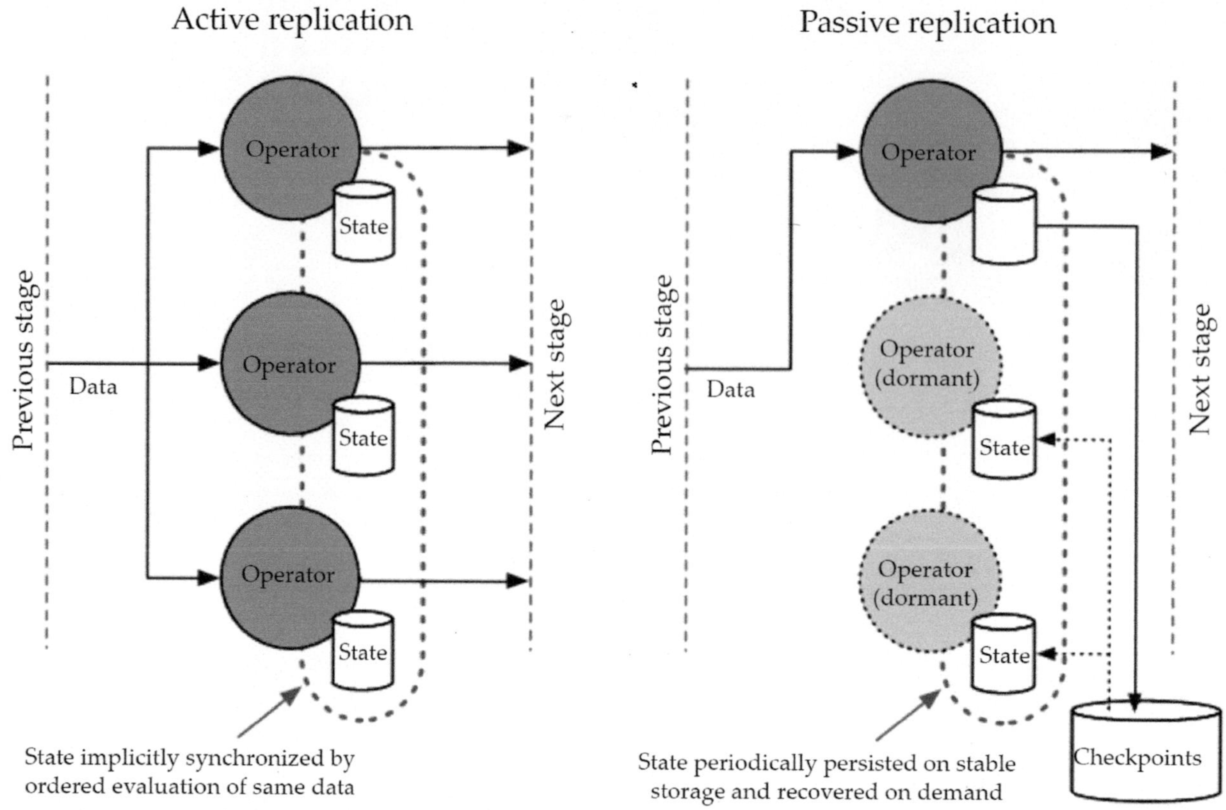

Figure 4.1. Schematic of data replication in distributed system.

Source: Hevo Data, Creative Commons License.

The propagation of updates among replicas is another area where replication techniques diverge. One choice is eager replication, also known as synchronous replication, which updates each replica as a component of a single atomic transaction. This method is used by consensus algorithms to accomplish solid consistency on a set of replicated data. The replication algorithm's main drawback is the quantity of coordination and communication needed. Consensus algorithms are implemented in the background of CP systems (Narasimhan, Moser, & Melliar-Smith, 1997). Lazy replication, also known as asynchronous replication, is an additional choice. Updates on replicas are carried out by lazy replication algorithms using separate transactions. They typically give it their best effort. In this way, the level of coordination between the replicas is reduced and data access is made more efficient. However, it is possible for replicas to diverge when a specific update is applied to some copies but not to others. Such issues can be solved using a variety of strategies, including read-repair, write-repair, and anti-entropy. Many AP systems use lazy replication strategies (Helal, Heddaya, & Bhargava, 2005).

There are two types of replications:

- **Data Replication:** When identical data is spread across several storage devices.
- **Computation Replication:** The ability for the same computing task to run on multiple servers.

Learning Objectives

At the end of this chapter, the reader will be able to understand:

- The importance of replication in distributed systems;
- The terms performance and reliability as they relate to replication;
- The cap theorem and its three properties: consistency, availability, and partition-tolerance;
- The trade-offs between consistency, availability, and partition-tolerance in distributed systems;
- Examples of cap theorems in distributed systems;
- How partition-tolerance affects the design of distributed systems;
- The different client-centric consistency models, including strict consistency, sequential consistency, causal consistency, FIFO consistency, entry and release consistency, and eventual consistency;
- The advantages and disadvantages of each client-centric consistency model;
- How scaling and replication affect the consistency of distributed systems.

Key Terms

- CAP theorem
- Causal consistency
- Client-centric consistency models
- Consistency
- Entry and release consistency
- Eventual consistency
- FIFO consistency
- NoSQL systems
- Partition-tolerance
- Sequential consistency
- Strict consistency

4.1. IMPORTANCE OF REPLICATION

4.1.1. Performance

We are able to utilize all of the resources accessible to those n machines for handling requests when our system is replicated on those n machines. On the other hand, if there is no expansion and we only have one machine, our options are constrained by its capabilities. For instance, if we only had one web server, it would only be capable of handling a certain number of requests per second. When it reaches the limit, it becomes saturated. We may boost the ability of our application to handle more inquiries per second by replicating it across multiple servers (Goel & Buyya, 2007).

4.1.2. Reliability

We need at least one replica in our distributed system to be able to handle server requests and guarantee that the data is still available even if one replica fails. If one of the database servers in a distributed system crash, for instance, and we have a replicated replica of the exact same data on a different database server, the data is still safe. We can direct the system to the second database replica and keep using it for accessing the data without any issues (Sandhu & Zhou, 1992).

4.2. CAP THEOREM

According to the CAP theorem, no distributed system can deliver more than two of its subsequent three guarantees at once (Figure 4.2).

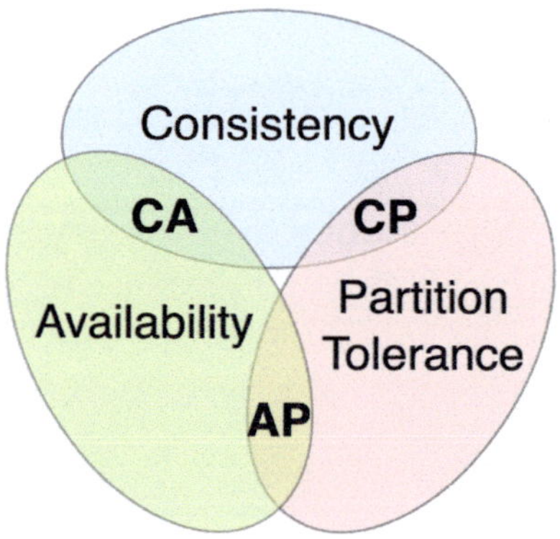

Figure 4.2. Image of CAP theorem.

Source: JamieMcCarthy, Creative Commons License.

4.2.1. Consistency (C)

If a replicated data item exists in multiple copies, they are all in sync and show up as a single, current item.

4.2.2. Availability

If there are node errors, they are accepted (Availability). In other words, even if one node fails, the system won't crash because other nodes have control over its function(s) (Gilbert & Lynch, 2012).

4.2.3. Partition-Tolerance (P)

The system keeps running even if there is a network error. The network is offline in this instance, but the nodes are still operational.

4.2.4. Examples of CAP Theorems

Single database, cluster database, LDAP, and xFS: consistency and availability. They rely on the network's dependability to ensure that messages aren't vanished.

TIPS

The CAP theorem highlights the challenges of achieving consistency, availability, and partition tolerance in a distributed system, and the trade-offs that must be made between them.

4.2.5. Partition Tolerance Plus Consistency

Distributed database, distributed locking. They presumptively believe the coordinator is infallible.

4.2.6. Availability plus Partition tolerance

Coda, DNS, and web caching. The propagation of a DNS update may require several days (Kleppmann, 2015).

4.2.7. CAP Properties

We should examine why it is challenging to achieve consistency when there is a network division. Think about a situation where we have two copies. To keep our system consistent, when we update one replica, it must notify the other replica that a change has been made. Consistency cannot occur if the network is down because the two replicas are unable to communicate. This indicates that there is a conflict between uniformity and network failures that is inherent. Similar defenses can be made for any set of properties (Andrikopoulos, Fehling, & Leymann, 2012).

4.2.8. NoSQL Systems and CAP

There is NoSQL database used by these systems. It is problematic when there are inconsistencies when there are network partitions (Han, Haihong, Le, & Du, 2011).

Both the first and second halves' nodes can communicate with one another, but only the second half's nodes can communicate with the first, despite the fact that both halves' nodes have clients that can communicate with either or both of them (Frank, Pedersen, Frank, & Larsson, 2014). These are copies in our case. Updates made to a node can spread to other nodes, but because the network is divided, nodes cannot communicate with one another until the problem with the network is resolved. If the messages aren't exchanging back and forth, the system won't function consistently (Sharma & Dave, 2012) (Figure 4.3).

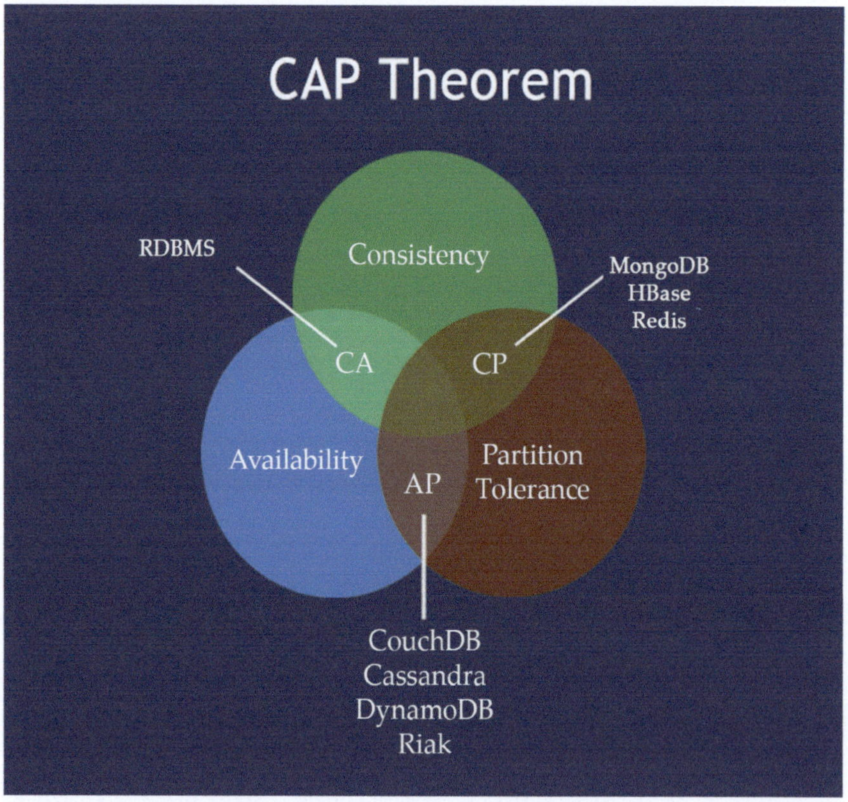

Figure 4.3. Depiction of NoSQL system in CAP theorem.

Source: w3resource, Creative Commons License.

4.3. SCALING AND REPLICATION

What kinds of consistency guarantees can we provide? We must first consider what kinds of overheads consistency imposes. Ideally, we want to offer the most robust guarantee we are still able to afford. For instance, if a file has been copied n times, we must update all of the replicas whenever it is changed. Consider that R is the frequency of read requests and W is the frequency of writes. Read and write frequency must be taken into account (Wang & Tang, 2012).

- **Scenario 1:** Consider a file on a well-liked new website. R > W because this file might be read once every second but current every 10 minutes. Since each written inform will be read several times in the future, we are probably willing to pay more for consistency in this case.
- **Scenario 2:** Consider, however, a file on a blog that no one devours. Although the read frequency for this file may be high, the write frequency is, so W > R. We have to put in a lot of extra effort to achieve consistency, but since so few reads actually see updates, there is no reward (Cattell, 2011).

Remember

NoSQL systems and CAP: when it comes to distributed databases, you can have consistency, availability, or partition tolerance - pick two.

4.4. CLIENT CENTRIC CONSISTENCY MODELS

In order to always retrieve the most recent version of a data item, we can examine various consistency models from the viewpoint of a client (Zaza & Nystrom, 2016).

4.4.1. Strict Consistency

All copies are constantly synchronized in strict consistency. We instantly update all copies of a data item whenever we render an update to it. We will never see out-of-date information in strict consistency. Implementing strict consistency is extremely difficult. A message must be delivered to other replicas after a copy is updated. The speed of light imposes a limit on the process's speed. It is therefore feasible for an additional request to make it to machine M between time if an update has been sent at time t and it takes time for the revised message to arrive at machine M. Therefore, we must take into account network delays and make the difficult assumption that each node receives the message on time in a real system (Liu, Mao, Van der Merwe, & Fernandez, 2011).

4.4.2. Sequential Consistency

Sequential consistency is weaker because it relaxes strict consistency's requirements. If we create a series of operations on one machine, replicas of it will see them in a certain sequential order and will carry out the operations in the same order as the original machine did. Any interleaving is acceptable as long as the program's order is maintained, and everyone observes it in that order. A situation in which one node observes a particular sequence and another observes a different order is not possible (Chalupa, Chatterjee, Pavlogiannis, Sinha, & Vaidya, 2017) (Figure 4.4).

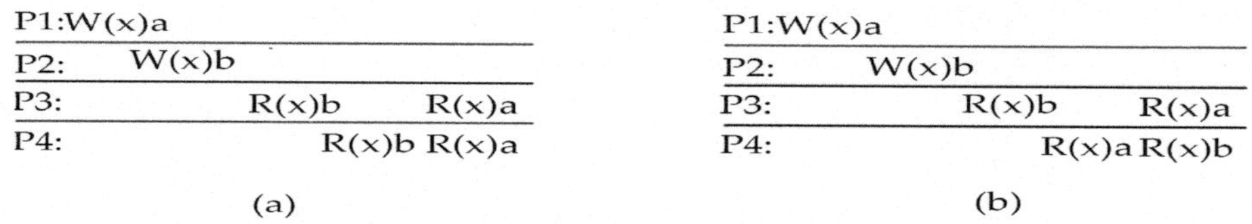

Figure 4.4. Illustration of sequential consistency.

Source: Prashant Shenoy, Creative Commons License.

Let's assume that 'x' in Figure 4.4 is a web page. Both process P1 and P2 write to the same variable, x, respectively. The value of 'x' is initially read by Process P3 as B, and then later as A. We could determine that P1 composed it first and then P2 if we had an international lock. Therefore, P3 shouldn't see b after seeing a. However, since P1 and P2 were not in touch with one another, we are unable to determine whether they are simultaneous occurrences because we lack a synchronized clock. As a result, we are unable to determine whether that is what actually occurred. Processes have just agreed that write P1 occurred before write P2. The processes in 4.4(a) concur on the sequence of words that P2 composed before P1 and that P3 and P4 read in. P3 and P4 are shown in different orders in Figure 4.4(b), which is not acceptable (Jarrahi, Memariani, & Guha, 2022).

4.4.2.1. Linearizability

Linearizability takes into account all of the demands of sequential consistency but provides the condition that interleaving must maintain that order if the timestamp of a write is shorter than another timestamp. Therefore, this must be maintained if two writes are somehow related. As long as there is a connection between the timestamps, any interleaving is acceptable. Sequential consistency is stronger than linearizability, but strict consistency is still stronger (Herlihy & Wing, 1990).

Every process reads one variable generated by the others

and writes one variable. As a result, the ordering is implicitly communicated here. When we print a 0 after giving a value to a variable that would be an invalid ordering. In the event that we reject the program order, there may be another scenario (Lee, Park, Kejriwal, Matsushita, & Ousterhout, 2015).

Did you Know?

Strict consistency is a crucial feature of distributed systems, ensuring that all nodes in the system see the same data at the same time, even in the face of failures and network partitions.

4.4.3. Causal Consistency

All processes must perceive causally ordered writes in the same order for there to be causal consistency. Causally ordered implies that because there was some form of communication, for instance, if P1 conveys a message to P2, the process's order must be preserved by interleaving. Sequential consistency, which is able to select any order, avoids this. Only if events are concurrent or independent can we choose any order according to causal consistency (Bailis, Ghodsi, Hellerstein, & Stoica, 2013) (Figure 4.5).

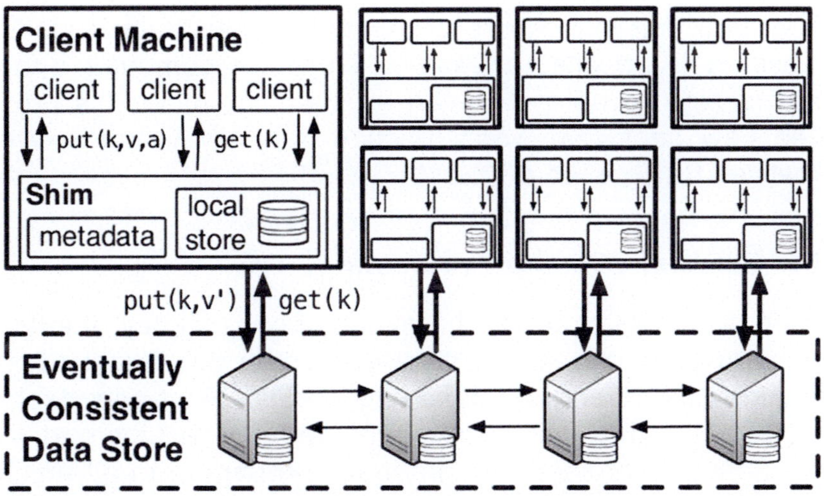

Figure 4.5. Schematic of casual consistency.

Source: Jan Lindstorm, Creative Commons License.

4.4.4. FIFO Consistency

Other consistency models, like FIFO consistency, don't care about how writes are interspersed among different machines. We reverence that ordering on a machine-by-machine basis if one machine is performing a series of updates. This is a weaker model than the others (George & Minet, 1997).

4.4.5. Entry and Release Consistency

We presume consistency at the entrance to critical sections in entry consistency, but not at the exit. The opposite is releasing consistency, in which data that is shared is made in line after leaving a crucial section (Iftode, Singh, & Li, 1996).

4.4.6. Eventual Consistency

Many systems operate via eventual consistency. We make no promises and presume that everything will eventually spread. We don't factor in the time it will take. The general idea is that our copies will eventually converge if we stop updating files. Our system will operate as expected if the user consistently accesses the same replica. Unlike more rigid forms of consistency, eventual consistency is simpler to attain and less expensive to implement (Burckhardt, 2014).

ACTIVITY 4.1:

How can a database administrator balance the need for strict consistency in a database system with the potential trade-offs in performance and scalability that can result from enforcing strict consistency across all transactions?

A system that makes use of eventual consistency is DNS. We can observe if we alter a password on one computer and then attempt to sign in right away on another computer. It's probable that the new password won't function right away, but it will in a short while (Balegas et al., 2015).

4.4.6.1. Epidemic/Gossip Protocols

Epidemic protocols simulate the eventual consistency of infectious disease transmission. As an illustration, you can infect someone by shaking their hand after having a cold. Pairwise exchange is the term for this. In our system, updates will spread in the same manner. Improvements gradually propagate to all machines because replicas connect and verify for updates on a regular basis. Since we accept a slight update delay, this is how many systems operate. Examples include GitHub, Dropbox, and any other type of cross-platform cloud storage (Montresor, 2017). If a server never communicates with an infected server, there is always a small chance that it won't be infected, which increases the chance that an update won't spread widely (Gupta, Kermarrec, & Ganesh, 2002).

- **Anti-Entropy:** A variant in which server P randomly chooses server Q, and the two exchange updates through pull requests, push requests, or both.

  Updates do not spread quickly using a pure push-based strategy. If we push, we might only be able to communicate with machines that already have the updates. In general, a push quickly spreads an update across most of the system, while a pull ensures that the update reaches the few remaining uninfected machines (Van Renesse, Dumitriu, Gough, & Thomas, 2008).

4.4.6.2. Rumor Mongerging

Another variation is where P pushes updates to Q when it receives them. We prevent promoting the latest information with probability if Q has already received it, providing us a probabilistic backoff. Similar to gossip, when something is "hot" it gets spread more, but when it gets "cold" it stops (Deb, Médard, & Choute, 2006).

4.5. SUMMARY

The chapter "Consistency and Replication" discusses the importance of replication in distributed systems and the trade-offs between consistency, availability, and partition-tolerance. The CAP theorem, which states that distributed systems can only guarantee two of these three properties at any given time, is explained. The chapter explores how partition-tolerance affects the design of distributed systems and the different client-centric consistency models, including strict consistency, sequential consistency, causal consistency, FIFO consistency, entry and release consistency, and eventual consistency. The advantages and disadvantages of each client-centric consistency model are also discussed. Finally, the chapter examines how scaling and replication affect the consistency of distributed systems.

REVIEW QUESTIONS

1. Why is replication important in distributed systems?
2. What is the difference between performance and reliability in the context of replication?
3. What is the CAP theorem and what are its three properties?
4. What trade-offs are involved between consistency, availability, and partition-tolerance in distributed systems?
5. Can you provide examples of how the CAP theorem applies to different distributed systems?
6. How does partition-tolerance affect the design of distributed systems?
7. What is the different client-centric consistency models and how do they differ?
8. What are the advantages and disadvantages of each client-centric consistency model?
9. How do scaling and replication impact the consistency of distributed systems?

MULTIPLE CHOICE QUESTIONS

1. Why is replication important in distributed systems?

a. To improve performance

b. To increase reliability

c. Both a and b

d. None of the above

2. Which term refers to the ability of a system to perform a certain function within a specified time frame?

a. Performance

b. Reliability
c. Consistency
d. Availability

3. The CAP theorem refers to which three properties of distributed systems?

a. Consistency, reliability, and availability
b. Consistency, availability, and partition-tolerance
c. Reliability, partition-tolerance, and scalability
d. Scalability, availability, and consistency

4. Which of the following is a trade-off between consistency, availability, and partition-tolerance in distributed systems?

a. Increased partition-tolerance can lead to decreased consistency
b. Increased availability can lead to decreased partition-tolerance
c. Increased consistency can lead to decreased availability
d. All of the above

5. Which distributed system is an example of the CAP theorem in action?

a. Google Spanner
b. Amazon DynamoDB
c. Apache Cassandra
d. All of the above

Answers to Multiple Choice Questions

1. (c); 2. (a); 3. (b); 4. (d); 5. (d)

REFERENCES

1. Andrikopoulos, V., Fehling, C., & Leymann, F., (2012). *Designing for CAP-The Effect of Design Decisions on the CAP Properties of Cloud-native Applications.* Paper presented at the CLOSER.
2. Bailis, P., Ghodsi, A., Hellerstein, J. M., & Stoica, I., (2013). *Bolt-on Causal Consistency.* Paper presented at the proceedings of the 2013 ACM SIGMOD international conference on management of data.
3. Balegas, V., Duarte, S., Ferreira, C., Rodrigues, R., Preguiça, N., Najafzadeh, M., & Shapiro, M., (2015). Putting consistency back into eventual consistency. In: *Proceedings of the Tenth European Conference on Computer Systems* (pp. 1–16).
4. Baumann, A., Peter, S., Schüpbach, A., Singhania, A., Roscoe, T., Barham, P., & Isaacs, R., (2009). *Your Computer is Already a Distributed System. Why Isn't Your OS?* Paper presented at the HotOS.

5. Burckhardt, S., (2014). Principles of eventual consistency. *Foundations and Trends® in Programming Languages, 1*(1, 2), 1–150.
6. Cattell, R., (2011). Scalable SQL and NoSQL data stores. *ACM Sigmod Record, 39*(4), 12–27.
7. Chalupa, M., Chatterjee, K., Pavlogiannis, A., Sinha, N., & Vaidya, K., (2017). Data-centric dynamic partial order reduction. *Proceedings of the ACM on Programming Languages, 2*(POPL), 1–30.
8. Deb, S., Médard, M., & Choute, C., (2006). Algebraic gossip: A network coding approach to optimal multiple rumor mongering. *IEEE Transactions on Information Theory, 52*(6), 2486–2507.
9. Dogra, N., & Singh, S., (2015). A survey of dynamic replication strategies in distributed systems. *International Journal of Computer Applications, 110*(11).
10. Frank, L., Pedersen, R. U., Frank, C. H., & Larsson, N. J., (2014). *The Cap Theorem Versus Databases with Relaxed Acid Properties.* Paper presented at the proceedings of the 8th international conference on ubiquitous information management and communication.
11. George, L., & Minet, P., (1997). *A FIFO Worst Case Analysis for a Hard Real-time Distributed Problem with Consistency Constraints.* Paper presented at the proceedings of 17th international conference on distributed computing systems.
12. Gilbert, S., & Lynch, N., (2012). Perspectives on the CAP theorem. *Computer, 45*(2), 30–36.
13. Goel, S., & Buyya, R., (2007). Data replication strategies in wide-area distributed systems *Enterprise Service Computing: From Concept to Deployment* (pp. 211–241). IGI Global.
14. Gupta, I., Kermarrec, A. M., & Ganesh, A. J., (2002). Efficient epidemic-style protocols for reliable and scalable multicast. In: *21st IEEE Symposium on Reliable Distributed Systems, 2002; Proceedings* (pp. 180–189). IEEE.
15. Han, J., Haihong, E., Le, G., & Du, J., (2011). *Survey on NoSQL Database.* Paper presented at the 2011 6th international conference on pervasive computing and applications.
16. Helal, A. A., Heddaya, A. A., & Bhargava, B. B., (2005). *Replication Techniques in Distributed Systems* (Vol. 4). Springer Science & Business Media.
17. Herlihy, M. P., & Wing, J. M., (1990). Linearizability: A correctness condition for concurrent objects. *ACM Transactions on Programming Languages and Systems (TOPLAS), 12*(3), 463–492.
18. Iftode, L., Singh, J. P., & Li, K., (1996). Scope consistency: A bridge between release consistency and entry consistency. In: *Proceedings of the Eighth Annual ACM Symposium on Parallel Algorithms and Architectures* (pp. 277–287).
19. Jarrahi, M. H., Memariani, A., & Guha, S., (2022). *The Principles of Data-Centric AI (DCAI).* arXiv preprint arXiv:2211.14611.

20. Kleppmann, M., (2015). *A Critique of the CAP Theorem*. arXiv preprint arXiv:1509.05393.
21. Lee, C., Park, S. J., Kejriwal, A., Matsushita, S., & Ousterhout, J., (2015). *Implementing Linearizability at Large Scale and Low Latency*. Paper presented at the proceedings of the 25th symposium on operating systems principles.
22. Liu, C., Mao, Y., Van, D. M. J., & Fernandez, M., (2011). *Cloud Resource Orchestration: A Data-Centric Approach*. Paper presented at the proceedings of the biennial conference on innovative data systems research (CIDR).
23. Milani, B. A., & Navimipour, N. J., (2017). A systematic literature review of the data replication techniques in the cloud environments. *Big Data Research, 10*, 1–7.
24. Montresor, A., (2017). Gossip and epidemic protocols. *Wiley Encyclopedia of Electrical and Electronics Engineering, 1*.
25. Narasimhan, P., Moser, L. E., & Melliar-Smith, P., (1997). Replica consistency of CORBA objects in partitionable distributed systems. *Distributed Systems Engineering, 4*(3), 139.
26. Oki, B. M., & Liskov, B. H., (1988). *View Stamped Replication: A New Primary Copy Method to Support Highly-Available Distributed Systems*. Paper presented at the proceedings of the seventh annual ACM symposium on principles of distributed computing.
27. Sandhu, H. S., & Zhou, S., (1992). Cluster-based file replication in large-scale distributed systems. *ACM SIGMETRICS Performance Evaluation Review, 20*(1), 91–102.
28. Sharma, V., & Dave, M., (2012). SQL and NOSQL databases. *International Journal of Advanced Research in Computer Science and Software Engineering, 2*(8).
29. Van, R. R., Dumitriu, D., Gough, V., & Thomas, C., (2008). Efficient reconciliation and flow control for anti-entropy protocols. In: *Proceedings of the 2nd Workshop on Large-Scale Distributed Systems and Middleware* (pp. 1–7).
30. Van, S. M., & Tanenbaum, A., (2002). Distributed systems principles and paradigms. *Network, 2*(28), 1.
31. Wang, G., & Tang, J., (2012). *The NOSQL Principles and Basic Application of Cassandra Model*. Paper presented at the 2012 international conference on computer science and service system.
32. Wu, J., (1998). *Distributed System Design*. CRC press.
33. Yu, H., (2000). Design and evaluation of a continuous consistency model for replicated services. In: *Fourth Symposium on Operating Systems Design and Implementation (OSDI 2000)*.
34. Zaza, N., & Nystrom, N., (2016). *Data-centric Consistency Policies: A Programming Model for Distributed Applications with Tunable Consistency*. Paper presented at the first workshop on programming models and languages for distributed computing.

CHAPTER 5

DISTRIBUTED FILE SYSTEM

UNIT INTRODUCTION

A distributed file system (DFS) is a system that enables multiple computers or nodes to share and access files and data across a network. It is a type of file system that allows multiple users to access and store data in a transparent and coordinated manner, irrespective of the location of the data or the users. The DFS provides a unified view of data and files that can be accessed and managed by users from multiple locations. The DFS is an essential component of modern computing systems, especially in environments where data is shared across multiple nodes or servers. It offers several advantages over traditional file systems, including increased scalability, reliability, and fault tolerance. It is integral to cloud computing, big data analytics, content delivery networks (CDNs), and scientific data management (Howard et al., 1988) (Figure 5.1).

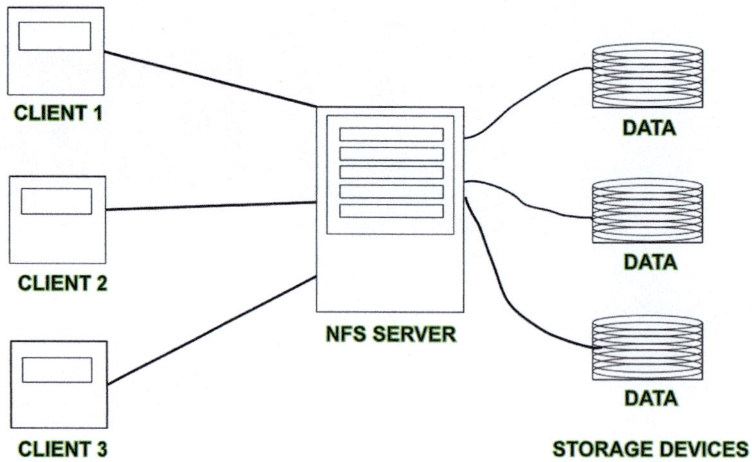

Figure 5.1. Illustration of the distributed file system.

Source: Geeks for Geeks, Creative Commons License.

Learning Objectives

At the end of this chapter, the reader will be able to understand:

- The importance and benefits of distributed file systems;
- The different types of distributed file systems and their characteristics;
- The architecture of distributed file systems and their components;
- The challenges in implementing distributed file systems and strategies for overcoming them;
- The case studies of distributed file system implementations;
- The applications and use cases of distributed file systems, such as big data analytics and cloud computing.

Key Terms

- Andrew file system (AFS)
- Big data analytics
- Ceph file system
- Cloud computing
- Content delivery networks
- Distributed file system
- Fault tolerance
- Gluster file system

- Google file system (GFS)
- Hadoop distributed file system (HDFS)
- High-performance computing
- Lustre file system
- Multimedia streaming
- Network file system (NFS)
- Scientific data management

5.1. IMPORTANCE OF DISTRIBUTED FILE SYSTEM (DFS)

The distributed file system (DFS) is an essential component of modern computing systems, especially in environments where data is shared across multiple nodes or servers. It offers several benefits over traditional file systems, including – scalability, fault tolerance, reliability, performance, and transparency.

TIPS

A distributed file system can improve the availability and reliability of data storage but must also address challenges such as consistency and scalability.

5.1.1. Scalability

The DFS can be easily scaled up or down to meet the changing demands of the users. It can handle large volumes of data and can support multiple users simultaneously.

5.1.2. Fault Tolerance

DFSs are designed to be fault tolerant. They can recover from failures and continue to operate without any interruption. They use various techniques such as redundancy, replication, and backup to ensure that data is always available (Gray & Cheriton, 1989).

5.1.3. Reliability

DFSs are designed to be reliable. They use various techniques such as data checksums and error detection to ensure that data is not corrupted or lost.

5.1.4. Performance

DFSs are designed to provide high-performance access to data. They use various caching and replication techniques to reduce latency and improve performance (Sur et al., 2010).

5.1.5. Transparency

DFSs provide a transparent and coordinated view of data and files. They enable users to access data from any location and provide a unified view of data and files, irrespective of their location.

In conclusion, the DFS is an essential component of modern computing systems. It provides a scalable, fault-tolerant, and reliable way to access and share data across multiple nodes or servers. It is a critical component of cloud computing, big data analytics, content delivery networks (CDNs), and scientific data management (Stroud, 1992).

5.2. TYPES OF DISTRIBUTED FILE SYSTEM (DFS)

There are various types of DFSs that are widely used in different computing environments. Some of the most popular types of DFSs are discussed in subsections.

5.2.1. Network File System (NFS)

Network file system (NFS) is a DFS that enables users to access and share files across a network. It was initially developed by Sun Microsystems in the 1980s and is widely used in Unix and Linux environments. NFS uses the client-server model, where the client requests data from the server, and the server responds with the requested data. NFS provides a transparent view of data and files across multiple platforms and operating systems. It allows users to access files as if they were stored locally, even if they are stored on remote servers. NFS supports multiple file-sharing protocols, including TCP/IP, UDP/IP, and remote procedure call (RPC).

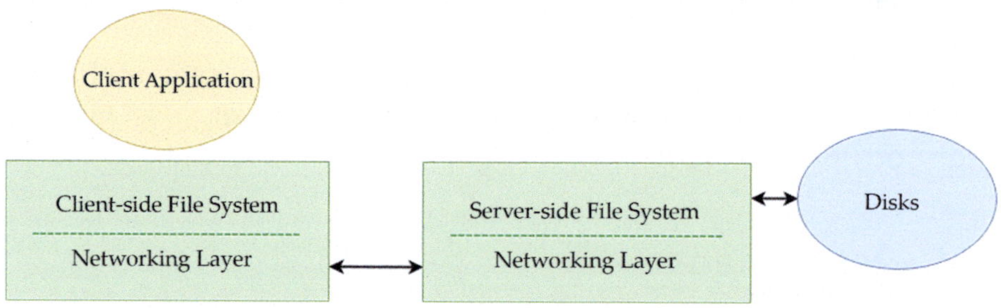

Figure 5.2. Schematic of network file system (NFS).

Source: Geeks for Geeks, Creative Commons License.

One of the primary benefits of NFS is its simplicity and ease of use. It is a well-established protocol that is widely supported in various operating systems and platforms. It also provides reliable data sharing and access over a network, which is essential for collaboration and productivity (Butt et al., 2006) (Figure 5.2).

5.2.2. Andrew File System (AFS)

Andrew file system (AFS) is a DFS that was developed at Carnegie Mellon University in the 1980s. AFS is designed to provide a transparent and coordinated view of data and files across multiple nodes or servers. AFS uses caching and replication techniques to improve performance and reduce latency.

Remember

Network file system (NFS) allows computers to share files as if they were on the same hard drive, making collaboration easier.

AFS is known for its scalability and reliability. It can handle large volumes of data and is designed to be fault tolerant. It uses a client-server model, where the client requests data from the server, and the server responds with the requested data. AFS uses a directory-based naming convention to organize and access files. The file names are hierarchical, and users can access files by navigating the directory structure. AFS also supports access control, where administrators can define permissions and access rights for different users and groups. AFS is widely used in scientific research, education, and corporate environments. It provides a reliable and efficient way to access and share data across multiple nodes or servers (Tobbicke, 1994).

5.2.3. Hadoop Distributed File System (HDFS)

Hadoop distributed file system (HDFS) is a DFS that is designed for big data analytics and processing. HDFS is a part of the Apache Hadoop project and is widely used in big data environments. HDFS uses a master-slave architecture, where the master node manages the file system's metadata, and the slave nodes store the data. HDFS is designed to be fault-tolerant and scalable. It uses replication to ensure that data is always available, even if some nodes fail. HDFS is optimized for large data sets and can handle terabytes or even petabytes of data. HDFS supports various data access models, including read, write, and append. It also supports distributed processing frameworks such as MapReduce and Spark, which enables parallel processing of data across multiple nodes.

HDFS is widely used in big data environments such as data warehousing, analytics, and machine learning. It provides a scalable and efficient way to store and process large data sets (Shvachko et al., 2010).

5.2.4. Google File System (GFS)

Google file system (GFS) is a DFS that was developed by Google in the early 2000s. GFS is designed to handle large volumes of data and is widely used in big data environments. GFS uses a master-slave architecture, where the master node manages the file system's metadata, and the slave nodes store the data. GFS is optimized for read-intensive workloads and supports large file sizes. It is designed to be fault-tolerant and uses replication to ensure that data is always available, even if some nodes fail. GFS also uses a distributed lock service to ensure that data is consistent across multiple nodes.

GFS supports various data access models, including read, write, and append. It also supports distributed processing frameworks such as MapReduce and Bigtable, which enables parallel processing of data across multiple nodes. GFS is widely used in big data environments such as data warehousing, analytics, and machine learning. It provides a scalable and efficient way to store and process large data sets (Ghemawat et al., 2003) (Figure 5.3).

Figure 5.3. Image of components of google file system (GFS).

Source: Praying, Creative Commons License.

5.2.5. Lustre File System

Lustre is a DFS that is designed for high-performance computing (HPC) environments. Lustre is an open-source file system and is widely used in scientific research and engineering environments. Lustre uses a distributed architecture, where the file system is spread across multiple nodes or servers. It uses a metadata server to manage the file system's metadata and multiple object storage targets to store the data. Lustre is designed to be scalable and can handle large volumes of data. Lustre supports various data access models, including read, write, and append. It also supports distributed processing frameworks such as MPI, which enables parallel processing of data across multiple nodes. Lustre is known for its high-performance capabilities and is optimized for large file sizes and high-throughput workloads. It is widely used in scientific research and engineering environments, where HPC is essential (Schwan, 2003).

Did you Know?

The google file system (GFS) revolutionized the field of distributed file systems, providing a scalable, fault-tolerant, and highly available solution for storing and accessing large datasets.

5.2.6. Ceph File System

Ceph is a DFS that is designed for cloud environments. Ceph is an open-source file system and is widely used in cloud computing environments. Ceph uses a distributed architecture, where the file system is spread across multiple nodes or servers. It uses a metadata server to manage the file system's metadata and multiple object storage targets to store the data. Ceph is designed to be scalable and can handle large volumes of data.

Ceph supports various data access models, including read, write, and append. It also supports distributed processing frameworks such as Hadoop, which enables parallel processing of data across multiple nodes. Ceph is known for its flexibility and scalability. It can be deployed on commodity hardware and can scale to handle petabytes of data. It is widely used in cloud computing environments, where flexibility and scalability are essential (Maltzahn et al., 2010).

5.2.7. Gluster File System

Gluster is a DFS that is designed for scale-out NAS environments. Gluster is an open-source file system and is widely used in storage and virtualization environments. Gluster uses a distributed architecture, where the file system is spread across multiple nodes or servers. It uses a metadata server to manage the file system's metadata and multiple storage bricks to store the data. Gluster is designed to be scalable and can handle large volumes of data. Gluster supports various data access models, including read, write, and append. It also supports distributed processing frameworks such as Hadoop and Spark, which enables parallel processing of data across multiple nodes.

Gluster is known for its simplicity and flexibility. It can be deployed on commodity hardware and can scale to handle petabytes of data. It is widely used in storage and virtualization environments, where flexibility and scalability are essential (Donvito et al., 2014).

5.3. ARCHITECTURE OF DISTRIBUTED FILE SYSTEM (DFS)

A DFS is a file system that is designed to provide access to files and directories that are stored on multiple networked computers. The architecture of a DFS is designed to allow files to be accessed and shared by users across multiple machines and locations. The architecture of a DFS typically consists of several components that work together to provide a unified file system interface (Lin et al., 2017) (Figure 5.4).

Figure 5.4. Schematic of distributed file system architecture.

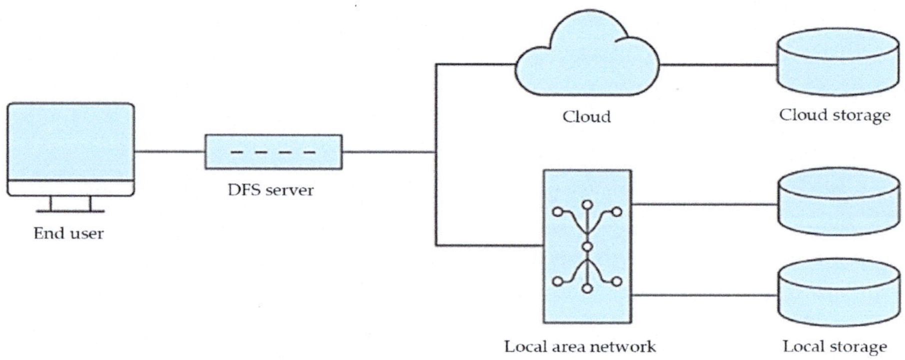

Source: Ryan Arel, Creative Commons License.

These components are discussed in subsections.

5.3.1. Components of Distributed File System (DFS)

The components of a DFS include:

- **Clients:** These are machines that access files in the DFS. They use standardized interfaces to access files and directories, just like a local file system.
- **Servers:** These are machines that store files in the DFS. They are responsible for managing the file system

metadata, handling file requests from clients, and providing data access mechanisms to clients.

- **Communication Protocols and Interfaces:** These are the standardized methods that clients and servers use to communicate with each other. They define how clients and servers send and receive data and how they interact with the file system metadata.
- **Name and Metadata Services:** These are responsible for managing the file system metadata. They use a distributed database to store metadata information, which allows them to scale and handle large volumes of data.
- **Data Storage and Access Mechanisms:** These are responsible for storing and retrieving data from the DFS. They can use a variety of storage technologies, including local disks, network-attached storage (NAS), or object storage systems.
- **Caching and Replication Techniques:** These are used to improve file system performance and reliability. Caching is used to store frequently accessed data in local memory, while replication is used to make copies of data on multiple servers to ensure data availability and reduce the impact of server failures (Sivaraman & Manickachezian, 2014).

5.3.2. Communication Protocols and Interfaces

Communication protocols and interfaces are standardized methods that clients and servers use to communicate with each other. The most commonly used protocols and interfaces in DFSs include:

- **Network File System (NFS):** It is a widely used protocol that allows clients to access files on remote servers as if they were local files.
- **Common Internet File System (CIFS):** It is a protocol that is used by Windows clients to access files on remote servers.
- **Remote Procedure Call (RPC):** It is a protocol that is used to enable clients and servers to communicate with each other.
- **Simple Network Management Protocol (SNMP):** It is a protocol that is used for monitoring and managing network devices (Gifford et al., 1991).

5.3.3. Name and Metadata Services

Name and metadata services are responsible for managing the file system metadata, which includes information such as file names, file sizes, and file permissions. The most commonly used name and metadata services in DFSs are discussed in subsections.

5.3.3.1. Network Information Service (NIS)

Network information service (NIS) is a directory service that is used to provide centralized authentication, authorization, and configuration information to networked computers.

5.3.3.2. Lightweight Directory Access Protocol (LDAP)

Lightweight directory access protocol (LDAP) is a protocol that is used to provide access to directory services, such as NIS (Salim et al., 2009).

5.3.3.3. Common Internet File System Distributed Namespace (CIFSDN)

Common internet file system distributed namespace (CIFSDN) is a namespace service that is used to manage the file system metadata in Windows environments.

5.3.4. Data Storage and Access Mechanisms

Data storage and access mechanisms are responsible for storing and retrieving data from the DFS. The most commonly used data storage and access mechanisms in DFSs are discussed in subsections.

5.3.4.1. Network-Attached Storage (NAS)

Network-attached storage (NAS) is a storage technology that is used to provide file-level storage to networked computers (Kumar, 2013).

5.3.4.2. Object Storage

Object storage is a storage technology that is used to store data as objects, rather than as files.

5.3.4.3. Distributed Block Storage

Distributed block storage is a storage technology that is used to provide block-level storage to networked computers.

5.3.5. Caching and Replication Techniques

Caching and replication techniques are used to improve file system performance and reliability. The most commonly used caching and replication techniques in DFSs are discussed in subsections.

5.3.5.1. Distributed File System Replication (DFSR)

Distributed file system replication (DFSR) is a replication technology that is used to synchronize data across multiple servers in a DFS (Sumirat et al., 2023).

5.3.5.2. File Caching

File caching is a technique that is used to store frequently accessed data in local memory, so that it can be accessed more quickly.

5.3.5.3. Server Load Balancing

Server load balancing is a technique that is used to distribute file system requests across multiple servers, to ensure that no single server becomes overloaded.

5.4. DISTRIBUTED FILE SYSTEM (DFS) IMPLEMENTATION

The implementation of a DFS involves designing and deploying the architecture, components, communication protocols, and services required to support the file system's functionality. The implementation process typically involves the following steps:

- Designing the architecture and selecting the appropriate components for the file system.
- Developing the communication protocols and interfaces that allow clients and servers to interact with each other.
- Implementing the name and metadata services that manage the file system metadata.
- Implementing the data storage and access mechanisms that store and retrieve data from the file system.
- Implementing caching and replication techniques to improve file system performance and reliability.
- Testing and optimizing the file system to ensure that it meets the performance and reliability requirements (Cheng & Sheu, 1991).

5.4.1. Challenges in Implementing Distributed File System (DFS)

Implementing a DFS can be challenging due to the following reasons:

- **Network Latency:** DFSs typically involve the transfer of large amounts of data over a network, which can result in network latency issues that affect performance.

- **Network Security:** Distributing data across multiple servers increases the risk of data breaches and other security threats, which must be addressed by implementing appropriate security measures.
- **System Complexity:** DFSs involve multiple components and services, which can make them complex to design, implement, and manage.
- **Synchronization:** Synchronizing data across multiple servers can be challenging, as it requires coordination between the servers to ensure that the data remains consistent (Huang et al., 2020).

5.4.2. Strategies for Implementing Distributed File System (DFS)

To overcome the challenges involved in implementing a DFS, the following strategies can be adopted:

- **Use of Distributed File System (DFS) Software:** Various DFS software, such as NFS, AFS, HDFS, GFS, Lustre, Ceph, and Gluster, provide a ready-made solution to implementing a DFS.
- **Use of Cloud-Based Storage Services:** Cloud-based storage services, such as Amazon S3, Azure Blob Storage, and Google Cloud Storage, provide an easy-to-use solution to implementing distributed file storage.
- **Use of Distributed File System (DFS) Architecture:** By adopting a DFS architecture, the system can be designed to handle the challenges of network latency, network security, system complexity, and synchronization (Devulapalli & Wyckoff, 2007).

5.4.3. Case Studies of Distributed File System (DFS) Implementation

There are many examples of successful DFS implementations, including:

- **Facebook's Haystack:** Haystack is Facebook's DFS that is used to store and serve billions of images to its users. It uses HDFS as its underlying storage system and relies on custom metadata management to optimize the retrieval of images.
- **Google's File System (GFS):** It is a DFS that is used to store and serve the company's massive data sets. It uses a master-slave architecture and a custom file access protocol to optimize data retrieval.

- **CERN's Ceph File System:** The European Organization for Nuclear Research, uses Ceph as its DFS to store and manage the vast amounts of data generated by its particle physics experiments. Ceph provides a scalable and fault-tolerant storage solution that can handle the large data volumes generated by the experiments (Levy & Silberschatz, 1990).

5.5. APPLICATIONS AND USE CASES OF DISTRIBUTED FILE SYSTEM (DFS)

DFSs are widely used in various applications and use cases that require the storage, management, and sharing of large volumes of data across multiple servers. Some of the common applications and use cases of DFSs are discussed in subsections.

5.5.1. Big Data Analytics

Big data analytics involves processing and analyzing large datasets to extract insights and value. DFSs such as HDFS, GFS, Lustre, and Ceph are commonly used in big data analytics to store and manage the massive amounts of data generated by organizations.

DFSs provide a scalable and fault-tolerant storage solution for big data, enabling organizations to store and manage petabytes or even exabytes of data across multiple servers. By distributing data across multiple servers, DFSs also enable high-speed data access and processing, which is critical for big data analytics (Mahmoud et al., 2018).

5.5.2. Cloud Computing

Cloud computing involves delivering computing resources over the internet. Cloud storage services, such as Amazon S3, Azure Blob Storage, and Google Cloud Storage, use DFSs to store and manage the data of their clients. DFSs enable cloud storage providers to provide a scalable and fault-tolerant storage solution for their clients' data, while also ensuring high-speed data access and processing. By distributing data across multiple servers, DFSs also enable cloud storage providers to achieve high levels of scalability and fault tolerance, which are critical for cloud computing.

5.5.3. Content Delivery Networks (CDNs)

Content delivery networks (CDNs) use DFSs to store and deliver content to users across the globe. CDNs, such as Akamai, Cloudflare, and Fastly, rely on DFSs to ensure that content is delivered quickly and reliably to users, regardless of their location. DFSs enable CDNs to store and manage large volumes of content, such as videos, images, and web pages, across multiple servers, which ensures high-speed content delivery and reduces latency (Borst et al., 2010).

5.5.4. High-Performance Computing (HPC)

High-performance computing (HPC) systems require high-speed data access and processing to handle complex computations and simulations. DFSs such as Lustre, Ceph, and Gluster are commonly used in HPC systems to store and manage large datasets. DFSs provide a scalable and fault-tolerant storage solution for HPC systems, enabling them to store and manage large datasets across multiple servers. By distributing data across multiple servers, DFSs also enable HPC systems to achieve high-speed data access and processing, which is critical for complex computations and simulations.

ACTIVITY 5.1:

In what ways has the Google File System (GFS) transformed the way large-scale data is managed and stored, and what are the implications of this technology for businesses and organizations across different industries?

5.5.5. Multimedia Streaming

Multimedia streaming applications require a scalable and reliable storage solution for large media files, such as videos and music. DFSs such as HDFS, GFS, and Ceph are commonly used in multimedia streaming applications to ensure that media files are delivered quickly and reliably to users. DFSs enable media streaming providers to store and manage large volumes of media files across multiple servers, which ensures high-speed media delivery and reduces latency.

5.5.6. Scientific Data Management

Scientific experiments generate large volumes of data that need to be stored and managed efficiently. DFSs such as Ceph, Gluster, and Lustre are commonly used in scientific data management to provide a scalable and fault-tolerant storage solution. By distributing data across multiple servers, DFSs enable scientists to store and manage large datasets across multiple servers, which ensures high-speed data access and processing. DFSs also provide fault tolerance, ensuring that data is not lost in the event of server failure (Lee et al., 2021).

5.6. SUMMARY

The chapter "Distributed File System" discusses the importance and benefits of using a DFS, which allows multiple computers to share data across a network. Different types of DFSs are presented, including NFS, common internet file system (CIFS), and Google file system (GFS), each with its own characteristics and features. The architecture and components of DFSs, such as metadata servers, data servers, and clients, are also explained.

The challenges in implementing DFSs, such as data consistency and fault tolerance, are identified and strategies for overcoming them are discussed. Case studies of DFS implementations, including HDFS and Microsoft Azure File Storage, are presented to illustrate how these systems are used in real-world scenarios.

Finally, the chapter explores the various applications and use cases of DFSs, such as big data analytics and cloud computing. Overall, the chapter provides a comprehensive overview of DFSs, their benefits, challenges, and real-world applications.

REVIEW QUESTIONS

1. What are the benefits of using a Distributed File System?
2. What are the different types of Distributed File Systems and what are their characteristics?
3. Describe the architecture of a Distributed File System and its components.
4. What are some challenges associated with implementing a Distributed File System, and what are some strategies for overcoming them?
5. Can you provide examples of case studies of Distributed File System implementations?
6. What are some common applications and use cases of Distributed File Systems, such as Big Data Analytics and Cloud Computing?

MULTIPLE CHOICE QUESTIONS

1. What is the importance of Distributed File Systems?

a. They enable users to access and share files from anywhere in the network.
b. They provide a centralized storage system for all network users.
c. They increase data security and reliability.
d. All of the above.

2. Which of the following is not a characteristic of Distributed File Systems?

a. Scalability
b. Fault tolerance

c. Centralized storage
d. High performance

3. What are the components of a Distributed File System?
a. Client, server, file metadata, and data storage
b. Client, server, file system cache, and backup storage
c. Client, server, file system cache, and data storage
d. Client, server, file metadata, and backup storage

4. What is a challenge in implementing Distributed File Systems?
a. Limited storage capacity
b. Difficulty in maintaining data consistency
c. Lack of security features
d. All of the above

5. Which Distributed File System is commonly used in cloud computing?
a. Hadoop Distributed File System (HDFS)
b. Network File System (NFS)
c. Andrew File System (AFS)
d. None of the above

6. Which application uses Distributed File Systems for large-scale data analysis?
a. Social media platforms
b. E-commerce websites
c. Big data analytics
d. Gaming platforms

Answers to Multiple Choice Questions

1. (d); 2. (c); 3. (c); 4. (b); 5. (a); 6. (c)

REFERENCES

1. Borst, S., Gupta, V., & Walid, A., (2010). Distributed caching algorithms for content distribution networks. In: *2010 Proceedings IEEE INFOCOM* (Vol. 1, pp. 1–9). IEEE.
2. Butt, A. R., Johnson, T. A., Zheng, Y., & Hu, Y. C., (2006). Kosha: A peer-to-peer enhancement for the network file system. *Journal of Grid Computing, 4*(3), 323–341.
3. Cheng, H. C., & Sheu, J. P., (1991). Design and implementation of a distributed file system. *Software: Practice and Experience, 21*(7), 657–675.

4. Devulapalli, A., & Wyckoff, P., (2007). File creation strategies in a distributed metadata file system. In: *2007 IEEE International Parallel and Distributed Processing Symposium* (Vol.1, pp. 1–10). IEEE.
5. Donvito, G., Marzulli, G., & Diacono, D., (2014). Testing of several distributed file-systems (HDFS, Ceph and GlusterFS) for supporting the HEP experiments analysis. In: *Journal of Physics: Conference Series* (Vol. 513, p. 42014). IOP Publishing.
6. Ghemawat, S., Gobioff, H., & Leung, S. T., (2003). The Google file system. In: *Proceedings of the Nineteenth ACM Symposium on OPERATING Systems Principles* (pp. 29–43).
7. Gifford, D. K., Jouvelot, P., Sheldon, M. A., & O'Toole, Jr. J. W., (1991). Semantic file systems. *ACM SIGOPS Operating Systems Review, 25*(5), 16–25.
8. Gray, C., & Cheriton, D., (1989). Leases: An efficient fault-tolerant mechanism for distributed file cache consistency. *ACM SIGOPS Operating Systems Review, 23*(5), 202–210.
9. Howard, J. H., Kazar, M. L., Menees, S. G., Nichols, D. A., Satyanarayanan, M., Sidebotham, R. N., & West, M. J., (1988). Scale and performance in a distributed file system. *ACM Transactions on Computer Systems (TOCS), 6*(1), 51–81.
10. Huang, H., Lin, J., Zheng, B., Zheng, Z., & Bian, J., (2020). When blockchain meets distributed file systems: An overview, challenges, and open issues. *IEEE Access, 8*, 50574–50586.
11. Kumar, K. L., (2013). Implementing network file system protocol for highly available clustered applications on network attached storage. In: *2013 5th International Conference and Computational Intelligence and Communication Networks* (Vol. 1, pp. 496–499). IEEE.
12. Lee, J. Y., Kim, M. H., Raza, S. S. A., Ahn, S. U., Yoon, H., & Noh, S. Y., (2021). Performance evaluations of distributed file systems for scientific big data in FUSE environment. *Electronics, 10*(12), 1471.
13. Levy, E., & Silberschatz, A., (1990). Distributed file systems: Concepts and examples. *ACM Computing Surveys (CSUR), 22*(4), 321–374.
14. Lin, Z., Li, K., Hou, H., Yang, X., & Li, H., (2017). MDFS: A mimic defense theory based architecture for distributed file system. In: *2017 IEEE International Conference on Big Data (Big Data)* (Vol. 1, pp. 2670–2675). IEEE.
15. Mahmoud, H., Hegazy, A., & Khafagy, M. H., (2018). An approach for big data security based on Hadoop distributed file system. In: *2018 International Conference on Innovative Trends in Computer Engineering (ITC)* (Vol. 1, pp. 109–114). IEEE.
16. Maltzahn, C., Molina-Estolano, E., Khurana, A., Nelson, A. J., Brandt, S. A., & Weil, S., (2010). Ceph as a scalable alternative to the Hadoop distributed file system. *Login: The USENIX Magazine, 35*, 38–49.
17. Salim, M., Akhtar, M. S., & Qadeer, M. A., (2009). Data retrieval and security using lightweight directory access protocol. In: *2009 Second International Workshop on*

Knowledge Discovery and Data Mining (Vol. 1, pp. 685–688). IEEE.

18. Satyanarayanan, M., Howard, J. H., Nichols, D. A., Sidebotham, R. N., Spector, A. Z., & West, M. J., (1985). The ITC distributed file system: Principles and design. *ACM SIGOPS Operating Systems Review, 19*(5), 35–50.
19. Schwan, P., (2003). Lustre: Building a file system for 1000-node clusters. In: *Proceedings of the 2003 Linux Symposium* (Vol. 2003, pp. 380–386).
20. Shvachko, K., Kuang, H., Radia, S., & Chansler, R., (2010). The Hadoop distributed file system. In: *2010 IEEE 26th Symposium on Mass Storage Systems and Technologies (MSST)* (Vol. 1, pp. 1–10). IEEE.
21. Sivaraman, E., & Manickachezian, R., (2014). High performance and fault tolerant distributed file system for big data storage and processing using Hadoop. In: *2014 International Conference on Intelligent Computing Applications* (Vol.1, pp. 32–36). IEEE.
22. Stroud, R., (1992). Transparency and reflection in distributed systems. In: *Proceedings of the 5th Workshop on ACM SIGOPS European Workshop: Models and Paradigms for Distributed Systems Structuring* (Vol. 1, pp. 1–5).
23. Sumirat, U., Setiawan, A., Wilyanti, S., & Al-Hakim, R., (2023). Analysis of distributed file system replication using the NDLC method with hyper-V virtual simulation machine. *SaNa: Journal of Blockchain, NFTs and Metaverse Technology, 1*(1), 11–23.
24. Sur, S., Wang, H., Huang, J., Ouyang, X., & Panda, D. K., (2010). Can high-performance interconnects benefit Hadoop distributed file system. In: *Workshop on Micro Architectural Support for Virtualization, Data Center Computing, and Clouds (MASVDC); Held in Conjunction with MICRO* (Vol. 1, p. 10).
25. Tobbicke, R., (1994). Distributed file systems: Focus on Andrew file system/distributed file service (AFS/DFS). In: *Proceedings Thirteenth IEEE Symposium on Mass Storage Systems; Toward Distributed Storage and Data Management Systems* (Vol. 1, pp. 23–26). IEEE.

CHAPTER 6

DATA STORAGE IN DISTRIBUTED SYSTEM

UNIT INTRODUCTION

Distributed systems refer to a network of interconnected computers that communicate with each other and work together to achieve a common goal. These computers are geographically dispersed and can be connected through local area networks (LANs) or wide area networks (WANs) such as the Internet. Distributed systems are widely used in various domains such as cloud computing, social networks, and e-commerce, to name a few. In a distributed system, data is often spread across multiple nodes, which can pose challenges for data storage, management, and retrieval. This is where the importance of data storage in distributed systems comes into play (Wang & Zhang, 2020) (Figure 6.1).

Data storage is a crucial component of any distributed system. The ability to store, manage, and retrieve data efficiently and reliably is essential for the proper functioning of a distributed system. The distributed nature of these systems requires data to be replicated and distributed across multiple nodes for fault tolerance, scalability, and performance. Moreover, distributed systems generate large volumes of data that need to be stored and processed in real-time. This data can come from various sources such as sensors, social media, and user interactions. Therefore, choosing the right data storage solution that can handle the data requirements of a distributed system is crucial for its success (Seitz et al., 2003).

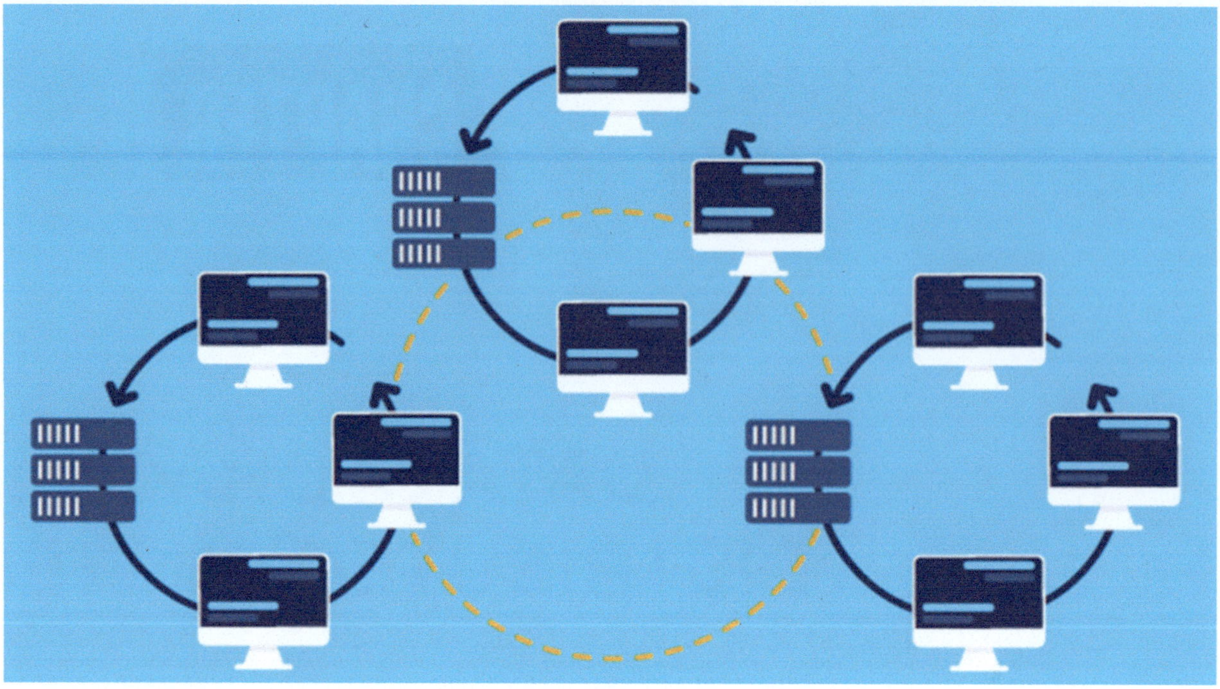

Figure 6.1. Image of wide area networks (WANs).

Source: Cisco, Creative Common license.

Learning Objectives

At the end of this chapter, the reader will be able to understand:

- The data storage requirements in distributed systems, including durability, availability, consistency, scalability, performance, and security.
- The types of data storage in distributed systems, such as distributed file systems (DFSs), key-value stores, column-family stores, and document-oriented databases.
- The reasons and techniques for data replication in distributed systems.
- Difference between the strong consistency, weak consistency, and eventual consistency models in distributed systems and their consistency levels in different data stores.
- The data partitioning techniques in distributed systems, such as horizontal partitioning, vertical partitioning, and hybrid partitioning.

Key Terms

- Data durability
- Data partitioning

- Data replication
- Distributed file systems
- Document-oriented databases
- Eventual consistency
- Horizontal partitioning
- Hybrid partitioning
- Key-value stores
- Security
- Strong consistency
- Vertical partitioning
- Weak consistency

6.1. DATA STORAGE REQUIREMENTS IN DISTRIBUTED SYSTEMS

Data storage is an essential component of any distributed system. However, the distributed nature of these systems requires data to be replicated and distributed across multiple nodes, which can introduce challenges in terms of data durability, availability, consistency, scalability, performance, and security. In this section, we will discuss each of these requirements in detail.

6.1.1. Data Durability

Data durability refers to the ability of a distributed system to ensure that data is not lost or corrupted, even in the event of hardware or network failures. In a distributed system, data is typically replicated across multiple nodes, which provides fault tolerance and resilience against data loss. However, this also means that data must be replicated consistently and reliably across all nodes. To ensure data durability, distributed systems use techniques such as data replication, which involves creating copies of data on multiple nodes. This ensures that even if one node fails, the data can still be retrieved from another node. In addition, distributed systems often use techniques such as data checksumming, data backups, and data redundancy to ensure data integrity and prevent data loss (Utard & Vernois, 2004).

6.1.2. Data Availability

Data availability refers to the ability of a distributed system to ensure that data is always accessible to users, even in the event of hardware or network failures. In a distributed system, data can be distributed across multiple nodes, and users may access different nodes to retrieve data. This can make it challenging to ensure that data is always available, as failures in one node can affect the availability of data. To ensure data availability, distributed systems use techniques such as load balancing, which involves distributing user requests across multiple nodes. This helps to ensure that no single node is overloaded with requests, which can cause it to fail. In addition, distributed systems often use techniques such as data replication, caching, and data partitioning to ensure that data is readily available to users (Federer et al., 2018).

6.1.3. Data Consistency

Data consistency refers to the ability of a distributed system to ensure that data is consistent across all nodes in the system. In a distributed system, data can be replicated across multiple nodes, and updates to data can occur on different nodes at different times. This can lead to inconsistencies in data across nodes, which can affect the reliability and accuracy of the system (Pitoura & Bhargava, 1999).

To ensure data consistency, distributed systems use techniques such as distributed transactions, which allow updates to data to occur across multiple nodes in a coordinated and consistent manner. In addition, distributed systems often use consistency models, which define the level of consistency that is acceptable for the system. Examples of consistency models include strong consistency, weak consistency, and eventual consistency (Oster et al., 2006) (Figure 6.2).

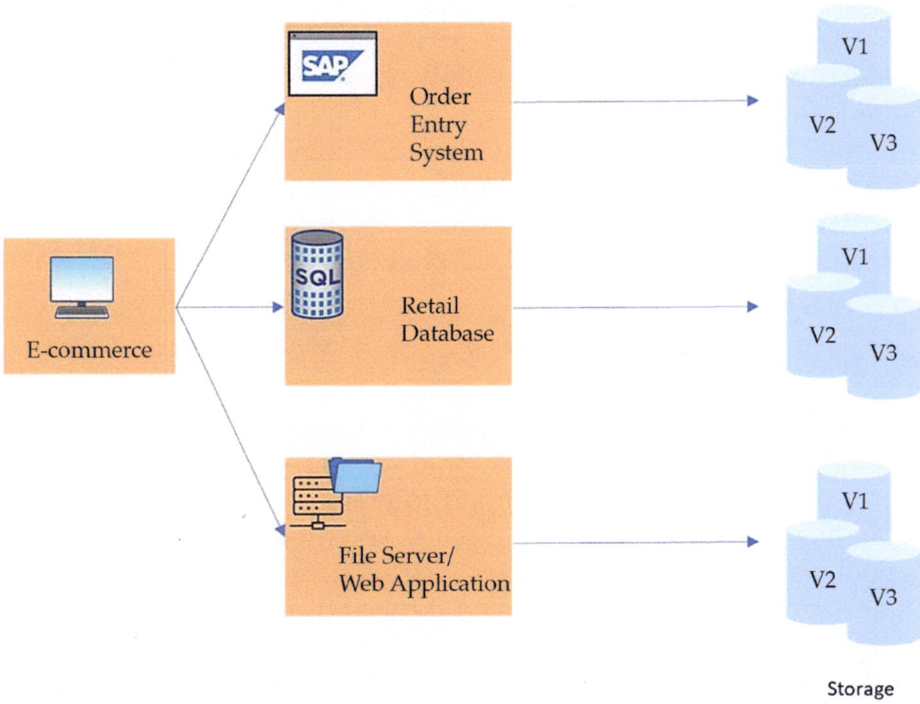

Figure 6.2. Illustration of data consistency.

Source: Ebin Kadai, Creative Commons License.

6.1.4. Scalability

Scalability refers to the ability of a distributed system to handle increasing amounts of data and users without sacrificing performance or reliability. In a distributed system, adding more nodes can increase the system's capacity to handle data and users. However, adding more nodes can also introduce complexity and overhead, which can affect the system's performance and reliability. To ensure scalability, distributed systems use techniques such as data partitioning, which involves dividing data into smaller subsets and distributing them across multiple nodes. This helps to ensure that each node only handles a subset of the data, which can improve performance and reduce overhead. In addition, distributed systems often use load balancing, caching, and horizontal scaling techniques to handle increasing amounts of data and users (Aguilera et al., 2007).

6.1.5. Performance

Performance refers to the ability of a distributed system to handle user requests and data processing in a timely and efficient manner. In a distributed system, performance can be affected by factors such as network latency, data access patterns, and load distribution. To ensure performance, distributed systems use techniques such as load balancing, which involves distributing user requests across multiple nodes. This helps to ensure that no single node is overloaded with requests, which can cause it to fail or slow down. In addition, distributed systems often use techniques such as caching, which involves storing frequently accessed data in memory for faster access. This can help to reduce the latency of data access and improve overall system performance. Additionally, distributed systems can also use data compression and parallel processing techniques to improve data processing speeds (Rohloff & Schantz, 2010).

6.1.6. Security

Security refers to the ability of a distributed system to protect data and resources from unauthorized access, data breaches, and other security threats. In a distributed system, security can be challenging to ensure, as data is replicated and distributed across multiple nodes. To ensure security, distributed systems use techniques such as authentication and authorization, which involves verifying the identity of users and controlling access to data and resources. In addition, distributed systems often use encryption, which involves converting data into a secure form that can only be accessed by authorized users with the proper decryption key. Other security measures such as firewalls, intrusion detection systems, and network monitoring can also be used to protect against security threats (Ni et al., 2013).

In conclusion, data storage is an essential component of any distributed system. However, the distributed nature of these systems requires data to be replicated and distributed across multiple nodes, which can introduce challenges in terms of data durability, availability, consistency, scalability, performance, and security. By understanding these requirements and using appropriate techniques, distributed systems can ensure that data is stored and accessed in a reliable, secure, and efficient manner (Kaufman, 2009).

6.2. TYPES OF DATA STORAGE IN DISTRIBUTED SYSTEMS

Distributed systems require specialized types of data storage to ensure data is stored, accessed, and processed efficiently across multiple nodes. Some of the most commonly used types of data storage in distributed systems are discussed in subsections.

6.2.1. Distributed File Systems (DFSs)

Distributed file systems (DFSs) allow for large files to be split across multiple nodes in a cluster, making it easier to manage and access the data. Here are some examples of popular DFSs used in distributed systems:

- **Hadoop Distributed File System (HDFS):** It is a DFS used in Apache Hadoop, an open-source big data processing framework. HDFS is designed to handle large data sets and is optimized for batch processing workloads.
- **GlusterFS:** It is an open-source DFS that can scale to petabytes of data. It is highly available and provides redundancy and failover capabilities.
- **Ceph:** It is a distributed storage system that provides object, block, and file storage. It is highly scalable and provides fault tolerance, data redundancy, and data availability (Maltzahn et al., 2010).

TIPS

Key-value stores can provide high-speed access to data but may not be suitable for complex queries or large data sets.

6.2.2. Key-Value Stores

Key-value stores are a type of NoSQL database that stores data as key-value pairs. Key-value stores are highly scalable and can handle large volumes of data. Here are some popular key-value stores used in distributed systems:

- **Redis:** It is an open-source, in-memory key-value store that is highly scalable and provides high-performance data access. It supports advanced data structures such as lists, sets, and hashes.
- **Riak:** It is a highly available, fault-tolerant key-value store that provides high scalability and fault tolerance. It is optimized for write-heavy workloads and is often used in real-time data processing applications.
- **DynamoDB:** It is a managed NoSQL database service

provided by Amazon Web Services (AWS). It is highly scalable, fault-tolerant, and provides high-performance data access. It is optimized for low-latency workloads and is often used in web and mobile applications (Liu et al., 2015) (Figure 6.3).

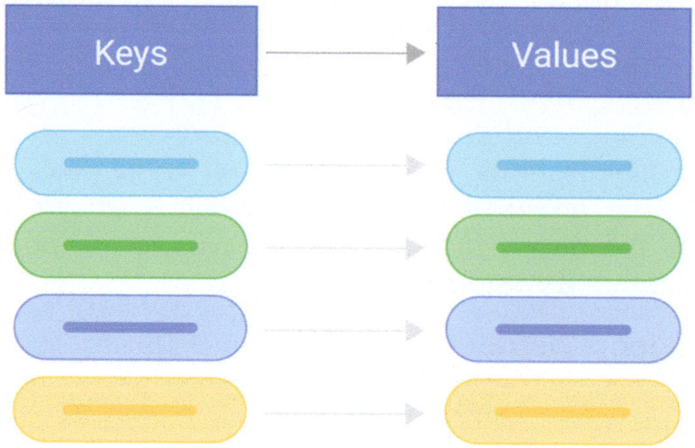

Figure 6.3. Depiction of key-value store template.

Source: Scylla, Creative Commons License.

6.2.3. Column-Family Stores

Column-family stores are a type of NoSQL database that stores data as column families, which are groups of columns that are frequently accessed together. Here are some popular column-family stores used in distributed systems:

- **Apache Cassandra:** Cassandra is a highly scalable, distributed NoSQL database that provides high availability and fault tolerance. It is optimized for write-heavy workloads and is often used in large-scale web applications.
- **HBase:** It is an open-source, distributed column-family store that is built on top of Apache Hadoop. It provides low-latency access to large datasets and is optimized for read-heavy workloads (Ho et al., 2015).

6.2.4. Document-Oriented Databases

Document-oriented databases are a type of NoSQL database that stores data as JSON-like documents. Document-oriented databases are highly scalable and can handle large volumes of unstructured data. Here are some popular document-oriented databases used in distributed systems:

- **MongoDB:** It is a popular open-source document-oriented database that is highly scalable and provides high-performance data access. It supports advanced features such as dynamic schema, secondary indexes, and sharding.
- **Couchbase:** It is a distributed document-oriented database that provides high scalability and fault tolerance. It is optimized for low-latency workloads and provides advanced features such as cross-data center replication and mobile synchronization.
- **CouchDB:** It is an open-source, distributed document-oriented database that is highly scalable and provides high-performance data access. It supports advanced features such as versioning, conflict resolution, and offline data synchronization (Gallinucci et al., 2018).

Remember

In distributed systems, data replication is like a game of telephone - the more copies you make, the less likely it is that the message will be lost or corrupted.

6.3. DATA REPLICATION IN DISTRIBUTED SYSTEMS

Data replication is an essential aspect of data storage in distributed systems. It involves copying data from one node to another to ensure data availability, fault tolerance, and performance. In this section, we will discuss the reasons for data replication and the techniques used for data replication in distributed systems (Kaskina, 2010).

6.3.1. Reasons for Data Replication

There are several reasons why data replication is important in distributed systems:

- **High Availability:** Data replication ensures that data is available even if one or more nodes fail. If one node fails, the replicated data can be accessed from other nodes.
- **Fault Tolerance:** Data replication provides fault tolerance by allowing data to be accessed even if one or more nodes fail or go offline. Replication also ensures that data is not lost if a node fails.
- **Performance:** Data replication can improve performance by allowing data to be accessed from the node closest to the client. Replicated data can be stored on multiple nodes, and the client can access the data from the node closest to it, reducing network latency.

- **Disaster Recovery:** Data replication is an important part of disaster recovery planning. If a disaster such as a fire or flood occurs, replicated data can be used to restore the system to its previous state (Serrano et al., 2007).

6.3.2. Techniques for Data Replication

There are several techniques for data replication in distributed systems. These include:

- **Master-Slave Replication:** In this technique, one node is designated as the master node, and all updates to the data are made on the master node. The updated data is then replicated to one or more slave nodes. The slave nodes can be used for read-only operations, and the master node is used for writing operations. This technique is simple to implement but can result in performance bottlenecks if the master node becomes overloaded.
- **Master-Master Replication:** In this technique, multiple nodes act as master nodes, and updates to the data can be made on any of the master nodes. The updated data is then replicated to all the other master nodes. This technique provides better performance and fault tolerance than master-slave replication, but it can be more complex to implement.
- **Multi-Master Replication:** This technique is similar to master-master replication, but it allows updates to be made on any node, and the updated data is replicated to all other nodes. This technique provides the best performance and fault tolerance but can be the most complex to implement.

In conclusion, data replication is an essential aspect of data storage in distributed systems. It ensures data availability, fault tolerance, and performance. There are several techniques for data replication, including master-slave replication, master-master replication, and multi-master replication. The choice of replication technique depends on the specific requirements of the distributed system, such as performance, fault tolerance, and complexity of implementation (Milani & Navimipour, 2016).

6.4. CONSISTENCY MODELS IN DISTRIBUTED SYSTEMS

Consistency models are an essential aspect of data storage in distributed systems. In a distributed system, consistency refers to the property that all nodes in the system see the same data at the same time. There are different levels of consistency that a distributed system can provide, depending on the specific requirements of the system and the application it supports (Aldin et al., 2019).

6.4.1. Strong Consistency

Strong consistency is a model that guarantees that all nodes in the system see the same data at the same time. In other words, if a node writes data to the system, any subsequent read operation on any node will return the latest written value. This model ensures that there is no data inconsistency or ambiguity in the system. To achieve strong consistency, the system must implement strict synchronization mechanisms to ensure that all nodes have access to the same data at the same time. This can be a costly process in terms of performance, especially in large-scale systems (Bannour et al., 2018).

6.4.2. Weak Consistency

Weak consistency is a model that allows for temporary inconsistencies in the system, where different nodes may have different versions of the same data. In this model, data updates are not immediately propagated to all nodes, and reads may return stale data. However, eventually, all nodes in the system will converge to the same data values. The weak consistency model provides better performance than strong consistency, as it reduces the synchronization overhead between nodes. However, it may not be suitable for applications that require immediate access to the latest data, as it may take some time to propagate updates across all nodes (Zhang et al., 2016).

6.4.3. Eventual Consistency

Eventual consistency is a model that allows temporary inconsistencies in the system but guarantees that all nodes in the system will eventually converge to the same data values. In this model, updates are propagated asynchronously, and nodes may temporarily see different versions of the same data. However, over time, updates will propagate to all nodes, and eventually, all nodes will have the same data values. The eventual consistency model provides the best performance among the three models, as it minimizes synchronization overhead between nodes. However, it may not be suitable for applications that require immediate access to the latest data, as it may take some time to propagate updates across all nodes (Burckhardt, 2014).

6.4.4. Consistency Levels in Different Data Stores

Different data stores may provide different levels of consistency depending on their specific design and implementation. For example, a distributed key-value store may provide eventual consistency, while a distributed relational database may provide strong consistency. Some data stores may allow users to configure the consistency level based on their specific requirements. It is important to choose a consistency model that meets the requirements of the application and the performance needs of the system. Applications that require immediate access to the latest data may require strong consistency, while applications that can tolerate temporary inconsistencies may benefit from eventual consistency. Ultimately, the choice of consistency model will depend on the specific requirements of the application and the characteristics of the distributed system in which it operates (Sivaramakrishnan et al., 2015).

Did you Know?

Consistency levels in different data stores vary widely, with some systems prioritizing strong consistency for data integrity while others may favor eventual consistency for better availability and performance.

6.5. DATA PARTITIONING IN DISTRIBUTED SYSTEMS

Data partitioning is a key aspect of data storage in distributed systems. It involves dividing the data across multiple nodes in the system, allowing for more efficient and scalable storage and retrieval of data. There are three main types of data partitioning: horizontal partitioning, vertical partitioning, and hybrid partitioning (Adoni et al., 2020).

6.5.1. Horizontal Partitioning

Horizontal partitioning, also known as sharding, involves dividing data horizontally based on some attribute, such as customer ID or region. Each shard is stored on a separate node in the distributed system, allowing for parallel processing of queries and improving performance. In a sharded system, a query can be executed on multiple shards in parallel, allowing for faster retrieval of data. Horizontal partitioning is often used in systems with large datasets, where storing all the data on a single node is not feasible.

One of the main advantages of horizontal partitioning is its scalability. As the dataset grows, new nodes can be added to the system, and the data can be partitioned across them, without affecting the performance of the system. However, horizontal partitioning can also lead to data skew, where some shards contain more data than others, leading to performance issues. It can also make it more difficult to maintain consistency across the system, as updates to the data may need to be propagated across multiple shards (Inan et al., 2007).

6.5.2. Vertical Partitioning

Vertical partitioning involves dividing data based on columns or attributes, with each partition containing only a subset of the columns in a given row. This type of partitioning is often used to improve the performance of queries that only access a subset of the columns in a table. In a vertically partitioned system, each node stores a subset of the columns for each row, allowing for more efficient storage and retrieval of data.

Vertical partitioning can lead to more efficient use of storage space, as each node only stores a subset of the data, but it can also lead to increased complexity in query processing, as queries may need to be executed across multiple nodes to retrieve all the required data. It can also be more difficult to maintain consistency across the system, as updates to a row may need to be propagated across multiple nodes (Son & Kim, 2004).

ACTIVITY 6.1:

How can different consistency levels in various data stores, such as relational databases, NoSQL databases, and distributed systems, impact data integrity and availability, and what trade-offs do developers need to consider when selecting a consistency model?

6.5.3. Hybrid Partitioning

Hybrid partitioning combines horizontal and vertical partitioning to divide data based on both rows and columns. This approach allows for more efficient storage and retrieval of data and can help to mitigate some of the drawbacks of horizontal and vertical partitioning. In a hybrid partitioned system, the data is first divided horizontally into shards, and then each shard is vertically partitioned into subsets of columns. Hybrid partitioning can lead to better performance than horizontal or vertical partitioning alone, as it allows for parallel processing of queries across shards and columns. It can also improve the efficiency of storage and reduce data skew, as the data is divided both horizontally and vertically. However, hybrid partitioning can be more complex to implement and manage than horizontal or vertical partitioning alone.

In conclusion, data partitioning is an important aspect of data storage in distributed systems. Horizontal partitioning, vertical partitioning, and hybrid partitioning are the three main types of data partitioning. Each type has its own advantages and disadvantages, and the choice of partitioning approach depends on the specific requirements of the system (Ye et al., 2010).

6.6. SUMMARY

The chapter on "Data Storage in Distributed Systems" discusses the various data storage requirements and techniques in distributed systems. The chapter covers different types of data storage in distributed systems, including DFSs, key-value stores, column-family stores, and document-oriented databases. It also explains the reasons and techniques for data replication in distributed systems. The chapter discusses the different consistency models in distributed systems, such as strong consistency, weak consistency, and eventual consistency, and their levels of consistency in different data stores. Additionally, the chapter covers the data partitioning techniques in distributed systems, such as horizontal partitioning, vertical partitioning, and hybrid partitioning. Overall, the chapter provides a comprehensive overview of data storage in distributed systems, including the various types of data stores, replication techniques, consistency models, and partitioning techniques. It is an essential read for anyone interested in distributed systems and data storage.

REVIEW QUESTIONS

1. What are the main data storage requirements in distributed systems? How do these requirements affect the design and implementation of data storage solutions?
2. Describe the different types of data storage used in distributed systems. What are the advantages and disadvantages of each type?
3. What are the reasons for data replication in distributed systems? What are some common techniques used for data replication, and what are their benefits and limitations?
4. Explain the differences between strong consistency, weak consistency, and eventual consistency models in distributed systems. How do these models impact the performance, availability, and scalability of data storage solutions?
5. What are the main data partitioning techniques used in distributed systems? Describe the differences between horizontal partitioning, vertical partitioning, and hybrid partitioning. What are the factors to consider when choosing a partitioning technique?

MULTIPLE CHOICE QUESTIONS

1. Which of the following is not a data storage requirement in distributed systems?

a. Durability

b. Performance

c. Cost-effectiveness

d. Availability

2. **Which type of data storage is suitable for storing large amounts of unstructured data in distributed systems?**
   a. Distributed file systems
   b. Key-value stores
   c. Column-family stores
   d. Document-oriented databases
3. **What is the reason for data replication in distributed systems?**
   a. To improve data consistency
   b. To improve data security
   c. To improve data performance
   d. All of the above
4. **Which consistency model in distributed systems provides the highest level of consistency?**
   a. Strong consistency
   b. Weak consistency
   c. Eventual consistency
   d. They all provide the same level of consistency
5. **Which data partitioning technique is suitable for storing data with a high degree of relationships between different entities?**
   a. Horizontal partitioning
   b. Vertical partitioning
   c. Hybrid partitioning
   d. None of the above

Answers to Multiple Choice Questions

1. (c); 2. (d); 3. (d); 4. (a); 5. (b)

REFERENCES

1. Adoni, H. W. Y., Nahhal, T., Krichen, M., Aghezzaf, B., & Elbyed, A., (2020). A survey of current challenges in partitioning and processing of graph-structured data in parallel and distributed systems. *Distributed and Parallel Databases, 38*, 495–530.
2. Aguilera, M. K., Merchant, A., Shah, M., Veitch, A., & Karamanolis, C., (2007). Sinfonia: A new paradigm for building scalable distributed systems. *ACM SIGOPS Operating Systems Review, 41*(6), 159–174.
3. Aldin, H. N. S., Deldari, H., Moattar, M. H., & Ghods, M. R., (2019). *Consistency*

Models in Distributed Systems: A Survey on Definitions, Disciplines, Challenges and Applications (pp. 300–305). arXiv preprint arXiv:1902.

4. Bannour, F., Souihi, S., & Mellouk, A., (2018). Adaptive state consistency for distributed ONOS controllers. In: *2018 IEEE Global Communications Conference (Globecom)* (Vol. 1, pp. 1–7). IEEE.
5. Burckhardt, S., (2014). Principles of eventual consistency. *Foundations and Trends® in Programming Languages, 1*(1, 2), 1–150.
6. Federer, L. M., Belter, C. W., Joubert, D. J., Livinski, A., Lu, Y. L., Snyders, L. N., & Thompson, H., (2018). Data sharing in PLOS one: An analysis of data availability statements. *PloS One, 13*(5), 194768.
7. Gallinucci, E., Golfarelli, M., & Rizzi, S., (2018). Schema profiling of document-oriented databases. *Information Systems, 75*, 13–25.
8. Ho, L. Y., Hsieh, M. J., Wu, J. J., & Liu, P., (2015). Data partition optimization for column-family NoSQL databases. In: *2015 IEEE International Conference on Smart City/SocialCom/SustainCom (SmartCity)* (Vol. 1, pp. 668–675). IEEE.
9. Inan, A., Kaya, S. V., Saygın, Y., Savaş, E., Hintoğlu, A. A., & Levi, A., (2007). Privacy preserving clustering on horizontally partitioned data. *Data & Knowledge Engineering, 63*(3), 646–666.
10. Kaskina, A., (2010). *Data Replication in Distributed Systems* (Vol. 2, No. 1, pp. 14–20). Doctoral dissertation, Oxford Brookes University.
11. Kaufman, L. M., (2009). Data security in the world of cloud computing. *IEEE Security & Privacy, 7*(4), 61–64.
12. Liu, S., Nguyen, S., Ganhotra, J., Rahman, M. R., Gupta, I., & Meseguer, J., (2015). Quantitative analysis of consistency in NoSQL key-value stores. In: *Quantitative Evaluation of Systems: 12th International Conference, QEST 2015, Madrid, Spain, September 1–3, 2015, Proceedings 12* (Vol. 2, pp. 228–243). Springer International Publishing.
13. Maltzahn, C., Molina-Estolano, E., Khurana, A., Nelson, A. J., Brandt, S. A., & Weil, S., (2010). Ceph as a scalable alternative to the Hadoop distributed file system. *Login: The USENIX Magazine, 35*, 38–49.
14. Milani, B. A., & Navimipour, N. J., (2016). A comprehensive review of the data replication techniques in the cloud environments: Major trends and future directions. *Journal of Network and Computer Applications, 64*, 229–238.
15. Ni, J., Yu, Y., Mu, Y., & Xia, Q., (2013). On the security of an efficient dynamic auditing protocol in cloud storage. *IEEE Transactions on Parallel and Distributed Systems, 25*(10), 2760–2761.
16. Oster, G., Urso, P., Molli, P., & Imine, A., (2006). Data consistency for P2P collaborative editing. In: *Proceedings of the 2006 20th Anniversary Conference on Computer Supported Cooperative Work* (Vol. 1, pp. 259–268).
17. Pitoura, E., & Bhargava, B., (1999). Data consistency in intermittently connected

distributed systems. *IEEE Transactions on Knowledge and Data Engineering, 11*(6), 896–915.

18. Rohloff, K., & Schantz, R. E., (2010). High-performance, massively scalable distributed systems using the MapReduce software framework: The SHARD triple-store. In: *Programming Support Innovations for Emerging Distributed Applications* (Vol. 1, pp. 1–5).
19. Seitz, L., Pierson, J. M., & Brunie, L., (2003). Key management for encrypted data storage in distributed systems. In: *Second IEEE International Security in Storage Workshop* (Vol. 1, pp. 20). IEEE.
20. Serrano, D., Patiño-Martínez, M., Jiménez-Peris, R., & Kemme, B., (2007). Boosting database replication scalability through partial replication and 1-copy-snapshot-isolation. In: *13th Pacific Rim International Symposium on Dependable Computing (PRDC 2007)* (Vol.1, pp. 290–297). IEEE.
21. Sivaramakrishnan, K. C., Kaki, G., & Jagannathan, S., (2015). Declarative programming over eventually consistent data stores. *ACM SIGPLAN Notices, 50*(6), 413–424.
22. Son, J. H., & Kim, M. H., (2004). An adaptable vertical partitioning method in distributed systems. *Journal of Systems and Software, 73*(3), 551–561.
23. Utard, G., & Vernois, A., (2004). Data durability in peer-to-peer storage systems. In: *IEEE International Symposium on Cluster Computing and the Grid, 2004; CCGrid 2004* (Vol. 1, pp. 90–97). IEEE.
24. Wang, M., & Zhang, Q., (2020). Optimized data storage algorithm of IoT based on cloud computing in distributed system. *Computer Communications, 157*, 124–131.
25. Ye, Y., Xiao, L., Yen, I. L., & Bastani, F., (2010). Cloud storage design based on hybrid of replication and data partitioning. In: *2010 IEEE 16th International Conference on Parallel and Distributed Systems* (Vol. 1, pp. 415–422). IEEE.
26. Zhang, J., Wu, Y., & Chung, Y. C., (2016). PROAR: A weak consistency model for Ceph. In: *2016 IEEE 22nd International Conference on Parallel and Distributed Systems (ICPADS)* (Vol.2, pp. 347–353). IEEE.

CHAPTER 7

SCALABILITY AND PERFORMANCE IN DISTRIBUTED SYSTEM

UNIT INTRODUCTION

Distributed systems have become an integral part of modern computing infrastructure, powering everything from web applications and cloud computing platforms to social networks and mobile apps. As these systems grow in size and complexity, ensuring scalability and performance becomes increasingly important. In this chapter, we will explore the concepts of scalability and performance in distributed systems, and how they impact the design, implementation, and management of these systems. Scalability and performance are two critical aspects of distributed systems. Scalability refers to the ability of a system to handle increasing workload and user traffic, while performance refers to the speed and efficiency with which the system can process requests and deliver results. In a distributed system, achieving both scalability and performance is crucial for ensuring that the system can meet the needs of its users and handle increasing demand over time. Without proper scalability and performance, a distributed system can experience slowdowns, outages, and other performance-related issues that can negatively impact the user experience and ultimately harm the reputation and success of the system (Zhang et al., 2003).

Scalability is the ability of a distributed system to handle increasing workload or user traffic by adding more resources to the system. This can be achieved through horizontal scaling (adding more nodes to the system) or vertical scaling (adding more resources to each node). Performance, on the other hand, refers to the speed and efficiency with which the system can process requests and deliver results. Key performance metrics include throughput (the amount of work the system can handle per unit of time), latency (the time it takes for a request to be processed), response time (the time it takes for the system to respond to a request), and resource utilization (the efficient use of system resources) (Aguilera et al., 2007).

In this chapter, we will first explore the concept of scalability, including the different types of scalabilities (horizontal, vertical, and hybrid) and the approaches used to achieve scalability (sharding, replication, caching, and load balancing). We will also examine the challenges associated with achieving scalability, including consistency, fault tolerance, and coordination (Rohloff & Schantz, 2010).

Next, we will delve into the concept of performance, including the key metrics used to measure performance (throughput, latency, response time, and resource utilization) and the techniques used to optimize performance (caching, compression, pipelining, batching, and parallelism). We will also examine the challenges associated with optimizing performance, including contention, network congestion, resource contention, and bottlenecks (Smith & Williams, 2002). Finally, we will discuss the tradeoffs between scalability and performance, and how to achieve a balance between these two critical aspects of distributed systems. We will also examine real-world case studies of distributed systems and how they achieved scalability and performance, along with lessons learned and best practices. Overall, this chapter will provide a comprehensive overview of the concepts of scalability and performance in distributed systems, along with practical strategies for achieving these critical goals (Yan et al., 2015).

Learning Objectives

At the end of this chapter, the reader will be able to understand:

- The concept of scalability in distributed systems and identify the different approaches to achieve it;
- The key metrics used to measure the performance of distributed systems and the techniques to optimize their performance;
- The tradeoffs between scalability and performance in distributed systems and recognize the challenges associated with both;
- The case studies of popular distributed systems such as Google's Bigtable, Facebook's TAO, and Amazon's DynamoDB to understand their scalability and performance design.

Key Terms

- Amazon's DynamoDB
- Facebook's TAO
- Google's Bigtable

- Horizontal scalability
- Hybrid scalability
- Load balancing
- Netflix's chaos monkey
- Twitter's snowflake
- Vertical scalability

7.1. SCALABILITY

Scalability is the ability of a distributed system to handle an increasing amount of load or traffic while maintaining its performance and availability. In other words, scalability refers to the ability of a system to scale up or scale out to meet the growing demands of its users (Jogalekar & Woodside, 2000).

7.1.1. Horizontal Scalability

Horizontal scalability refers to the ability of a distributed system to handle more traffic or users by adding more nodes or servers to the system. This approach is also known as scaling out because it involves adding more computing resources to the system horizontally. Horizontal scalability is achieved by partitioning data or workload across multiple nodes or servers, thereby allowing the system to handle more requests in parallel. This approach is well-suited for applications with a high read-to-write ratio, such as content delivery networks (CDNs), search engines, and social media platforms (Chapuis et al., 2017).

7.1.2. Vertical Scalability

Vertical scalability refers to the ability of a distributed system to handle more traffic or users by adding more resources, such as memory or processing power, to the existing nodes or servers in the system.

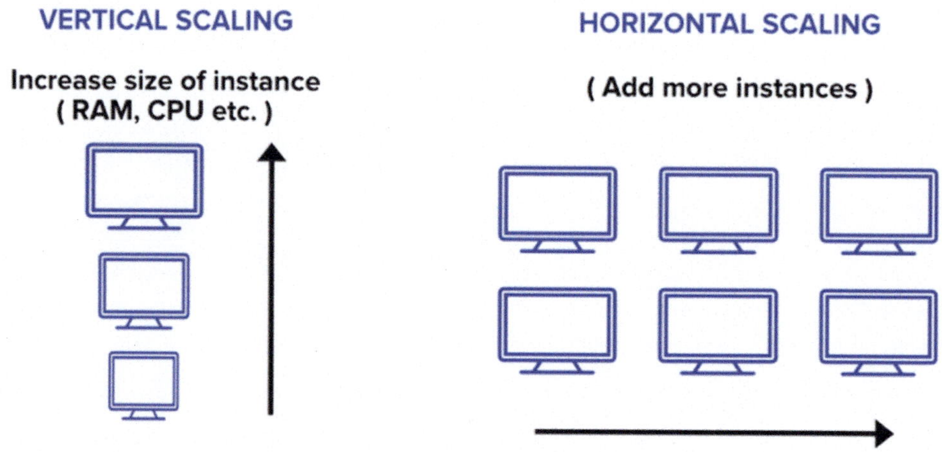

Figure 7.1. Illustration of difference between horizontal and vertical scalability.

Source: Anuupadhyay.

This approach is also known as scaling up because it involves adding more resources to the system vertically. Vertical scalability is achieved by upgrading the hardware of the existing nodes or servers in the system, thereby allowing them to handle more requests. This approach is well-suited for applications that require high throughput and low latency, such as financial trading systems and real-time analytics (Garcia et al., 2008) (Figure 7.1).

7.1.3. Hybrid Scalability

Hybrid scalability refers to a combination of horizontal and vertical scalability. In this approach, the system can scale up by adding more resources to existing nodes, or it can scale out by adding more nodes to the system. Hybrid scalability is achieved by partitioning data or workload across multiple nodes or servers and then vertically scaling each node to handle more requests. This approach is well-suited for applications that require both high throughput and low latency, such as online gaming platforms and e-commerce sites (Wu et al., 2015).

Did you Know?

Vertical scalability remains a viable option for organizations seeking to increase their computing power, but it is limited by the physical constraints of hardware and is generally less cost-effective than horizontal scaling.

7.1.4. Approaches to Achieve Scalability

- **Sharding:** It involves breaking down a large dataset into smaller pieces and distributing them across multiple nodes or servers. By doing so, the system can handle more data and traffic in a distributed manner, thereby achieving better scalability. Each node or server is responsible for a subset of the data, and requests are routed to the appropriate node based on the data's partition key (Karakus & Durresi, 2017) (Figure 7.2).
- **Replication:** It involves creating multiple copies of data and distributing them across multiple nodes or servers. By doing so, the system can handle more read requests, as multiple nodes can serve the same data. Each node or server is responsible for a replica of the data and read requests can be served from any replica (Chen et al., 2014).
- **Caching:** It involves storing frequently accessed data in memory or disk for faster access. By doing so, the system can reduce the number of requests to the backend storage system, thereby improving scalability. Cache is used to store data that is frequently accessed but does not change frequently (Yang et al., 2009).

- **Load Balancing:** It involves distributing incoming traffic across multiple nodes or servers to ensure that no single node is overloaded. By doing so, the system can handle more traffic and avoid bottlenecks. Load balancers can be implemented as hardware or software and can distribute traffic based on various algorithms, such as round-robin, least connections, and IP hash (Abuarqoub, 2020).

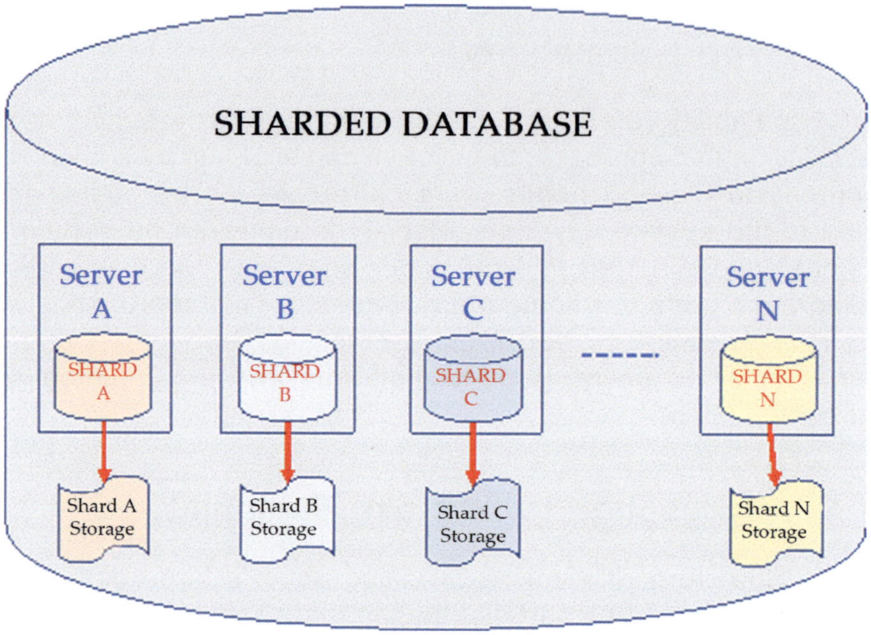

Figure 7.2. Schematic of a sharding template.

Source: Shelby Klingerman, Creative Commons License.

7.1.5. Challenges in Achieving Scalability

- **Consistency:** Maintaining consistency in a distributed system, especially in the face of failures or network partitions, is a challenging task. Achieving consistency in a distributed system is not trivial, as data can be stored in multiple nodes, and updates to the data must be propagated to all replicas. Consistency models such as strong consistency, eventual consistency, and causal consistency can be used to achieve consistency in a distributed system.
- **Fault Tolerance:** In a distributed system, nodes or servers can fail due to various reasons, such as hardware failure, network failure, or software bugs. Achieving fault tolerance in a distributed system is crucial to ensure high availability and

reliability. Fault tolerance can be achieved through techniques such as replication, redundancy, and error detection and recovery (Worley & Skjellum, 2018) (Figure 7.3).

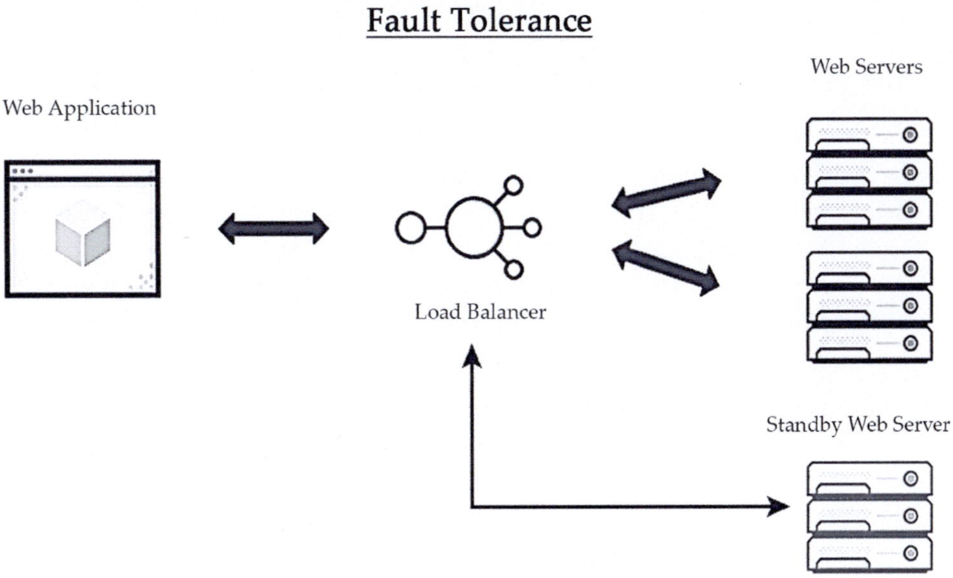

Figure 7.3. Image of fault tolerance.

Source: AVI Networks, Creative Commons License.

- **Coordination:** In a distributed system, multiple nodes or servers must coordinate with each other to ensure correct operation. Coordination can be a challenging task, as nodes can fail, messages can be lost or delayed, and the network can be partitioned. Techniques such as distributed consensus algorithms, such as Paxos and Raft, can be used to achieve coordination in a distributed system.

In summary, scalability is a critical factor in the design and operation of distributed systems. Different types of scalabilities, such as horizontal, vertical, and hybrid, can be used to achieve scalability. Various approaches, such as sharding, replication, caching, and load balancing, can be used to achieve scalability, while consistency, fault tolerance, and coordination remain significant challenges (Khan et al., 2021).

7.2. PERFORMANCE

Performance is a key metric that measures the efficiency and effectiveness of a system in completing a task within a certain timeframe while meeting the desired level of quality. In distributed systems, performance is a critical aspect that determines how well a system can handle the workload and deliver the expected response time (Tierney et al., 1998).

7.2.1. Key Metrics to Measure Performance

There are several key metrics used to measure performance in distributed systems:

- **Throughput:** It is the number of requests a system can handle per unit time. It is an important metric for high-traffic applications and indicates the capacity of a system to handle a large number of requests. Throughput is typically measured in requests per second or transactions per second.
- **Latency:** It is the time it takes for a request to be completed from the time it was sent. It is an important metric for applications that require real-time response, such as financial trading or gaming. Latency is typically measured in milliseconds or microseconds (Wybranietz & Haban, 1988).
- **Response Time:** It is the time it takes for a system to respond to a request, including network latency, processing time, and queuing time. It is an important metric for providing a good user experience. Response time is typically measured in milliseconds or seconds.
- **Resource Utilization:** It is the amount of resources a system uses to process requests, including CPU, memory, and network bandwidth. High resource utilization can lead to performance degradation or even system failure. Resource utilization is typically measured as a percentage of available resources (Haban & Wybranietz, 1990).

TIPS

Hybrid scalability allows a system to scale both horizontally (by adding more nodes) and vertically (by increasing the resources of individual nodes), providing a balance between performance and cost.

7.2.2. Techniques to Optimize Performance

To optimize performance in distributed systems, there are several techniques that can be used:

- **Caching:** It involves storing frequently accessed data in memory to reduce the time it takes to retrieve it from a database or disk. Caching can significantly reduce response time and improve throughput.
- **Compression:** It involves reducing the size of data transmitted over the network to reduce network bandwidth

usage and improve response time. Compression can be used to optimize network performance in systems that transmit large amounts of data.

- **Pipelining:** It involves breaking down a request into smaller, independent sub-requests that can be processed in parallel, reducing overall response time. Pipelining can be used to optimize performance in systems that process large amounts of data.
- **Batching:** It involves combining multiple requests into a single request to reduce network overhead and improve throughput. Batching can be used to optimize performance in systems that process a large number of small requests (Nudd et al., 2000).
- **Parallelism:** It involves dividing a task into smaller sub-tasks that can be executed in parallel on multiple CPUs or nodes to improve throughput. Parallelism can be used to optimize performance in systems that require high computational power (Weigle & Feng, 2002).

7.2.3. Challenges in Optimizing Performance

Optimizing performance in distributed systems can be challenging due to several factors, including:

- **Contention:** It occurs when multiple requests compete for the same resources, leading to delays and reduced performance. Contention can occur in systems that process a large number of requests or in systems that share resources.
- **Network Congestion:** It occurs when network bandwidth is limited or congested, leading to increased latency and reduced throughput. Network congestion can occur in systems that transmit large amounts of data or in systems that are distributed across multiple nodes.
- **Resource Contention:** It occurs when multiple processes or nodes compete for the same system resources, such as CPU or memory, leading to reduced performance (Liu et al., 2017). Resource contention can occur in systems that require high computational power or in systems that share resources.
- **Bottlenecks:** It occur when a single component or process limits the overall performance of the system, such as a slow disk or a slow database query. Bottlenecks can significantly reduce the performance of a system and may require redesigning the system architecture to remove the bottleneck.

In summary, optimizing performance in distributed systems is crucial for delivering a high-quality user experience and handling a large number of requests. To achieve this, it is important to measure key metrics such as throughput, latency, response time, and resource utilization, and use techniques such as caching, compression, pipelining, batching, and parallelism to optimize performance. However, challenges such as contention, network congestion, resource contention, and bottlenecks can hinder performance optimization and require careful consideration in the system design (Zhu et al., 2013).

7.3. SCALABILITY VS. PERFORMANCE TRADE-OFFS

Scalability and performance are two key aspects of distributed systems that are often in tension with each other. While scalability refers to the ability of a system to handle increasing amounts of data or users, performance relates to the speed and efficiency with which the system performs its functions. In order to achieve optimal results, it is necessary to strike a balance between these two factors, which requires an understanding of the tradeoffs involved (Holmquist et al., 2021).

Remember

The scalability and performance of distributed systems are like a balancing act between resources, demand, and efficiency.

One of the main tradeoffs between scalability and performance is that improving one often comes at the expense of the other. For example, adding more nodes to a system can increase its scalability by increasing its capacity to handle more users or data, but it may also decrease its performance due to increased network traffic and coordination overhead. Similarly, optimizing for performance by reducing latency and response time may limit the system's ability to scale by putting more pressure on the underlying infrastructure (Yilmaz & Matta, 2002).

To achieve a balance between scalability and performance, it is important to carefully analyze the requirements of the system and identify the key factors that contribute to its overall performance. This may involve testing the system under different scenarios and analyzing the results to determine the optimal configuration. For example, it may be necessary to choose between horizontal scaling (adding more nodes) or vertical scaling (upgrading existing nodes) depending on the specific needs of the system (Cincilla et al., 2016).

Common pitfalls to avoid when optimizing for scalability and performance include over-optimizing for one factor at the expense of the other, failing to properly test and monitor the system, and underestimating the impact of network latency and coordination overhead. It is also important to consider the long-term implications of any changes to the system, as scalability and performance requirements may change over time (Mamidala et al., 2007). In summary, achieving a balance between scalability and performance requires careful analysis, testing, and monitoring of the system, as well as an understanding of the tradeoffs involved. By avoiding common pitfalls and taking a holistic approach to optimization, it is possible to create a distributed system that is both scalable and high-performing (Suárez-Varela & Barlet-Ros, 2018).

7.4. CASE STUDIES

7.4.1. Google's Bigtable

- Description of the system and its requirements.
- Approach to achieve scalability: sharding and replication.
- Techniques used to optimize performance: compression, caching, and batching.
- Lessons learned and best practices: use of distributed lock services, importance of monitoring and metrics, and balancing consistency with performance (Chang et al., 2008) (Figure 7.4).

Figure 7.4. Picture of Google' Bigtable.

Source: Andreas Bender, Creative Commons License.

7.4.2. Facebook's TAO

- Description of the system and its requirements.
- Approach to achieve scalability: sharding and caching.

- Techniques used to optimize performance: use of in-memory caches and asynchronous replication.
- Lessons learned and best practices: importance of schema design and access patterns, use of multiple levels of caching, and tradeoffs between consistency and performance (Cheng et al., 2021).

7.4.3. Netflix's Chaos Monkey

- Description of the system and its requirements.
- Approach to achieve scalability: horizontal scaling and fault tolerance.
- Techniques used to optimize performance: use of auto-scaling and canary releases.
- Lessons learned and best practices: embracing failure as a feature, designing for failure, and using chaos engineering to improve system resilience (Tseitlin, 2013).

7.4.4. Amazon's DynamoDB

- Description of the system and its requirements.
- Approach to achieve scalability: partitioning and replication.
- Techniques used to optimize performance: use of local secondary indexes and adaptive capacity.
- Lessons learned and best practices: importance of partitioning design and consistent hashing, use of consistent and eventual consistency models, and tradeoffs between cost and performance (Elhemali et al., 2022).

ACTIVITY 7.1

What are some of the challenges and advantages of vertical scalability in modern cloud computing architectures, and how can businesses make informed decisions about when and how to scale up or down to meet changing demand?

7.4.5. Twitter's Snowflake

- Description of the system and its requirements.
- Approach to achieve scalability: distributed generation of unique IDs.
- Techniques used to optimize performance: use of stateless servers and fast network communication.
- Lessons learned and best practices: importance of simple and stateless design, focus on operational simplicity and ease of deployment, and use of high-precision timekeeping (Jianmin et al., 2020) (Figure 7.5).

Figure 7.5. Picture of twitter snowflake.

Source: Github, Creative Commons License.

7.5. SUMMARY

The chapter "Scalability and Performance in Distributed System" focuses on the key concepts related to scalability and performance in distributed systems. The chapter discusses the different approaches that can be used to achieve scalability, including horizontal and vertical scaling, sharding, and load balancing. It also explores the key metrics that are used to measure the performance of distributed systems, such as response time, throughput, and scalability. The chapter highlights the tradeoffs between scalability and performance and the challenges associated with achieving both. Finally, the chapter provides case studies of popular distributed systems such as Google's Bigtable, Facebook's TAO, and Amazon's DynamoDB to understand their scalability and performance design.

REVIEW QUESTIONS

1. What is scalability in distributed systems, and why is it important? What are the different approaches to achieving scalability?
2. What are the key metrics used to measure the performance of distributed systems, and how are they calculated? What techniques can be used to optimize the performance of distributed systems?
3. What are the tradeoffs between scalability and performance in distributed systems? How do these tradeoffs impact the design and implementation of distributed systems?
4. What are some of the challenges associated with achieving scalability and performance in distributed systems? How can these challenges be addressed?
5. Describe the scalability and performance design of popular distributed systems such as Google's Bigtable, Facebook's TAO, and Amazon's DynamoDB. What approaches do they use to achieve scalability and optimize performance?

MULTIPLE CHOICE QUESTIONS

1. Which of the following is true about scalability in distributed systems?

a. It refers to the ability of a system to handle increasing workload by adding resources

b. It refers to the ability of a system to handle decreasing workload by removing resources

c. It refers to the ability of a system to handle a fixed workload without any changes

d. None of the above

2. Which of the following is a key metric used to measure the performance of distributed systems?

a. CPU usage

b. Memory usage

c. Network bandwidth

d. All of the above

3. **Which of the following techniques can be used to optimize the performance of distributed systems?**

a. Caching

b. Load balancing

c. Parallel processing

d. All of the above

4. **Which of the following is a tradeoff between scalability and performance in distributed systems?**

a. Increased scalability can result in decreased performance

b. Increased performance can result in decreased scalability

c. Both a and b

d. None of the above

5. **Which of the following is an example of a popular distributed system that has been designed for scalability and performance?**

a. Google's Bigtable

b. Facebook's TAO

c. Amazon's DynamoDB

d. All of the above

Answers to Multiple Choice Questions

1. (a); 2. (d); 3. (d); 4. (c); 5. (d)

REFERENCES

1. Abuarqoub, A., (2020). A review of the control plane scalability approaches in software defined networking. *Future Internet, 12*(3), 49.
2. Aguilera, M. K., Merchant, A., Shah, M., Veitch, A., & Karamanolis, C., (2007). Sinfonia: A new paradigm for building scalable distributed systems. *ACM SIGOPS Operating Systems Review, 41*(6), 159–174.
3. Chang, F., Dean, J., Ghemawat, S., Hsieh, W. C., Wallach, D. A., Burrows, M., & Gruber, R. E., (2008). Bigtable: A distributed storage system for structured data. *ACM Transactions on Computer Systems (TOCS), 26*(2), 1–26.
4. Chapuis, B., Garbinato, B., & Mourot, L., (2017). A horizontally scalable and reliable

architecture for location-based publish-subscribe. In: *2017 IEEE 36th Symposium on Reliable Distributed Systems (SRDS)* (Vol. 1, pp. 74–83). IEEE.

5. Chen, K., Liu, P., & Zhang, Y., (2014). Achieving accuracy and scalability simultaneously in detecting application clones on android markets. In: *Proceedings of the 36th International Conference on Software Engineering* (Vol. 1, pp. 175–186).
6. Cheng, A., Shi, X., Pan, L., Simpson, A., Wheaton, N., Lawande, S., & Stoica, I., (2021). RAMP-TAO: Layering atomic transactions on Facebook's online TAO data store. *Proceedings of the VLDB Endowment, 14*(12), 3014–3027.
7. Cincilla, P., Hicham, O., & Charles, B., (2016). Vehicular PKI scalability-consistency trade-offs in large scale distributed scenarios. In: *2016 IEEE Vehicular Networking Conference (VNC)* (Vol. 1, pp. 1–8). IEEE.
8. Elhemali, M., Gallagher, N., Tang, B., Gordon, N., Huang, H., Chen, H., & Vig, A., (2022). Amazon {DynamoDB}: A scalable, predictably performant, and fully managed {NoSQL} database service. In: *2022 USENIX Annual Technical Conference (USENIX ATC 22)* (Vol. 1, pp. 1037–1048).
9. Garcia, D. F., Rodrigo, G., Entrialgo, J., Garcia, J., & Garcia, M., (2008). Experimental evaluation of horizontal and vertical scalability of cluster-based application servers for transactional workloads. In: *8th International Conference on Applied Informatics and Communications (AIC'08)* (Vol. 1, pp. 29–34).
10. Haban, D., & Wybranietz, D., (1990). A hybrid monitor for behavior and performance analysis of distributed systems. *IEEE Transactions on Software Engineering, 16*(2), 197–211.
11. Holmquist, J. R., Schile-Beers, L., Buffington, K., Lu, M., Mozdzer, T. J., Riera, J., & Megonigal, J. P., (2021). Scalability and performance tradeoffs in quantifying relationships between elevation and tidal wetland plant communities. *Marine Ecology Progress Series, 666*, 57–72.
12. Jianmin, W., Wenbin, Z., Tongrang, F., Shilong, Y., & Hongwei, L., (2020). An improved join□free snowflake schema for ETL and OLAP of data warehouse. *Concurrency and Computation: Practice and Experience, 32*(23), e5519.
13. Jogalekar, P., & Woodside, M., (2000). Evaluating the scalability of distributed systems. *IEEE Transactions on Parallel and Distributed Systems, 11*(6), 589–603.
14. Karakus, M., & Durresi, A., (2017). A survey: Control plane scalability issues and approaches in software-defined networking (SDN). *Computer Networks, 112*, 279–293.
15. Khan, D., Jung, L. T., & Hashmani, M. A., (2021). Systematic literature review of challenges in blockchain scalability. *Applied Sciences, 11*(20), 9372.
16. Liu, Y., Fieldsend, J. E., & Min, G., (2017). A framework of fog computing: Architecture, challenges, and optimization. *IEEE Access, 5*, 25445–25454.
17. Mamidala, A. R., Narravula, S., Vishnu, A., Santhanaraman, G., & Panda, D. K., (2007). On using connection-oriented vs. connection-less transport for performance and scalability of collective and one-sided operations: Trade-offs and impact. In:

Proceedings of the 12th ACM SIGPLAN symposium on Principles and Practice of Parallel Programming (Vol. 1, pp. 46–54).

18. Nudd, G. R., Kerbyson, D. J., Papaefstathiou, E., Perry, S. C., Harper, J. S., & Wilcox, D. V., (2000). PACE—A toolset for the performance prediction of parallel and distributed systems. *The International Journal of High Performance Computing Applications, 14*(3), 228–251.
19. Rohloff, K., & Schantz, R. E., (2010). High-performance, massively scalable distributed systems using the MapReduce software framework: The SHARD triple-store. In: *Programming Support Innovations for Emerging Distributed Applications* (Vol. 1, pp. 1–5).
20. Smith, C. U., & Williams, L. G., (2002). Performance and scalability of distributed software architectures: An SPE approach. *Parallel and Distributed Computing Practices, 3*(4), 74106–0700.
21. Suárez-Varela, J., & Barlet-Ros, P., (2018). Flow monitoring in software-defined networks: Finding the accuracy/performance tradeoffs. *Computer Networks, 135*, 289–301.
22. Tierney, B., Johnston, W., Crowley, B., Hoo, G., Brooks, C., & Gunter, D., (1998). The NetLogger methodology for high performance distributed systems performance analysis. In: *Proceedings; The Seventh International Symposium on High Performance Distributed Computing (Cat. No. 98TB100244)* (Vol. 1, pp. 260–267). IEEE.
23. Tseitlin, A., (2013). The antifragile organization. *Communications of the ACM, 56*(8), 40–44.
24. Weigle, E., & Feng, W. C., (2002). A comparison of TCP automatic tuning techniques for distributed computing. In: *Proceedings 11th IEEE International Symposium on High Performance Distributed Computing* (Vol.1, pp. 265–272). IEEE.
25. Worley, C., & Skjellum, A., (2018). Blockchain tradeoffs and challenges for current and emerging applications: Generalization, fragmentation, sidechains, and scalability. In: *2018 IEEE International Conference on Internet of Things (iThings) and IEEE Green Computing and Communications (GreenCom) and IEEE Cyber, Physical and Social Computing (CPSCom) and IEEE Smart Data (SmartData)* (Vol.1, pp. 1582–1587). IEEE.
26. Wu, W., Bouteiller, A., Bosilca, G., Faverge, M., & Dongarra, J., (2015). Hierarchical Dag scheduling for hybrid distributed systems. In: *2015 IEEE International Parallel and Distributed Processing Symposium* (Vol.2, pp. 156–165). IEEE.
27. Wybranietz, D., & Haban, D., (1988). Monitoring and performance measuring distributed systems during operation. *ACM SIGMETRICS Performance Evaluation Review, 16*(1), 197–206.
28. Yan, F., Ruwase, O., He, Y., & Chilimbi, T., (2015). Performance modeling and scalability optimization of distributed deep learning systems. In: *Proceedings of the 21th ACM SIGKDD International Conference on Knowledge Discovery and Data Mining* (Vol. 1, pp. 1355–1364).

29. Yang, J., Qiu, J., & Li, Y., (2009). A profile-based approach to just-in-time scalability for cloud applications. In: *2009 IEEE International Conference on Cloud Computing* (Vol.1, pp. 9–16). IEEE.
30. Yilmaz, S., & Matta, I., (2002). Scalability-performance tradeoffs in MPLS and IP routing. In: *Scalability and Traffic Control in IP Networks II*. SPIE. (Vol. 4868, pp. 69–77).
31. Zhang, X., Freschl, J. L., & Schopf, J. M., (2003). A performance study of monitoring and information services for distributed systems. In: *High Performance Distributed Computing, 2003: Proceedings; 12th IEEE International Symposium* (Vol. 1, pp. 270–281). IEEE.
32. Zhu, Q., Zeng, H., Zheng, W., Natale, M. D., & Sangiovanni-Vincentelli, A., (2013). Optimization of task allocation and priority assignment in hard real-time distributed systems. *ACM Transactions on Embedded Computing Systems (TECS), 11*(4), 1–30.

CHAPTER 8

DISTRIBUTED SYSTEM SECURITY

UNIT INTRODUCTION

Many security risks in one system of computers can be mitigated by installing specialized hardware that prevents processes from interfering with one another (Standard, 1977). These hardware protection mechanisms are unable to be used in communications systems, and the foundation of any security system is typically cryptographic techniques (Summers, 1984).

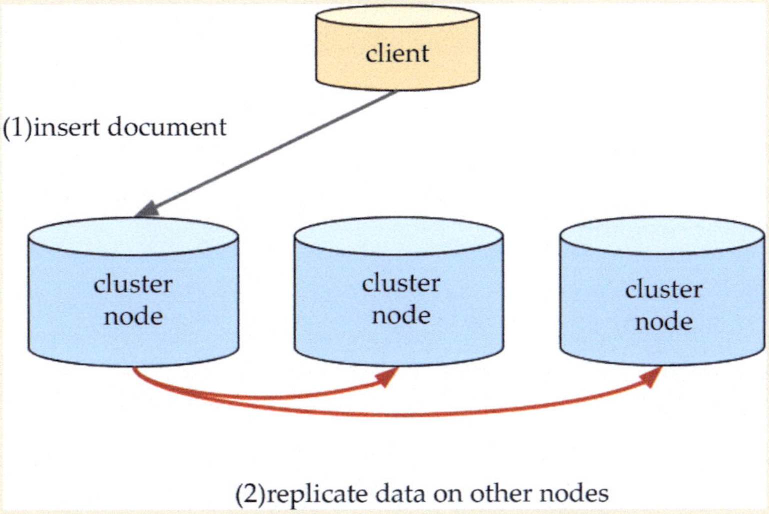

Figure 8.1. Illustration of security system of distributed system.

Source: Search Guard, Creative Commons License.

These notes will examine distributed system threats before moving on to fundamental encryption mechanisms. The system's security depends on how these are used, and several techniques that have been developed will be covered. Keys are essential to cryptographic systems, and participants must be given access to them (Biham, 2005). This will also be covered. Key storage is possibly one of the trickiest issues in communications security (Wilbur, 2000). Finally, many systems contain numerous autonomous administrations. Dealing with them while remaining skeptical of the reliability of every aspect of the system is a rising concern and has been the focus of papers such as (Botting, 1986) (Figure 8.1).

Learning Objectives

At the end of this chapter, the reader will be able to understand:

- The aspects of security in distributed systems;
- The access control and its importance in distributed systems security;
- The various security threats to distributed systems and ways to mitigate them;
- The authentication and its role in ensuring secure access to distributed systems;
- The concept of non-repudiation and its importance in distributed systems security;
- The basics of cryptography and its role in ensuring secure communication in distributed systems;
- The different ciphers and their use in cryptography;
- The block and stream cipher security and their differences;
- The key distribution techniques and their importance in cryptography.

Key Terms

- Access control
- Block cipher
- Breaking ciphers
- Ciphers
- Cryptographic sealing
- Cryptography
- Encryption algorithms
- Non-repudiation
- Security threats
- Stream cipher

8.1. ASPECTS OF SECURITY

Following are four extensive categories of security systems (Jones, 2005):

- Access control;
- Security threats;
- Authentication; and
- Notarization (Landwehr, 1981).

8.1.1. Access Control

The server may want to restrict access to resources in a straightforward client-server interaction. Standard methods for doing this include:

- Matrix for access control;
- Capabilities;
- Labels.

The access control medium, which divides the world into the "owner" of the source, "friends," and "the rest of the world," is well-known from many systems. A small number of operations, such as Read, Write, Delete, shift Protection, etc., may be subject to the controls. Classically, each resource will keep its permissions matrix secure, and before access is granted, the client should first establish its individuality and be classified. Although there may be more than one principal, the person who uses the client process, or the client's principal, is typically the one who is authenticated. Extensions to such systems are also available, such as UNIX, which uses the "set UID" bit to let a program's developer or installer exercise their (superior) authority even when someone with fewer privileges runs the client application (Li & Tripunitara, 2006).

Unforgeable tokens called capabilities contain information about the operations that can be carried out on a resource. Such tokens aren't ever passed to processes in a single-machine environment; the operating system securely stores them (Denning & Sacco, 1981). Only references to such tokens are passed out. They must be transmitted over the network in a distributed system, and changes to them must be impossible without being noticed. Additionally, it is preferable for a procedure to be able to transfer a limited set of rights to a different process via a potential, preferred without first seeking permission from the capability's creator. In other words, it should be possible for regular processes to lower but not increase the access rights provided by capabilities. There are methods for doing this.

In supposedly mandatory security systems, labels are used. The aforementioned methods are employed in optional security systems. Military and high safety measures use mandatory control. Only individuals or processes with the appropriate rank could access information resulting from other high-security information, which would be classified as high security. Rules would govern the categorization of new documents obtained from currently classified sources. Declassification must occur on a regular basis in such systems because there is a propensity for all fresh knowledge (Tourani et al., 2017).

8.1.2. Security Threats

Think about a client and server that are linked by a network. Such links present a number of pressures, including (Boehm, 1984):

- Passive tap;
- Active tap;
- Denial of service;
- Faking;
- Replay;
- Traffic analysis;
- Accidental access.

Did you Know?

Security threats are a persistent and evolving challenge in modern computing, requiring constant vigilance, adaptation, and innovation to mitigate the risk of cyberattacks and protect sensitive data.

The *passive tap* lets the intrusive party watch traffic moving along the linkage. While it cannot alter the messages that have been noted, it may be capable to use the data to have unauthorized right to use. For instance, if a password has been seen, it could be utilized to log in as some other person. Passive tapping is incredibly simple on a few networks, such as shared Ethernet (Jouini et al., 2014).

The interloper can place an operation between the initial client and server in a situation known as an *active tap*. This could be done solely to obtain information, such as passwords ("Trojan Horse"), or it could be done to alter messages, typically to the intrusive party's advantage (Chaum, 1985).

Denial of service is a risk that is frequently overlooked. Even though ongoing efforts to approach a server, even ones that may be poorly formed messages, can clog the protocol manager and hinder authorized approach in some circumstances, it can be a serious threat to do so. A Bruce Springsteen concert is said to have caused a telephone exchange in Washington to become congested for several hours in the past. We received assurances that crucial US Government lines were not in danger (Shaikh & Haider, 2011) (Figure 8.2).

Figure 8.2. Illustration of network security threat.

Source: The AME Group, Creative Commons License.

Fake messages could be sent to a server by a process. These could be modified versions of earlier, valid messages with key fields altered. Replay happens when the fields are left alone, and if the fraud can, for example, receive numerous deposits into its bank account, it may be advantageous. Secure systems typically use audit trails to keep track of all transfers, but by the time the culprit is identified, it might be too late to undo the damage. Audit trails in computer systems must keep track of information about people, processes, and machines, though it can be very challenging to do so on LANs (Hu et al., 2021). Traffic analysis is typically used to predict where and when an engagement of military will occur. It depends on the presumption that message movement is going to rise links to the front-line forces will experience heavy traffic. There are some comparable situations in business. The typical defense is to maintain all links packed with at accidental messages and only send them when necessary. Several errors, such as crossed lines, software flaws, etc., can result in accidental access. The failure of software to completely disconnect a call, allowing a subsequent caller to connect without any formalities to the previous caller's session, is the most frequent issue with dial-up computer connections. Packet protocols can experience similar issues (Pearce et al., 2013).

8.1.3. Authentication

The requirement for client and server authentication has already been determined. Principal authentication typically involves client authentication as well (Bellovin & Merritt, 1990). In addition to the danger of active tapping (Trojan Horse), server authentication is crucial because many RPC binders only provide clue as to the location of a service. When it collides, another entirely different server might take its place, but the client must be made aware of this discrepancy so that the binder can be consulted again. Such uses are possible for cryptography (Birrell et al., 1986).

Message integrity, also known as message authentication, is a related concept. Confirming that a message hasn't been tampered with during transit is crucial. Sometimes the confidentiality of the message while it is in transit is unnecessary, and other times it is. For these reasons, a strong sumcheck utilizing cryptographic methods is appended to messages. This is also known as a message authentication code (MAC) or a digital signature (Barkadehi et al., 2018).

8.1.4. Non-Repudiation

Occasionally, an even stricter requirement forbids the sender from denying sending a message (Smid & Branstad, 1988). In these situations, messages are recorded by a notary so neither party may opt out of a transaction and disagreements can be settled by showing pertinent signatures (Birrell, 1985) (Figure 8.3).

Figure 8.3. Image of non-repudiation.

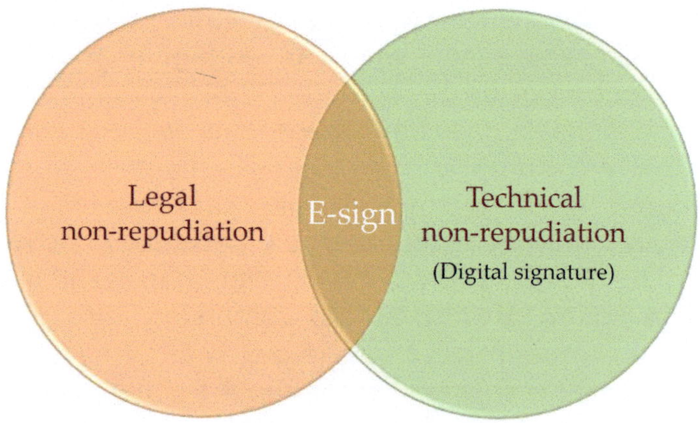

Source: Wentz Wu, Creative Commons License.

8.2. CRYPTOGRAPHY

8.2.1. Ciphers

The goal of encryption or encipherment is to change a message or text into a presumably chance pattern, or ciphertext, making it extremely challenging to decrypt the ciphertext without the knowledge of the proper algorithm (Diffie & Hellman, 2022). For a typical two-way cipher, there should be complementary encryption and decryption algorithms; however, for a one-way cipher, the encryption algorithm will not have a known opposite, making it impossible to change ciphertext to plaintext algorithmically (Shujun et al., 2001).

The Caesar cipher, which shifts every letter of the message by a certain number of positions, say three, is an illustration of a straightforward two-way cipher. Such shifts are regarded as circular. In order to decrypt, a three-position move is applied in the other direction, for example.

VENI VIDI VICI

might become:

YHQL YLGL YLFL

It is typically essential to, on occasion, alter the encryption algorithm to maintain secrecy. Many algorithms must be decided upon beforehand if this was done daily or hourly. Because of this, keys are typically used to change algorithms (Ehrsam et al., 1978). For instance, in the example above, the key was 3 (which was one of a total of 26 keys). A good system will have many keys, making it difficult to crack the code by thoroughly examining the key space, which entails decrypting the ciphertext with each key conceivable until recognizable cleartext is produced (Kerckhof et al., 2012).

TIPS

Ciphers can help protect sensitive data from unauthorized access but must be implemented correctly and kept up to date to remain effective.

Matching or related keys are employed for encryption and decryption in the popular systems, also called secret key cryptography (SKC). Therefore, security would be compromised if the algorithm and key were known (Matyas & Meyer, 1978). Due to this, it is crucial that the keys remain a secret, even though the algorithm may be made public. If the encoding process took just 5 microseconds and the typical key is 56 bits long, a comprehensive search will still take 11,000 years even if the algorithm is made public!

Public key cryptography (PKC) is a substitute. The goal is to create a two-key system, where one key is utilized for encryption and the other for decryption. It is obvious that the two keys are connected, but the system is built in a way that understanding 1 key provides little insight into the other. It will take hundreds or thousands of years to compute the other key using the best available algorithms. If so, only one key—the public key—can be shared and only one key—the personal or secret key—must be kept by the owner. A message is encrypted when sent utilizing the recipient's public key, and only the recipient can decrypt it. This mechanism has an intriguing twist in that it can be used to confirm the sender's legitimacy encrypted with the confidential key of the sender. The originator has been verified if it decrypts correctly and the keys that are published are reliable. Secrecy and authentication can be provided by combining the two methods (Jakimoski & Kocarev, 2001) (Figure 8.4).

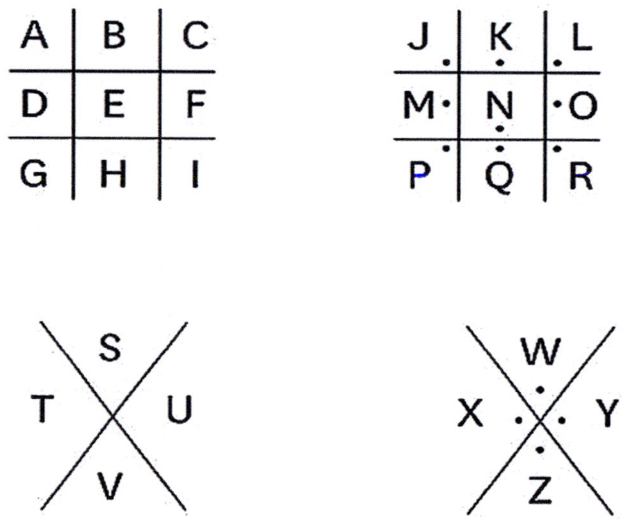

Figure 8.4. Image of ciphers.

Source: Bryn Mawr, Creative Commons License.

8.2.2. Block and Stream Cipher Security

It is possible to use cipher block chaining (CBC) to get around this. In addition to the encryption tool, a 64-bit buffer is added to the system. Prior to the message is sent, this is stuffed with an initialization vector (IV) that has been previously agreed upon (Popek & Kline, 1979). The buffer's contents are XORed with the message's first 64 bits, and the outcome is encrypted before it is transmitted to the receiver and saved in the buffer. Repeating the procedure results in additional 64-bit blocks. As a result, each block depends on the one before it (or the IV), making systematic analysis more challenging. The recipient should know both the key and the IV and have a complementary decryption scheme (De Canniere, 2006) (Figure 8.5).

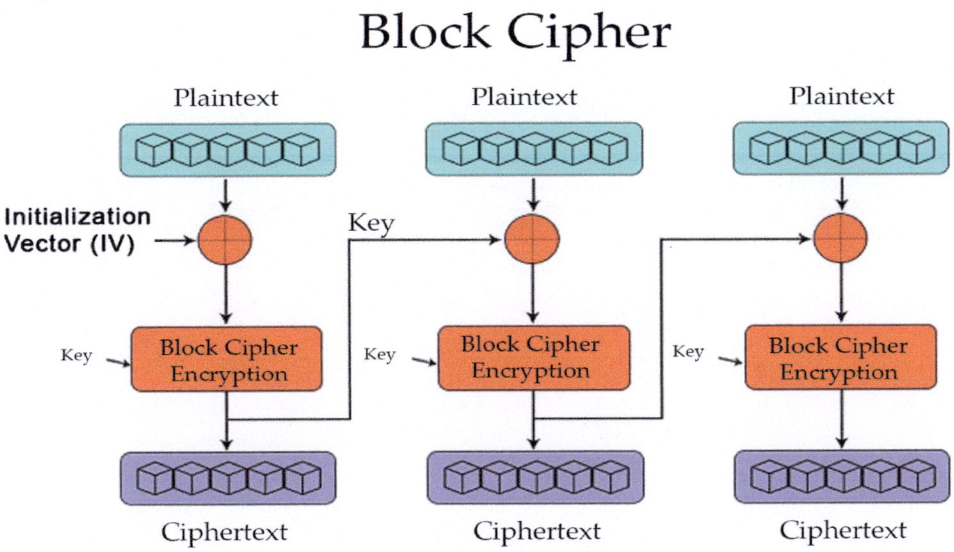

Figure 8.5. Depiction of block cipher template.

Source: Java T Point, Creative Commons License.

The result of the select buffer is directly provided back to the IV buffer in the second stream cipher, known as output feedback (OFB). Additionally, the chosen value is XORed with the characters of the message, but the result is only given to the recipient. As a result, a random sequence generator is formed by the IV buffer, encryption, and chosen buffer independent of the message's contents. A system like this could be helpful for broadcasting video and other types of content because it is a lot faster and broadcast errors do not spread.

The methods mentioned above are included in the DES norms but also work with other block ciphers (Wang et al., 2011).

8.2.3. Encryption Algorithms

8.2.3.1. DES Algorithm

The data encryption standard (DES), a block cipher which uses a 56-bit key to encrypt 64-bit data blocks, is not an ISO standard. In the diagrams that are attached, the algorithm is outlined (Figure 8.6).

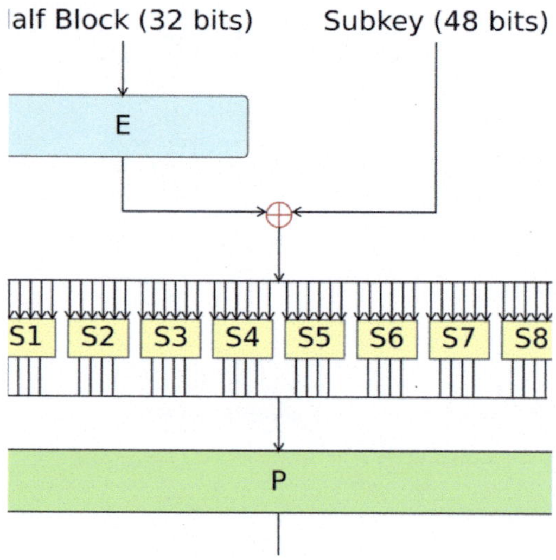

Figure 8.6. Illustration of data encryption standard (DES).

Source: Hellisp, Creative Commons License.

8.2.3.2. RSA Algorithm

The Rivest, Shamir, and Adleman (RSA) algorithm (Rivest et al., 1978) is a member of the exponentiation cipher family. They depend on the relatively simple exponential computation and the challenging logarithmic computation. Additionally, they employ modular arithmetic, in which the modulus is typically an extremely great number. Thus, using 'e,' a message M can be encrypted to ciphertext C and then decrypted back to M (Zhou & Tang, 2011).

$$C = (M^e) \bmod N \qquad (1)$$

and

$$M = (C^d) \bmod N \qquad (2)$$

where; 'N' is a large integer; 'e' and 'd' stand for the encryption and decryption keys, correspondingly. 'N' typically has a length of 500 to 1,000 bits (Zimmermann, 1986).

We need to first understand a little bit of mathematics in order to fully understand the RSA approach. According to Fermat's Theorem, if p is prime and gcd(a,p)=l (where "gcd" stands for greatest common divisor), then:

$$a^{p-1} \bmod p = 1$$

The aforementioned relationship holds true if a and p do not share any factors, i.e., and is not a multiple of p.

According to Euler's Generalization, whenever a and n are such that gcd(a,n)=l, then:

$a^{\varphi(n)} \bmod n = 1$ (3)

where (n) is the Euler Totient Function, or the number of positive integers less than 'n' that are relatively prime to 'n.' For n = 10, where (n) = 4, the relative primes are (1, 3, 7, 9). (p) = p–1 if p is prime.

Now, to use encryption, we use Eqns. (1), (2), and (3), which gives us the following:

$M^{\varphi(n)} \bmod n = 1$

from this it can be displayed that:

$e * d \bmod \varphi (n) = 1.$ (4)

We can now use the Pohlig-Hellman Scheme to create a straightforward exponentiation cipher. Since the modulus in this case is a prime number p, (p) = p–1. With p = 11 and d = 7 as the decryption key, we obtain (Goshwe, 2013):

$7 * e \bmod 10 = 1$

Evidently, e = 3 fulfills this. If wecurrently encipher a message, say M = 5, we acquire:

$C = 5^2 \bmod 11 = 4$

and decrypting it provides:

$M = 4^2 \bmod 11 = 5$

But for this scheme to work, the sender and the recipient must be aware of the modulus p; one requires e, the other requires d. Knowing p also makes it known that (p) (p–1), and given one key, Eqn. (4) makes it simple to find the other. It is obvious that this is inappropriate for a publicly accessible key system. Similar methods, such as RSA, but RSA picks the modulus n as the product of two prime numbers, p and q. Thus:

$n = p * q$

and

$\varphi (n) = (p–1) * (q–1)$

If we proceed as p=5 and q=7, we obtain n=35 and φ (n) = 4*6 = 24. Picking a key d=11, e can be calculated by Eqn. (4), i.e.:

$e = inv (11, 24) = 11.$

For a message M = 2:

C = 2 mod 35 = 2048 mod 35 = 18

and

M = 18 mod 35 = 2

Naturally, 'e' and 'd' rarely end up being the same. Compared to the Pohlig-Hellman scheme, this one has the following level of security. Both parties must be aware of n (but not necessarily its factors), one must be aware of e, and the other must be aware of d. However, it is very challenging to calculate (n) and subsequently separate the additional key from the one in your ownership unless the factors of n are known. The period required to calculate separate logarithms, that the quickest known algorithm requires, is inversely proportional to the difficulty of factoring integers.

T = O (exp (sqrt (ln (n). ln (ln (p))))

Factorization might take two to three days for a 200-bit value of p at a rate of one per microsecond, but it would take many billions of years for a 200-decimal digit key (664 bits). However, constructing n from its component primes is simple because it is quick and simple to demonstrate that a number is a prime (Rahman et al., 2012).

8.2.4. Breaking Ciphers

The one-time-pad is the only type of encryption that cannot be cracked. In order to encrypt the data units being sent, both parties to the communication have the same extensive list of chance values. The code cannot be cracked if the values are completely arbitrary, not the result of an algorithm.

Other codes are built using algorithms, making them theoretically breakable. They are typically made to be very difficult to decipher and to take up a lot of time and space. The "brute force" method entails a thorough search. The ciphertext is subjected to a series of key trials until both the known simple text and a plaintext that can be recognized appears. A 56-bit key would require hundreds of years to decrypt using this method, even with quick encryption. According to a US study from the early 1980s, it can be possible by 1990 to have a mechanism that can identify a key in a day, but it will be extremely expensive, use a tremendous amount of power, and there is only a 10–20% chance that it will ever be built.

Finding the key may be made possible if the cryptanalyst can introduce some simple text into the system in order to monitor the ciphertext. These are referred to as chosen-plaintext attacks.

Some criticisms may be leveled based on the modes of communication. For instance, it wouldn't take much to decode the encodings of just two messages, such as the rise or fall of financial shares. It is obvious that the key must be altered for each message or that another method of whitening is required (Kumar et al., 2006).

8.3. TECHNIQUES

8.3.1. Passwords

Personal identification numbers (PINS), passwords, and passphrases are the main ways to authenticate users of computing equipment. Passwords serve as an example of the idea that sound operational procedures are just as important for system security as sound algorithms. No matter how a computer system stores passwords, selecting: (a) a brief password; (b) one that can be easily guessed (such as the spouse's name); and (c) one with a very limited character set, such as a phone number (Narayanan & Shmatikov, 2005).

The NIST guidelines (FIPS, 1985) outline 10 characteristics that must be carefully taken into account when scheming a password system, including:

- Length;
- Character set;
- Lifetime;
- The source, i.e., user or administrator generated;
- Ownership, preferably individual;
- Distribution;
- Storage;
- Entry (e.g., keyboard; display; potential for oversight), etc. (Denning, 1992).

Problems with transmission and storage can arise. Nowadays, many systems (like UNIX) use a one-way encryption to store passwords. The checking program encrypts the cleartext password before comparing it to the stored value. The advantage of this strategy is that since decryption is "impossible," no additional security measures are required for the password file. However, thorough search methods may be employed, which is why it's important to manage passwords carefully. In situations where passwords must be sent over insecure channels, neither the plain text nor the one-way enciphered forms are safe; in the former, the password could be seen by an observer, while in the latter, the enciphered password is publicly accessible in a file, rendering a system that uses it by means of a link completely insecure. Passwords must be transmitted while being further encrypted during the transmission process (Boklan, 2009).

8.3.2. Capabilities

In a system that is object-based, access could be restricted using a bit map of the permitted operations, an arbitrary constituent blocked by the bits in the capacity, or some other means of object identification. If this is to be safe, the algorithm that produces the element of chance should be kept a secret. A public algorithm can be used the random component—that acts as a way of noticing incorrect changes—is produced using the other constituents and a key kept on the server. The server makes keys and validates their usability before using them, so the distribution of keys is not complicated. Because a client must send a network request to the server asking it to create a new capability each time it desires to move a limited capability to a different process in a distributed system, this solution is time-consuming.

In order to circumvent this, Mullender & Tanenbaum (1987) presented an intriguing plan that only used one-way cryptography. In a simple case where all rights have been provided, the system is alike to that previously described because the server key is then utilized to encrypt the constant fields of the ability. It is entered into the verification (random) field and saved on the server for later use (Laprie, 1995). Every bit in the right field, Ri, has a one-way algorithm, Ai, which corresponds to it. Rj decreases the rights after the correct permission bit is cleaned and the algorithm is used to the check field. Application of the algorithms must be commutative, i.e.:

$$A_i (A_j(X)) = A_j(A_i (X))$$

in order to produce an identical appreciation in the check field, rights can be reduced in any order.

With this system, it is possible for clients to lower their rights before transferring their abilities to others without contacting the issuing server and for all machines to be equipped with a set of AI (Srivastava & Bhatia, 2018).

8.3.3. Cryptographic Sealing

The capability system described beyond is appropriate when an object-oriented strategy is being utilized, i.e., when attempting to restrict access to legal functions to avoid access to objects (Gifford, 1982). Proposed an alternative strategy to deal with controlling right to use to data items. Instead of applying access control with physical barriers near to the item's storage location, it is cryptographically concluded and complete publicly accessible. However, only authorized users are given access to keys. Let's consider how this might be done. We'll write this down as (Sandhu, 1987):

$$\{x\}k$$

To imply that the key k has been used to encrypt the plaintext x, which serves as our fundamental "sealing" operation. The decryption algorithm is used in conjunction with key k to unlock x. The data is therefore sealed into Sx in the most basic scenario, i.e.,

Sx = {x}k

and only possessors of key k can contact it. An indirect key I can be made as described follows:

$I = \{k_1\}\ k_2$

$Sx = \{x\}k_1$

So, to open Sx, you must first open I in order to get k1. This can only be done by people who have k2. With indirect keys, it's possible to seal with more power. For example, if you want to seal 'x' so that only k1 or k2 can open it, you can use two indirect keys:

$I1 = \{k\}\ k_1$

$I2 = \{k\}\ k_2$

Sx= {x}k

A logical AND practical can be attained by double stopping of data (or an indirect key), e.g.:

$I = \{\{k\}\ k_1\}\ k_2$

Sx = {x}k

Remember

Cryptographic sealing is like locking a secret message in a safe, ensuring that only the intended recipient can access it.

The dual encryption would ideally be commutative to allow for the application of sealing or unsealing in any order. It is obvious that using this technique, mechanisms for access control can be created that are perfect for read access. However, two issues must be resolved:

- Key distribution; and
- Update access.

Key distribution is problematic since giving out a new key to authorized users may be essential after a key has been compromised (Voydock & Kent, 1983). This system's use of free read access does not work well with updates. Intruders may substitute data items with junk and at the very slightest, prevent others from using the legitimate service if all users have the ability to overwrite files freely. It would be feasible to grant some users read and write access using an asymmetric cipher, like a public key system, and to grant read-only access to others using only one of the keys. However, a further safeguard is required to stop unauthorized data overwriting by key holders (Moran & Naor, 2005).

8.3.4. Authentication

8.3.4.1. SKC Approach

Let's say that a client, A, wants to show a server, B, that it is real and also wants to be sure that B is not a Trojan Horse. Needham and Schroeder (Needham & Schroeder, 1978). Came up with the standard plan for this, which uses an authorized authentication server, AS. Before data can be sent from A to B, there needs to be a conversation of the following form. Let's start with SKC.

1. A → AS: A, B, Ia Message (1)
2. AS → B: {Ia, B, Kc, {Kc, A} Kb} Ka Message (2)
3. A → B: (Kc, A) Kb Message (3)
4. B → A: (Ib) Kc Message (4)
5. A → B: {f(Ib)} Kc

The client sends Message 1 in plain text to the AS. The Ia is on hand to prevent frauds, and this message can be read and replayed. The integers Ia and Ib are referred to as "nonces," and they are limited to use once. This means that playing a previous version of message 2 won't be helpful. The names of the relevant information principals on the client and server are essentially contained in parts A and B of the message. For instance, A could be the client's username and B could be the server's name (Butun et al., 2012).

The authentication server is trustworthy and is equipped with all of the principals' keys. It can therefore create messages that are sealed with these keys and that are only accessible to the right principal. Only the client can break the outer seal on Message 2 and view Ia, B, and Kc. The remaining portions are covered so that "only B can see it." The client now determines whether the principles for Ia and B align with those in the request (Hong & Su, 1982). The client then stores the session or conversation key, Kc, if they do. The rest of the message is delivered to the server as message 3. The server may open message 3 when it comes in and obtain A's IP address and the session key. The name of A is written on the package in case a Trojan Horse altered the message. Frauds are less likely to occur when the opened return address is used instead of the one from the protocol package header. Now, the server sends a message (4) encrypted with Kc back to the client's device. A send back an encrypted message with a small change to Ib, like

Ib–1, which can only be done by someone with Kc, demonstrating that it is A. This serves as evidence that A is A. Clients and servers can send and receive encrypted data thanks to Kc.

The significance of the session key is that each time it is used, it could be used to find the key. So, users' personal keys are utilized solely to give each party their session key. This session key is utilized after that. For the same reason, a distinct session key may be utilized for each interaction, which means that session keys will change at odd times.

The above plan can be made to work with more than one authentication server in case the client and the server are in different administrations. In this case, one AS might recognize the client's key, and another might know the server's key. We presume the ASs have utilized the session key, Kas, to set up a secure channel. This would be the plan as earlier, then:

1. A → AS1: A, B, Ial
2. AS1 → AS2: {Kc, A, B, Ia2, A}Kas
3. AS2 → AS1: {{Kc, A}Ka, Ia2, A}Kas
4. AS1 → A: {Ial, B, Kc, {Kc, A}Kb} ka

Remind that both the client and the server can't tell the difference between this protocol and the case of a single authentication server. Note that AS1 selects a conversation key and gives it to AS2, which seals it with B's key. So, AS2 doesn't have to believe AS1 regarding B's key. But AS1 has to believe that AS2 won't share the conversation key. To make it harder to fake, dissimilar nonces are employed for the conversations between A and AS1 and between ASI and AS2 (Meena & Sharma, 2022).

8.3.4.2. PKC Approach

Structure for a single AS by public keys is as following:

1. A → AS: A, B
2. AS → A: {PKb, B}SKas
3. A → B: {Ia, A}PKb
4. B → AS: B, A
5. AS → B: {PKa, A)SKas
6. B → A: {Ia, Ib}PKa
7. A → B: {Ib}PKb

Data Phase:

a. A → B: {{Mab}SKa} Pkb

b. B → A: {{Mba} SKb}PKa

Messages 1, 2, 4, and 5 are just ways to determine the other person's public key. Since these are public keys, the purpose for encryption is not to keep them secret, but to prove that they came from the verification server, public key is extensively and unfalsifiably published. Aside from that, the procedure is easy to follow. During the data phase, double encryption is employed to prove and seal a message is real (Chuchaisri & Newman, 2012).

8.3.4.3. Asynchronous Communication

In order to establish A and B's authenticity to their mutual satisfaction, a dialogue was possible in the aforementioned synchronous authentication cases. This may not be feasible in some situations, such as with electronic mail systems, where there may be significant delays or parties who are not available at the same time. Even though the plan put forth by Needham and Schroeder is not the only option, it is practical. It makes use of timestamps and self-authenticating messages. When A wishes to send to B it asks its As to create a conversation key and wrap it up in B's key, i.e.: Token = {Kc, A}Kb.

The message body is then directed with this token, but it is encrypted using Kc in the following manner:

Seg1 = Token, {TS, S1, Mess1)Kc

Seg2 = {S2, Mess2}Kc Seg3 = (S3, Mess3}Kc, etc.

Mess1, Mess2, etc., are the message fragments and TS is a special timestamp that A added. Sequence numbers are S1, S2, etc., and transport service packets are Seg1, Seg2, etc. The recipient maintains a table of the TS values and related foundations for a set amount of time-based on the anticipated movement time of messages via the network. Each distinct message coming from the source is assigned a distinct TS. Thus, any outdated or rehearsed (duplicate) messages may be deleted (Vonderwell, 2003).

8.3.5. Message Integrity

In order for a message to be considered authentic, it frequently needs to be verified that it is complete and came from the specified source. The whole message does not have to be encrypted because maintaining secrecy may not always be necessary depending on the application. To verify the authenticity of messages, a code or signature known as a MAC is added. Such a MAC can be created by encrypting the message with a key that is unique to the sender using an algorithm like DES, then choosing the most crucial k bits from the last block of the ciphertext. This check gives a 2-k possibility that the message is real. To provide the required degree of integrity, one can choose (Davies et al., 1981). The message may be concealed once more using a different key if confidentiality is also required (Jueneman, 1987). When the message is decrypted, shifts to the ciphertext that are typically invisible might take place. In order to prevent this, a Using manipulation Detection Code (MDC) is included to the cleartext before encipherment. It might be a fundamental CRC or something comparable. An invalid MDC is produced when the message is decrypted as a consequence of changes to the ciphertext (Jutla, 2001).

Popek & Kline (1979) offers an alternative plan of action. A one-way function F is then applied to the message M, resulting in F(M), which has a smaller number of bits than the original message. F(M') must possess the property that it is hard to discover another message M' with a similar integrity code to its own for F(M') to be equivalent to F(M). As both the client and server (as well as the rest of the world) must be aware of F, it is imperative to enlist the help of a trustworthy third party to securely bind the integrity code. The authentication server can be appropriate, and the protocol may be appropriate:

1. A: Sig = F (Mess)
2. A → AS: A, {Sig}Ka
3. AS → A: {A, Sig}Kas
4. A → B: Mess, {A, Sig} Kas
5. B: Bsig = F{Mess}
6. B → AS: B, {A, Sig}Kas
7. AS → B: {A, Sig}Ka
8. B: Bsig = Sig ==> Authentic

Remember that the authentication server's key (Kas), used to verify both the sender's and the message's authenticity, is how the signature is transferred from point A to point B. The sender's and recipient's public keys are Kn and Ka, respectively. The message from A to B will be encrypted using PKC:

A → B: {{Mess} Ksa} Kpb

Kpb is B's general key and Ksa is A's secret key. B can therefore confirm with the help of an impartial third party that the meaning has not played with and that it originated from A if it keeps both Mess and MessKsa. This is especially helpful if A tries to break the terms of an electronic contract (Cagalj et al., 2006).

ACTIVITY 8.1:

How can organizations protect against emerging security threats, such as ransomware attacks and data breaches, while also balancing the need for open access to data and collaboration across different departments and stakeholders?

8.4. KEY DISTRIBUTION

Some of the processes for key distribution were covered in the section before this one. Initial key distribution frequently takes place through out-of-band methods, such as face-to-face meetings or the postal service. It might be possible to transmit new keys using the data distribution system (encrypted) after the initial keys have been distributed. However, human weakness is common, keeping users from seeing their keys is best (Burmester & Desmedt, 1995). Otherwise, they might be persuaded to share the clear text via email!

Key storage must be managed similarly, and it is wise to make sure that keys are kept encrypted even within programs so that, in the event of a program, machine, or file store clatter, plain text keys are difficult to locate among the wreckage (Bauer et al., 1983).

8.5. SUMMARY

The chapter "Distributed System Security" focuses on the various aspects of security in distributed systems. It covers the importance of access control and the different security threats to distributed systems. It also discusses the role of authentication and non-repudiation in ensuring secure access to distributed systems. The chapter provides an introduction to cryptography and its role in ensuring secure communication in distributed systems. It describes the different ciphers used in cryptography and their respective uses. The chapter also highlights the security differences between block and stream ciphers. Finally, it covers key distribution techniques and their importance in cryptography. Overall, the chapter provides a comprehensive overview of the security measures necessary for distributed systems.

REVIEW QUESTIONS

1. What are the important aspects of security in distributed systems?
2. Why is access control important for ensuring security in distributed systems?
3. What are the various security threats to distributed systems and what are some ways to mitigate them?
4. What is authentication and how does it help ensure secure access to distributed systems?
5. Why is non-repudiation important for ensuring security in distributed systems?
6. What are the basics of cryptography and how does it help ensure secure communication in distributed systems?
7. What are the different ciphers used in cryptography and what are their specific uses?
8. What are the differences between block and stream cipher security?
9. What are key distribution techniques and why are they important in cryptography?

MULTIPLE CHOICE QUESTIONS

1. Which of the following is an aspect of security in distributed systems?

a. Confidentiality
b. Reliability
c. Availability
d. All of the above

2. What is the importance of access control in distributed systems security?

a. It prevents unauthorized access to the system
b. It ensures system reliability
c. It enhances system performance

   d. None of the above

3. **Which of the following is NOT a security threat to distributed systems?**
   a. Denial of Service (DoS) attacks
   b. Malware attacks
   c. Physical theft of the server
   d. All of the above are security threats
4. **What is the role of authentication in ensuring secure access to distributed systems?**
   a. It ensures confidentiality of data
   b. It ensures integrity of data
   c. It ensures the identity of the user
   d. None of the above
5. **What is the importance of non-repudiation in distributed systems security?**
   a. It ensures confidentiality of data
   b. It ensures integrity of data
   c. It ensures accountability of users
   d. None of the above
6. **What is cryptography in the context of distributed systems security?**
   a. It is the science of secure communication over insecure channels
   b. It is the science of secure access control in distributed systems
   c. It is the science of secure storage of data in distributed systems
   d. None of the above
7. **Which of the following is a type of cipher used in cryptography?**
   a. Encryption cipher
   b. Decryption cipher
   c. Symmetric cipher
   d. All of the above

Answers to Multiple Choice Questions

1. (d); 2. (a); 3. (c); 4. (c); 5. (c); 6. (a); 7. (c)

REFERENCES

1. Barkadehi, M. H., Nilashi, M., Ibrahim, O., Fardi, A. Z., & Samad, S., (2018). Authentication systems: A literature review and classification. *Telematics and Informatics, 35*(5), 1491–1511.

2. Bauer, R. K., Berson, T. A., & Feiertag, R. J., (1983). A key distribution protocol using event markers. *ACM Transactions on Computer Systems (TOCS), 1*(3), 249–255.
3. Bellovin, S. M., & Merritt, M., (1990). Limitations of the Kerberos authentication system. *ACM SIGCOMM Computer Communication Review, 20*(5), 119–132.
4. Biham, E., (2005). On modes of operation: (Abstract) February 22, 1994. In: *Fast Software Encryption: Cambridge Security Workshop Cambridge, UK, December 9–11, 1993 Proceedings* (Vol.1, pp. 116–120). Berlin, Heidelberg: Springer Berlin Heidelberg.
5. Birrell, A. D., (1985). Secure communication using remote procedure calls. *ACM Transactions on Computer Systems (TOCS), 3*(1), 1–14.
6. Birrell, A. D., Lampson, B. W., Needham, R. M., & Schroeder, M. D., (1986). A global authentication service without global trust. In: *1986 IEEE Symposium on Security and Privacy* (Vol. 1, pp. 223–223). IEEE.
7. Boehm, B. W., (1984). Verifying and validating software requirements and design specifications. *IEEE Software, 1*(1), 75.
8. Boklan, K. D., (2009). Large key sizes and the security of password-based cryptography. *International Journal of Information Security and Privacy (IJISP), 3*(1), 65–72.
9. Botting, R., (1986). Novel security techniques for online systems. *Communications of the ACM, 29*(5), 416–417.
10. Burmester, M., & Desmedt, Y., (1995). A secure and efficient conference key distribution system. In: *Advances in Cryptology—EUROCRYPT'94: Workshop on the Theory and Application of Cryptographic Techniques Perugia, Italy, May 9–12, 1994 Proceedings 13* (Vol. 3, pp. 275–286). Springer Berlin Heidelberg.
11. Butun, I., Wang, Y., Lee, Y. S., & Sankar, R., (2012). Intrusion prevention with two–level user authentication in heterogeneous wireless sensor networks. *International Journal of Security and Networks, 7*(2), 107–121.
12. Cagalj, M., Capkun, S., Rengaswamy, R., Tsigkogiannis, I., Srivastava, M., & Hubaux, J. P., (2006). Integrity (I) codes: Message integrity protection and authentication over insecure channels. In: *2006 IEEE Symposium on Security and Privacy (S&P'06)* (Vol. 1, p. 15). IEEE.
13. Chaum, D., (1985). Security without identification: Transaction systems to make big brother obsolete. *Communications of the ACM, 28*(10), 1030–1044.
14. Chuchaisri, P., & Newman, R., (2012). Fast response PKC-based broadcast authentication in wireless sensor networks. *Mobile Networks and Applications, 17*, 508–525.
15. Davies, D. W., Holler, E., Jensen, E. D., Kimbleton, S. R., Lampson, B. W., LeLann, G., & Watson, R. W., (1981). *Distributed Systems—Architecture and Implementation: An Advanced Course* (Vol. 4, p. 147). Berlin, Heidelberg: Springer Berlin Heidelberg.
16. De Canniere, C., (2006). Trivium: A stream cipher construction inspired by block cipher design principles. In: *Information Security: 9th International Conference, ISC 2006, Samos Island, Greece, August 30-September 2, 2006; Proceedings 9* (Vol. 1, pp. 171–186). Springer Berlin Heidelberg.

17. Denning, D. E., & Sacco, G. M., (1981). Timestamps in key distribution protocols. *Communications of the ACM, 24*(8), 533–536.
18. Denning, P. J., (1992). The science of computing: Passwords. *American Scientist, 80*(2), 117–120.
19. Diffie, W., & Hellman, M. E., (2022). New directions in cryptography. In: *Democratizing Cryptography: The Work of Whitfield Diffie and Martin Hellman* (Vol. 1, pp. 365–390).
20. Ehrsam, W. F., Matyas, S. M., Meyer, C. H., & Tuchman, W. L., (1978). A cryptographic key management scheme for implementing the data encryption standard. *IBM Systems Journal, 17*(2), 106–125.
21. FIPS, N., (1985). *113–Computer Data Authentication* (Vol. 29, p. 124). National Institute of Standards and Technology, Federal Information Processing Standards.
22. Gifford, D. K., (1982). Cryptographic sealing for information secrecy and authentication. *Communications of the ACM, 25*(4), 274–286.
23. Goshwe, N. Y., (2013). Data encryption and decryption using RSA algorithm in a network environment. *International Journal of Computer Science and Network Security (IJCSNS), 13*(7), 9.
24. Hong, Y. C., & Su, S. Y. W., (1982). A mechanism for database protection in cellular-logic devices. *IEEE Transactions on Software Engineering*, (6), 583–596.
25. Hu, Y., Kuang, W., Qin, Z., Li, K., Zhang, J., Gao, Y., & Li, K., (2021). Artificial intelligence security: Threats and countermeasures. *ACM Computing Surveys (CSUR), 55*(1), 1–36.
26. Jakimoski, G., & Kocarev, L., (2001). Chaos and cryptography: Block encryption ciphers based on chaotic maps. *IEEE Transactions on Circuits and Systems I: Fundamental Theory and Applications, 48*(2), 163–169.
27. Jones, A. K., (2005). Protection mechanisms and the enforcement of security policies. *Operating Systems: An Advanced Course, 2*, 228–251.
28. Jouini, M., Rabai, L. B. A., & Aissa, A. B., (2014). Classification of security threats in information systems. *Procedia Computer Science, 32*, 489–496.
29. Jueneman, R. R., (1987). Electronic document authentication. *IEEE Network, 1*(2), 17–23.
30. Jutla, C. S., (2001). Encryption modes with almost free message integrity. In: *Advances in Cryptology—EUROCRYPT 2001: International Conference on the Theory and Application of Cryptographic Techniques Innsbruck, Austria, May 6–10, 2001 Proceedings 20* (Vol. 1, pp. 529–544). Springer Berlin Heidelberg.
31. Kerckhof, S., Durvaux, F., Hocquet, C., Bol, D., & Standaert, F. X., (2012). Towards green cryptography: A comparison of lightweight ciphers from the energy viewpoint. In: *Cryptographic Hardware and Embedded Systems–CHES 2012: 14th International Workshop, Leuven, Belgium, September 9–12, 2012; Proceedings 14* (Vol. 1, pp. 390–407). Springer Berlin Heidelberg.
32. Kumar, S., Paar, C., Pelzl, J., Pfeiffer, G., & Schimmler, M., (2006). Breaking

ciphers with COPACOBANA–a cost-optimized parallel code breaker. In: *Cryptographic Hardware and Embedded Systems-CHES 2006: 8th International Workshop, Yokohama, Japan, October 10–13, 2006; Proceedings 8* (Vol. 1, pp. 101–118). Springer Berlin Heidelberg.

33. Landwehr, C. E., (1981). Formal models for computer security. *ACM Computing Surveys (CSUR), 13*(3), 247–278.
34. Laprie, J. C., (1995). Dependable computing: Concepts, limits, challenges. In: *Special Issue of the 25th International Symposium on Fault-Tolerant Computing* (Vol. 1, pp. 42–54).
35. Li, N., & Tripunitara, M. V., (2006). Security analysis in role-based access control. *ACM Transactions on Information and System Security (TISSEC), 9*(4), 391–420.
36. Matyas, S. M., & Meyer, C. H., (1978). Generation, distribution, and installation of cryptographic keys. *IBM Systems Journal, 17*(2), 126–137.
37. Meena, U., & Sharma, P., (2022). Secret dynamic key authentication and decision trust secure routing framework for internet of things based WSN. *Wireless Personal Communications, 125*(2), 1753–1781.
38. Moran, T., & Naor, M., (2005). Basing cryptographic protocols on tamper-evident seals. In: *Automata, Languages and Programming: 32nd International Colloquium, ICALP 2005, Lisbon, Portugal, July 11–15, 2005; Proceedings 32* (Vol. 1, pp. 285–297). Springer Berlin Heidelberg.
39. Mullender, S. J., (1987). Distributed operating systems. *Computer Standards & Interfaces, 6*(1), 37–44.
40. Narayanan, A., & Shmatikov, V., (2005). Fast dictionary attacks on passwords using time-space tradeoff. In: *Proceedings of the 12th ACM conference on Computer and Communications Security* (Vol. 1, pp. 364–372).
41. Needham, R. M., & Schroeder, M. D., (1978). Using encryption for authentication in large networks of computers. *Communications of the ACM, 21*(12), 993–999.
42. Pearce, M., Zeadally, S., & Hunt, R., (2013). Virtualization: Issues, security threats, and solutions. *ACM Computing Surveys (CSUR), 45*(2), 1–39.
43. Popek, G. J., & Kline, C. S., (1979). Encryption and secure computer networks. *ACM Computing Surveys (CSUR), 11*(4), 331–356.
44. Rahman, M. M., Saha, T. K., & Bhuiyan, M. A. A., (2012). Implementation of RSA algorithm for speech data encryption and decryption. *IJCSNS International Journal of Computer Science and Network Security, 12*(3), 74–82.
45. Rivest, R. L., Shamir, A., & Adleman, L., (1978). A method for obtaining digital signatures and public-key cryptosystems. *Communications of the ACM, 21*(2), 120–126.
46. Sandhu, R. S., (1987). On some cryptographic solutions for access control in a tree hierarchy. In: *Proceedings of the 1987 Fall Joint Computer Conference on Exploring Technology: Today and Tomorrow* (Vol. 1, pp. 405–410).
47. Shaikh, F. B., & Haider, S., (2011). Security threats in cloud computing. In: *2011*

International Conference for Internet Technology and Secured Transactions (pp. 214–219). IEEE.

48. Shujun, L., Xuanqin, M., & Yuanlong, C., (2001). Pseudo-random bit generator based on couple chaotic systems and its applications in stream-cipher cryptography. In: *Progress in Cryptology—INDOCRYPT 2001: Second International Conference on Cryptology in India Chennai, India, December 16–20, 2001 Proceedings 2* (Vol. 1, pp. 316–329). Springer Berlin Heidelberg.
49. Smid, M. E., & Branstad, D. K., (1988). Data encryption standard: Past and future. *Proceedings of the IEEE, 76*(5), 550–559.
50. Srivastava, S., & Bhatia, A., (2018). On the learning capabilities of recurrent neural networks: A cryptographic perspective. In: *2018 IEEE International Conference on Big Knowledge (ICBK)* (Vol. 1, pp. 162–167). IEEE.
51. Standard, D. E., (1977). *National Bureau of Standards FIPS Publication, 46*, 125–127.
52. Summers, R. C., (1984). An overview of computer security. *IBM Systems Journal, 23*(4), 309–325.
53. Tourani, R., Misra, S., Mick, T., & Panwar, G., (2017). Security, privacy, and access control in information-centric networking: A survey. *IEEE Communications Surveys & Tutorials, 20*(1), 566–600.
54. Vonderwell, S., (2003). An examination of asynchronous communication experiences and perspectives of students in an online course: A case study. *The Internet and Higher Education, 6*(1), 77–90.
55. Voydock, V. L., & Kent, S. T., (1983). Security mechanisms in high-level network protocols. *ACM Computing Surveys (CSUR), 15*(2), 135–171.
56. Wang, X., Wang, X., Zhao, J., & Zhang, Z., (2011). Chaotic encryption algorithm based on alternant of stream cipher and block cipher. *Nonlinear Dynamics, 63*, 587–597.
57. Wilbur, S., (2000). *Distributed Systems Security, 21*(3), 25–29.
58. Zhou, X., & Tang, X., (2011). Research and implementation of RSA algorithm for encryption and decryption. In: *Proceedings of 2011 6th International Forum on Strategic Technology* (Vol. 2, pp. 1118–1121). IEEE.
59. Zimmermann, P., (1986). A proposed standard format for RSA cryptosystems. *Computer, 19*(09), 21–34.

INDEX

D

G

H

I

J

K

L

M

N

O